PARTICIPATORY

METHODOLOGIES

Sara Miller McCune founded SAGE Publishing in 1965 to support the dissemination of usable knowledge and educate a global community. SAGE publishes more than 1000 journals and over 800 new books each year, spanning a wide range of subject areas. Our growing selection of library products includes archives, data, case studies and video. SAGE remains majority owned by our founder and after her lifetime will become owned by a charitable trust that secures the company's continued independence.

Los Angeles | London | New Delhi | Singapore | Washington DC | Melbourne

PARTICIPATORY

VISUAL

METHODOLOGIES

SOCIAL CHANGE, COMMUNITY AND POLICY

Claudia Mitchell

Naydene de Lange

Relebohile Moletsane

Los Angeles | London | New Delhi
Singapore | Washington DC | Melbourne

Los Angeles | London | New Delhi
Singapore | Washington DC | Melbourne

SAGE Publications Ltd
1 Oliver's Yard
55 City Road
London EC1Y 1SP

SAGE Publications Inc.
2455 Teller Road
Thousand Oaks, California 91320

SAGE Publications India Pvt Ltd
B 1/I 1 Mohan Cooperative Industrial Area
Mathura Road
New Delhi 110 044

SAGE Publications Asia-Pacific Pte Ltd
3 Church Street
#10-04 Samsung Hub
Singapore 049483

Editor: Jai Seaman
Assistant Editor: Alysha Owen
Production editor: Sushant Nailwal
Copyeditor: Rosemary Morlin
Proofreader: Derek Markham
Indexer: Authors
Marketing manager: Susheel Gokarakonda
Cover design: Shaun Mercier
Typeset by: C&M Digitals (P) Ltd, Chennai, India
Printed in the UK

Library of Congress Control Number: 2017933485

British Library Cataloguing in Publication data

A catalogue record for this book is available from the British Library

ISBN 978-1-4739-4730-6
ISBN 978-1-4739-4731-3 (pbk)

At SAGE we take sustainability seriously. Most of our products are printed in the UK using FSC papers and boards. When we print overseas we ensure sustainable papers are used as measured by the PREPS grading system. We undertake an annual audit to monitor our sustainability.

In memory of Marianne Adam

22/06/1955 – 06/11/2016

CONTENTS

LIST OF FIGURES

ABOUT THE AUTHORS

Claudia Mitchell is a James McGill Professor in the Faculty of Education, McGill University where she is the Director of the McGill Institute for Human Development and Well-being and the founder and Director of the Participatory Cultures Lab. She is an Honorary Professor in the School of Education, University of KwaZulu-Natal, South Africa. She was the 2016 recipient of the Social Sciences and Humanities Research Council Gold Medal awarded for the impact of her research which cuts across a number of areas including girlhood studies, youth, sexuality, and HIV and AIDS, gender violence, and teacher identity, and in a number of countries including Canada, South Africa, Russia, Ethiopia, and Kenya. As a methodologist, she is particularly interested in participatory visual research, memory-work and material culture, and autoethnography. She has 25 books published or in press, many of which pertain to visual and other arts based methodologies: *Doing Visual Research*; *Researching Children's Popular Culture* (with Jacqueline Reid-Walsh), *Putting People in the Picture* (with Naydene DeLange and Jean Stuart); *Drawing as Visual Methodology* (with Linda Theron, Ann Smith and Jean Stuart), *Handbook of Participatory Video* (with EJ Milne and Naydene DeLange), *Participatory Visual Methodologies in Global Public Health* (with Marni Sommers) and *Visual Encounters in the Study of Rural Childhoods* (with April Mandrona). She is a co-founder and Editor-in-Chief of the award winning journal *Girlhood Studies: An Interdisciplinary Journal*.

Naydene de Lange is Emeritus Professor in the Faculty of Education at the Nelson Mandela Metropolitan University, Port Elizabeth, South Africa. She previously held the HIV and AIDS Education Research Chair in the Faculty of Education at the same university. Her research focuses on using participatory visual methodologies in addressing gender and HIV&AIDS issues, and integrating HIV&AIDS into Higher Education curricula. Her Educational Psychology background and interest in Inclusive Education provides a frame for working towards the inclusion of those who are marginalized – using a 'research as social change' approach. Besides peer reviewed articles and book chapters, she has co-edited three books, *Putting People in the Picture: Visual Methodologies for Social Change* (with Claudia Mitchell and Jean Stuart), *School-University Partnerships for Educational Change in Rural South Africa* (with Faisal Islam, Claudia Mitchell, Robert Balfour and Martin Combrinck), and *The Handbook of Participatory Video* (with EJ Milne and Claudia Mitchell), and has also co-authored a book *Picturing Hope* (with Tilla Olivier and Lesley Wood). She is the 2014 runner-up in the Distinguished Women in Science: Social Sciences and Humanities Award (awarded by the South African National Department of Science and Technology) and a

South African National Research Foundation rated researcher. She is co-founder and co-editor of the journal, *Educational Research for Social Change*.

Relebohile Moletsane is Professor and the John Langalibalele Dube Chair in Rural Education in the School of Education, University of KwaZulu-Natal in Durban, South Africa. Her areas of research include curriculum studies, rural education, gender and education, sexual and reproductive health education, girlhood studies and girls education in Southern African contexts. She is the Co-PI (with Claudia Mitchell, McGill University) on the Networks for Change and Wellbeing project (Networks for Change and Well-being (www.networks4change.co.za/). The project uses participatory visual methodologies, including photo-voice, participatory video (cellphilm), digital storytelling and drawing to address sexual violence with girls in rural KwaZulu-Natal. She is the co-author (with Claudia Mitchell, Ann Smith and Linda Chisholm) of the book: *Methodologies for Mapping a Southern African Girlhood in Age of Aids*. Rotterdam/New York/Taipei: Sense Publishers. Moletsane was the 2012 winner of the Distinguished Women in Science: Social Sciences and Humanities Award (awarded by the South African National Department of Science and Technology). She was a 2014 Echidna Global Scholar at Brookings Institutions' Centre for Universal Education, where she completed a research report: *The Need for Quality Sexual and Reproductive Health Education to Address Barriers to Girls' Educational Outcomes in South Africa*. Washington, DC: Centre for Universal Education, The Brookings Institution.

ACKNOWLEDGEMENTS

This book has been a project-in-the-making for some time, based on our fieldwork in Canada, Ethiopia, Rwanda, Swaziland and Vietnam, and of course in South Africa where we are attached to Nelson Mandela Metropolitan University and the University of KwaZulu-Natal. In working in the various communities, we have drawn inspiration from the many participants, and especially from our longstanding involvement in the Vulindlela district of KwaZulu-Natal and rural communities in Eastern Cape.

There are several people we want to single out in expressing our gratitude, starting with Dr Ann Smith for her meticulous and sharp editing skills. Having Ann's skill in smoothing out the voices and writing of three authors writing from three geographic locations is, in and of itself, a major contribution to the book. We would also like to thank Fatima Khan, Pamela Lamb, Lisa Wiebesiek, and Vimbiso Okafor for their excellent assistance in preparing the manuscript.

We thank our lovely students and colleagues at McGill University, the University of KwaZulu-Natal, Nelson Mandela Metropolitan University, the University of British Columbia, Carleton University, and Mid-Sweden University. For their generous Personal Communications we would like to thank Patti Alison, Bronson Chau, Ashley DeMartini, Sarah Flicker, Huyen Do, Linda Liebenberg, Mitchell Maclarnon, Katie MacEntee, Liz Miller, Xuan Thuy Nguyen and Jen Thompson.

We gratefully acknowledge the support of the International Partnerships for Sustainable Societies (IPaSS), jointly funded by Social Sciences and Humanities Research Council of Canada (SSHRC) (award number 895-2013-3007) and the International Development Research Centre (IDRC) (award number 107777-001) to our project, 'Networks for Change and Well-being: Girl-led "From the Ground Up" policy making to address sexual violence in Canada and South Africa'. The focus of this initiative, co-led by McGill University and the University of KwaZulu-Natal provided a compelling argument for why we needed to bring together in one book many of the ideas about participatory visual methods, community, and policy dialogue and the significance of local knowledge.

In addition, we would like to acknowledge the support of funders of various other projects about which we write in this book: the Canadian Institutes for Health Research, the Challenge Fund, Global Affairs Canada, HEAIDS, other projects funded by IDRC, the Interagency Coalition on AIDS in Development, the National Research Foundation (South Africa), and the support of SSHRC to several other research projects.

Finally, we thank Jai Seamen and Alysha Owen of SAGE Publications. They have been wonderfully supportive throughout the process and managed more-or-less to keep us to our deadlines.

Claudia Mitchell
Naydene de Lange
Relebohile Moletsane

1

INTRODUCTION: A FRAMEWORK FOR SOCIAL CHANGE THROUGH PARTICIPATORY VISUAL RESEARCH

CHAPTER CONTENTS

INTRODUCTION

There is a story behind every book and many books tell a story or a set of stories. We make every attempt in this book to tell the story of how participatory visual methodologies invoke stories which in turn can contribute, potentially, to changing stories and narratives in communities and at the policy table. Our own story – or the story behind this book – has a history that dates back to 2003 and even earlier, but 2003 is when the three of us started to work together as researchers attached to a university in South Africa. As a threesome, we more or less met over a typical academic exercise – a deadline for a grant application – except that it did not feel like a typical academic exercise. Even though none of us was really that familiar at the time with the term academic activists, we more or less saw our task of writing an academic research proposal as an act of activists. The time in South Africa was fraught given the AIDS pandemic. While it remains so 13 years later, in 2003 activists were calling for an ARV roll out, access to locally patented drugs, and, within the world of the social and educational, a recognition that schools had to be doing more. Young people were dying at an alarming rate. For example, the highest mortality rates were estimated to be among the 30–39 year age group (16.2%) during the period 2006 to 2010 (Skingsley, Takuva, Brown, Delpech, & Puren, 2014).

When we met as a trio, Relebohile had just been involved in a local conference convened by the medical faculty to address HIV and AIDS and education, except that she was the only person in Education at the conference, and worse, nobody there seemed to think there was anything unusual about the absence of educationalists at the conference. Claudia had just been involved in working with a group of young people in Khayelitsha, a township in Cape Town, who had been active in the Treatment Action Campaign and who were now keen to do something in schools. For them it was clear that doing something about HIV and AIDS meant producing something, creating something, making something – posters, videos, poetry books. Somehow, when the three of us connected it seemed as though we already had a multi-pronged agenda. All three of us in our work as teacher educators in an education faculty were indignant about how educators and educational researchers were being left out of school-based interventions and discussions about HIV and AIDS, and at the same time we were also outraged that so much of the work related to adolescents (and especially what was even then already referred to as 'AIDS fatigue'), seemed not to involve adolescents at all. It had been just a year earlier at the International AIDS conference in Barcelona that there were banners and placards asking 'Where are the youth?' So if you take out the teachers and you take out young people in designing and implementing what needs to happen in schools, who is left? Our first project together – the proposal, participatory and visual, that we were writing when we met in March 2003 – was perhaps a leap of faith, but it was based on a fundamental recognition that people who need to be talking together were not talking to each other. The project, *Learning Together,* was a modest study. All we wanted to do was see what would happen if teachers and community health-care workers all dealing with young people would learn together. To do this we built on tools and methods such as drawing and photovoice, and even before we started working with teachers and community health workers, we learned together ourselves by bringing together 20 or more colleagues and postgraduate students who were willing to try out drawing and photovoice as research methods. What we lacked in sophistication we made up for in enthusiasm and a good strong dose of what Low, Brushwood, Salvio, and Palacios (2012) refer to as celebration. It was hard not to be enthusiastic when people who never talk to each other – indeed had never met even professionally, though they lived down the road from each other–actually started listening and started viewing each other's work. What we found but did not know exactly what to do with, was a tremendous amount of goodwill and excitement, and although we knew it was not enough to change the world, it was enough to convince us and a few others around us that we needed to do even more of this kind of work and to broaden it into tools and methods such as participatory video, digital story-telling, and cellphilming.

Thirteen years later it would be wonderful to be able to offer the pat expression the rest is history and claim that we have somehow solved the world's problems through photovoice, drawing, participatory video, and digital story-telling, but of course we have not. What these methods have done is put into practice what visual theorists like Susan Sontag (2003) have said about the power of images to haunt us as we have seen in the types of images that are seen in humanitarian crises. Notwithstanding the controversies surrounding the use of provocative images in public settings as Batchen, Gidley, Miller, and Prosser (2012) explore in *Picturing Atrocity: Photography in Crisis,* these methods have pushed to the front of the line the vast inequalities and injustices in research. In participatory visual research these inequalities are highly visible: Who owns the images? Who sees the images? What happens to the images? Who decides? As a community of scholars we have become attuned to making sure that we talk about these things – often they are the whole point of a conference presentation or article or book or series of books and journals. But more importantly, they are the starting point for this work. In this book, we seek to shift the conversation towards outcomes and the ever-present question 'What difference does this make?' What possibilities are there for dialogue – community dialogue and policy dialogue?

POLICY, POLICY, POLICY

Everyone, it seems, in the social research community, wants to influence policy. It is a legitimate aspiration given the need to challenge inequities in schools, health care, agriculture, and other community settings, and particularly in relation to such persistent concerns as sexual violence, bullying, safety and security in housing, water and sanitation, food insecurity, environmental issues, HIV and AIDS, and related health and social issues. However, as Ray Rist (2003) observes:

There is no broad-based and sustained tradition within contemporary social science of focusing qualitative work specifically on policy issues, especially given the real time constraints that the policy process necessitates. Yet it is also clear that the opportunities are multiple for such contributions to be made. (p. 641)

3

Participatory visual research is an area of research where, quite clearly, there are contributions to be made in order to influence policy dialogue. The use of photography in photovoice, participatory video (including the use of mobile phone devices), digital story-telling and drawing and mapping have all been shown to be effective in engaging community participants, and especially in altering some of the typical power dynamics related to the researched/researcher, and to ensuring spaces for marginalized populations to both speak about and then speak back through interactive workshop sessions to social conditions. The products – photo exhibitions, video productions (live screenings and postings on YouTube) – are ideally suited to be seen. While there are hefty debates about process versus product, and the sometimes exaggerated claims that are often made for the overall effectiveness of such methods, especially as seen in what Low et al. (2012) refer to as celebratory writing, there are few who would argue against the power of the visual to engage multiple audiences. This book takes up the issue of ways of ensuring that visual data reaches critical audiences, providing new entry points for social change. Gubrium and Harper's (2013) book, *Participatory Visual and Digital Methods,* also calls for more explicit work in this area. One book that takes up some of the critical issues of beyond engagement is Laverack's (2013) *Health Activism: Foundations and Strategies.* However, it has a very specific activist agenda that is broader, and that has a narrower, albeit critical, policy focus in the area of health. It is clear, therefore, that much more is needed. In conference presentations, the issue of participatory research-into-policy change is one of the areas where we are bombarded with variations of the question, 'So what?'

Despite the popularity of terms such as youth-led policy-making or participant-led change, there remains a paucity of critical (and practical) work that maps out fully what this means in relation to influencing (and documenting) social change. While events and changes can happen without the intervention of researchers thinking of what happens beyond engagement, this type of change typically does not just happen as can be seen in an emerging field within participatory research that seeks to study, critique, and enhance possibilities for change. The concern is not with the generative possibilities for engaging participants in representing the issues through participatory visual methods; these possibilities are covered well in many books and articles on the use of the visual. Rather, this book seeks to offer perspectives, tools, and methods that can take us into the space beyond engagement with the overall aim of influencing community dialogue and the policy-making process. At the same time it also seeks to contribute to creating new pathways for participatory visual arts-based methods in policy-making as a field of study in itself.

COMMUNITY AND POLICY DIALOGUE

An overarching concern of this book relates to the impact of participatory visual research on community and policy dialogue. Often the most we see on impact are a few lines that appear at the end of the book, thesis, chapter, or article calling for action or suggesting implications for policy or policy dialogue. This is changing as we see in collections such as Gubrium, Harper, and Otañez's (2015) *Participatory Visual and Digital Research in Action,* in which strategies for taking action are highlighted. However, it is also important to recognize that the idea of social change is multi-faceted and so are the appropriate audiences. Sometimes the audience for the visual productions, as we highlight in Chapter 3 on speaking back, are the participants themselves. At other points the audiences may be community members or various policy makers, and often a combination of both. There may be many legitimate reasons for the fact that there is less documentation on the engagement process, not the least of which is the fact that community dialogue is not typically a once off affair (and when does it begin and end?), and policy dialogue and policy-making are seldom overnight activities. As we know from the rich body of work on policy cycles (see Bowe, Ball, & Gold, 1992), the task of policy uptake work often extends long beyond a project and, in the case of funded research, often beyond the life of the funding. In addition, there may be many intervening circumstances such as elections, a change of government or administration, or critical events that take place in the community or country. While the focus of the work of participation using visual media is commonly on the actual production process, increasingly there is also an interest in the images themselves (e.g. photos, videos, vlogs, and cellphilms) as a way of developing an understanding of the phenomenon under study, and the influence of power relations among those involved. There is also an increased emphasis on the idea of knowledge-production. This is something we see in the body of work on youth as knowledge producers, or work with community health-care workers as cultural producers and so on. A central premise of this chapter – and indeed, of the book as a whole – is the idea that the meaningful engagement of the various social groups who participate in participatory visual research necessitates an understanding of the meaningful engagement of communities and various stakeholders as audiences in relation to this work. As such, we argue that if we are to take seriously participatory visual research and the potential of this work to influence social change, we are obliged to go full circle to study the idea of engaging audiences.

Paradoxically, much less has been written in the area of participatory visual research about engaging audiences or the impact of participatory visual work on various communities and stakeholders. It is worth noting that in an analysis of a decade of articles in *Visual Studies,* the *Journal of Visual Culture* and *Visual Communication,* relatively few articles take up the idea of audience in an explicit way although, of course, audiences are often implicit.[1] Our analysis started with a keyword search using terms such as *audience, reception, and viewers/ship.* In the *Journal of Visual Culture,* a search for the term *audience* called up 201 entries, with only one including the term in the main title of the article (Chalfen, Sherman, & Rich, 2010). The keyword *reception* called up 157 entries, but was never located within the title of the publications. Finally, the term *viewers* or *viewership* located 337 and 1 entries respectively, with both terms combined within the same article only

---

[1] We acknowledge the assistance of Lukas Labacher in carrying out this keyword analysis.

once (Luce, 2011). Of those that cited *viewers*, only two (Halasz, 2010; Luce, 2011) included the term in the title of the article. Together, where *audience, reception, community engagement, and viewers/ship* were referenced in the journal *Visual Studies*, a combined 837 times located within book reviews, editorials, and primary journal articles, only five entries (0.005%) included the identifying terms in the titles of the works. In a second keyword search in the *Journal of Visual Culture, audience* located 177 entries, *reception* located 88, *community* AND *engagement* found 51, and *viewers* or *viewership* located 177 entries. Surprisingly, no entries from 493 initially located within an all-fields search had these keywords in the title of the entries. Finally, in the journal *Visual Communication*, a search for *audience, reception, community* AND *engagement, and viewers/ship* located 1/156 (Lobinger & Brantner, 2015), 1/51 (Bucher & Niemann, 2012), 0/56, and 1/156 (Lick, 2015) entries published between January 2005 and December 2015.

In our analysis it appears that notions of audience, community engagement, reception, and viewership are similarly hidden from the main titles of articles that, on a deeper analysis, do sometimes present a discussion on these topics. Surprisingly, the study of online audiences in these journals does not fare much better. While online work on audiences reveals terminology that suggests a much more nuanced notion of the interplay of uses, producers, and audiences, there still remains relatively little known about online audiences. As Carpentier, Schrøder, and Hallett (2013) observe:

… paradoxically, when user, producer and audience become more conflated, the user component dominates the chain of equivalence, and all audiences become articulated as passive participants. (As cited in de Ridder et al., 2016, p. 131)

At the same time, as Lunt and Livingstone (2013) point out, the idea of public sphere, is one that has become prominent in media studies as they found in an analysis of references to public sphere – a term which implies audience – in the journal *Media, Culture and Society*. Similarly, the idea of a public sociology located within the notion of 'Engaging Tactics' as it is termed at Goldsmith's College in the UK[2] brings with it a rich sense of audience, dialogue and engagement, and as such points to the possibilities for a stronger sense of audience in participatory visual research.

CRITICAL AUDIENCE ENGAGEMENT

In this section we embark upon mapping out a framework for what we term Critical Audience Engagement. In developing this we are strongly influenced by Gillian Rose's framework for a Critical Visual Methodology which, as a critical approach to interpreting visual images includes: (1) the idea of taking images seriously; (2) consideration of the

---

[2]https://engagingtactics.wordpress.com/

social conditions and effects of visual objects; and (3) a level of reflexivity on the part of the researcher which 'considers [their] own ways of looking at images' (Rose, 2001, p. 16). We take as an entry point the work of the French sociologist, Robert Escarpit (1958), well known for his formulation in the sociology of literature, 'Who reads what, why, how, and with what effect?' to develop a new extended question: 'Who looks at what, where, when, why, how and with what effect?' To respond to Escarpit, we have identified several bodies of literature and studies of visual practices that, while typically taken to be very separate (and that arise out of different disciplinary areas), have great potential to be complementary in contributing to a deeper understanding of the issues of engagement and impact in participatory visual studies. These include: (1) audience engagement research, as an area to which we have already alluded in reference to Rose's work, and as a research area that encompasses work across visual studies, media, and digital studies; (2) political listening as an important area of inquiry for studying policy dialogue; and (3) literature on reflexivity both in relation to researchers but also participants. Emerging from the interaction among these three elements is community engagement and dialogue which enhance opportunities for social change (see Figure 1.1).

Our work takes as a starting point the idea that the populations who typically are involved in participatory visual research occupy a marginal position and so their visual productions may also be marginalized. Darcy Alexandra (2015) in her compelling essay, *Are We Listening Yet? Participatory Knowledge-Production through Media Practices; Encounters of Political Listening*, draws on the work of well-known media theorist, Jean Burgess: 'The question that we ask about "democratic" media participation can no longer be limited to "Who gets to speak?" We must also ask "Who is heard and to what end?"' (Burgess, 2006, as cited

Figure 1.1   Framework for critical audience engagement and dialogue for social change

Diagram developed by Claudia Mitchell

in Alexandra, 2015, p. 43). Extensive work in the areas of childhood and youth studies, for example, draws attention to the fact that young people may not have a voice even in a project that sets out to give them voice. Researching and testing out the material and social conditions that are necessary for ensuring that community members or policy makers respond meaningfully to video productions or digital stories produced by homeless young people, young women who have been victims of gender violence, women farmers, or children in an informal settlement in Nairobi, are what make this work critical.

As a second key point, the viewers themselves for this work may also occupy varying positions that challenge conventional notions of audience. What does it mean to be a community member viewing the images produced by other community members who occupy the same status? Participatory work can both disrupt the idea of who is an artist, film maker, or photographer but also who and how audiences are meant to view the work. Participating in community exhibitions or screenings is a very context-specific social activity. This is highlighted by Mitchell's (2016) discussion of an exhibition in a community centre in the middle of an informal settlement in Nairobi, where community members arrive at the community centre but are uncertain about what they should do next. There is no obvious beginning. Should they sit down as they typically do for a community consultation and wait for events to start? But most of the benches have been removed to maximize viewing space. It is not just about how to look at the actual photos, but the idea of walking around freely in a public building and looking at things on the walls. Is it even allowed?

Closely related to the points noted above, there is still the researcher – I/we – and we might need to continue to think about the question 'Where are we in the picture?' Notwithstanding a consideration of the emerging body of work in participatory visual research on such issues as power and ownership, there is sometimes too much of researcher reflexivity and not enough of the participants' reflexivity. At the same time, this is typically not DIY work, and researchers are implicated. As Delgado (2015) reminds us in his comprehensive review of photovoice work with urban youth, we may be implicated in not doing enough or not being sufficiently strategic. As he observes, 'Having an exhibition boycotted because of its controversial content, or, even worse, simply ignored, with minimal attendance and no media coverage, can have a long lasting impact on the participants' (p. 99). Perhaps the most compelling point is one that he shares from the work of Haw (2008) and the idea that the opposite of having a voice is being silenced. Failure (on the part of researchers) to come up with a way for photos or other visual images and productions to reach appropriate audiences is part of that silencing.

Audience Research

Audience research is a legitimate area of study in Television Studies, Cultural Studies, and Communication Studies and indeed, in the context of digital and social media has become increasingly diversified and more complex. This is highlighted in several new collections

(Carpentier et al., 2013; Zeller, Ponte, & O'Neill, 2014) alongside relatively new journals such as *Participations: The Journal of Audience and Reception Studies*. To date, however, audience research in participatory visual research has not received in-depth attention. There are two notable exceptions, the work of visual theorist Gillian Rose and the work of media and cultural studies theorist John Fiske, although in both cases, the work has not been adapted to talk about audiencing in participatory visual research. Fiske and Rose have produced work that has important overlaps. In his work in critical television studies, Fiske maps out a triangle of the primary text (the television show or series), the producer text (based on all the levels of production), and the audience text. Fiske argues that meaning is somewhere in the middle of these three layers of textuality and that these three layers leak into each other. The producers then create the text taking into consideration particular viewers. Viewers may find many ways to insert themselves into this production text in everything from fandom to other critical reception activities. Various researchers have adapted Fiske's work to the production of cellphilms and participatory video (Doyon, 2009; MacEntee, 2016a; Mitchell, 2011; Yang, 2012). In these studies, the primary text is typically the image (cellphilm, photo, digital story, exhibition), the producers are the participants in the study; and the viewers would be the various audiences (participants viewing each other's work, community members, peers, academic audiences, policy makers) (see Figure 1.2).

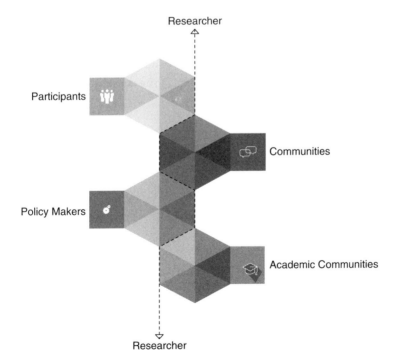

Figure 1.2 Engaging audiences

Diagram developed by Claudia Mitchell

Drawing on Fiske's work on audiencing (1994), Rose (2001) developed a critical visual framework in which she identified three overlapping sites in visual research: (1) the site of the image; (2) the site of producing the image; and (3) the site of audiencing. A particularly useful aspect of Rose's work is that it offers a set of questions for each site. Of particular relevance to this discussion, she includes 19 questions related to audiencing, eight of which we offer here as indicative of the rich possibilities for studying audience interactions:

Who were the original audience for this image? Where and how would the text have been displayed originally? How is it circulated? How is it stored? How is it redisplayed? Who are the more recent audiences for this text? Where is the spectator positioned in relation to the components of the image? What relation does this produce between the image and the viewers? Is the image one of a series...? (2001, pp. 189–190)

Rose notes that the questions are in no particular order of significance and that some will be more applicable to a situation than others. They are not questions that rule out application to participatory visual research. It is also clear that both Fiske's and Rose's frameworks are useful to studying audiencing in participatory visual studies.

Political Listening

Our journey to considering the idea of political listening comes out of Darcy Alexandra's (2015) work with asylum seekers in Ireland in which she considers the tensions in a longitudinal digital story-telling project. As she notes:

The practice of producing stories unfolds within a field of diverse and, at times, conflicting interests. Participants, facilitators, researchers, and collaborating and funding agencies have different ideas about which stories to tell, who is best positioned to tell them, how they 'should' and 'should not' be told and what is at stake. Within this nexus of interdependent yet unequal relationships, a methodological attention to the politics of listening offers conceptual inroad into addressing the power asymmetries inherent in participatory knowledge projection through media practice. (p. 43)

Taking into consideration the almost invariable power differentials that might exist between and among participants, communities and policy makers and the various tensions (and sometimes silences) that we were seeing in many of the participatory visual projects in which we have been involved, we became interested in building political listening/political viewing into our work. We have long argued that one of the strengths of the visual is that it is what might be described as right there such that it is difficult for audiences to look away. But of course, as we know from a vast range of work with media and art, it is not at all difficult to look away or to see only what we want to see. Our example in Chapter 4 of a college dean who willingly viewed a photo exhibition produced by his students and interpreted a photograph of a half-eaten meal placed on a chair in the cafeteria as a transgression on the part of the students who should just clean up the mess is a good example of this. The idea of political listening/viewing at least takes into account the obvious tensions that are likely to exist. Citing Bickford as the person who coined the term political listening, Alexandra observes:

Political listening is not primarily a caring or amicable practice, and I emphasize this at the outset because 'listening' tends immediately to evoke ideas of empathy and compassion. We cannot suppose that political actors are sympathetic towards one another in a conflictual context, yet is it precisely the presence of conflict and differences that makes communicative interaction necessary. This communicative interaction – speaking and listening together – does not necessarily resolve or do away with the conflicts that arise from uncertainty, inequality or identity. Rather it enables political actors to decide democratically how to act in the face of conflict, and to clarify the nature of the conflict at hand. (Bickford, 1996, as cited in Alexandra, 2015, p. 44)

The asylum seekers about whom Alexandra writes, report concern about whether their digital stories would be believed, 'repeatedly asking if their story was "okay", if they could "really" tell it' (p. 45). There was some question on the part of the participants about whether they could tell anything but positive stories and whether they ought to express their gratitude to Ireland. There was also a concern about whether the story happened to the storyteller directly or whether he or she could narrate the story of someone else. Again there is a concern: 'Did that really happen?' Alexandra suggests the need for different questions: 'Instead of asking "Is it truth?" we might ask instead: In what ways is it true? What does the story mean to the storyteller and the viewer? What does the story do?' (p. 48). Typically the images, and related captions, curatorial statements, policy posters, and other artefacts produced by participants are in response to conditions that frame their views of social conditions and what needs to happen. While not all images produced in digital stories, videos, cellphilms, drawings and photos are of atrocities, some of the images may be ones that are not easy for the target audiences (especially policy makers) to look at since the images are typically a critique of social inequalities. Indeed, our own work and many of the studies we report on in this book are ones that are often directed at 'a public that disbelieves' (Alexandra, 2015, p. 45) and who might ask 'did that really happen?' We are reminded here of a project in South Africa involving children's drawings of sexual violence. As we explore further in Chapter 7, many of the policy makers who viewed the images wondered if these violations really happened to the young artists. We are also reminded of one of the first 'feeling safe/feeling not so safe' photovoice projects we carried out with seventh grade students in Swaziland (Mitchell, 2009). Responding to the images of unsafe toilets produced by the girls, several of the teachers commented that the girls shouldn't have taken such pictures and why didn't they take pictures of something nicer. At the same time, as McNay (2009) also reminds us, images can have an afterlife, particularly the kind of images that are produced in participatory visual studies. In our own archive of what we regard as provocative and disturbing photos, some of which we have written about elsewhere, we think of the photovoice image produced by a group of Grade 9 boys in a rural school in South Africa on stigma in which they stage a hanging (see Mitchell, 2011; Moletsane, Mitchell, De Lange, Stuart, Buthelezi & Taylor, 2009), or the drawing produced by a girl in Rwanda of an unwanted baby dropped into a toilet pit (Mitchell, 2008), or the various videos of gender violence produced by secondary school students (De Lange & Mitchell, 2014; Moletsane, Mitchell, Smith & Chisholm, 2008). The idea is not to just tell positive stories, but rather to create an environment in which participants and audiences can listen to each other. Not all occasions will be perfect arenas for this. We are aware, for example, that the image of the boys who staged the hanging scene may be very disturbing. In the same way that there is a context (the boy who seems to be hanging is standing on a chair), there also needs to be a broader context for viewing images produced by children in an era of AIDS. As Bickford (1996) observes, we may need to 'decide democratically how to act in the face of conflict' (p. 2).

Reflexivity

'There's nothing wrong with standing back and thinking', writes Susan Sontag (2003, p. 118). It is with this in mind that, in this section, we explore the links between participatory visual research and reflexivity. As an underpinning to the various aspects of spectatorship, listening/viewing, following, looking, visiting, reception, and audiencing in participatory visual studies, we consider the cross-cutting role of reflexivity, particularly in relation to the participants, audiences, and researchers. Most of the scholarship in the field of participatory visual research emphasizes the need for reflexivity on the part of the researchers, if indeed we are concerned about democratizing the research space so as to optimize participant engagement throughout the process. However, less is written about maximizing researcher, participant, and audience reflexivity, an element we view as key in ensuring that the work involves the full participation of all stakeholders and promotes continuous dialogue and reflection for social change. Thus, we take as our entry point the notion that using such methods as participatory video, cellphilms, digital story-telling, and photovoice, enables researcher and participant reflexivity, geared towards confronting 'existing power dynamics prior to the initiation of research and encouraging the constant questioning and re-evaluating of the ways in which a more equitable balance of power can be achieved' (Darroch & Giles, 2014, p. 30). Participatory visual research encourages 'reflexivity on the part of the participants to learn about their own [lives, as well as] a more reflexive understanding of research practices' on the part of researchers (Whiting, Symon, Roby, & Chamakiotis, 2016, p. 19).

Specifically, the questions that inform reflexivity in participatory visual research include those that guide the producer: What am I trying to do? What do I want to say and to whom? What will move this audience to questions that guide the viewer/audience? What is it about these images and captions that are so provocative? What do I take away from this screening or exhibition? Sometimes, as we highlight in many of the chapters in this book, we as researchers might plant some of these questions as we see in speaking back activities, for example, but ultimately it is up to the producers and viewers to engage with the questions. Often, as researchers we are one of the first audiences alongside the participants to produce, watch, and respond to cellphilms, photos, and digital stories. As Alexandra (2015, p. 45) observes, often the questions about a story revolve around the question: 'Is it okay to tell this story?' and as facilitators or researchers we may advertently or inadvertently play a role in determining which stories get told.

To illustrate, almost a decade ago the three of us were involved in a series of participatory video workshops with young people in rural schools in South Africa. What was remarkable about the workshops, as we have explored elsewhere, is that almost all the young people, working in small groups, independently chose to produce videos about some aspect of sexual violence. One group of boys decided that they needed the participation of a girl from one of the other groups so that they could film a gang rape scene. As a team involved in facilitating, researching, and making sure that all the equipment would work for screening the videos as soon as each group finished, it was only when it was time to screen the video at the end of the day that we saw what had been produced. The girl is depicted lying down on a large sheet of paper on the cement floor of the classroom. One by one each boy in the group makes the motions of raping the girl, but unlike other groups who chose to have a rape scene take place behind closed doors, this group films the work graphically. Nothing is left to the imagination of the audience.

At this point, several questions confronted us as researchers. We have written about the scene, and we have discussed the scene many times among ourselves. The questions that concerned us included: Do we interact with the girl? Do we find out if she is okay? How might we have reflexively addressed these issues? One approach would be to re-consider Linda Finlay's (2002) framework for reflexivity in research, published in an essay, titled, *Negotiating the Swamp: The Opportunity and Challenge of Reflexivity in Research Practice* (see also Pillow, 2002). First, as researchers we engaged in what Finlay (2002) referred to as 'reflexivity as introspection', which involves 'self-dialogue and discovery' and our 'own reflecting, intuiting and thinking [were] used as primary evidence' (p. 213). Beyond this, we screened the video on occasion to talk about some of the risks and ethical considerations in participatory visual research. But one question continued to bother us: Could we talk about ethical issues and risk without ever screening this particular video?

Thus, going back to Rose's (2001) notion of researcher reflexivity which 'considers your own ways of looking at images' (p. 16) and watching participatory videos and digital stories, we recognize that we are seldom in the position of looking at images in participatory visual projects without being in a particularized and highly contextualized position of audience. As Sultana (2007) argues, if we are to conduct ethical research, as participatory visual scholars we must pay particular attention to our own and our participants' positionality, as well as to 'reflexivity, the production of knowledge and the power relations that are inherent in research processes' (p. 382). According to her, informed by an understanding that positionality and subjectivity change with changing time and space, such a process of reflection has to be continuous throughout the research process and beyond and has to involve both the researchers and the participants. However, we do not uncritically claim that to acknowledge 'positionality, reflexivity, identity, and representation [will] necessarily result in politically engaged research and writing, or in destabilizing existing power relations...' (Sultana, 2007, p. 383). Instead, we believe that if we engage in a continuous process of reflexivity, negotiated and re-negotiated with our participants, ethical relations within the research context are enhanced and the research process itself is democratized.

Second, if, indeed, we were co-constructing knowledge with the participants, including the producers of this video (as participatory visual research demands), what was their role in deciding what stories could be made public and therefore, which videos could audiences outside the research setting see? What was our responsibility in engaging in what Finlay (2002) called 'reflexivity as intersubjective reflection' in which we might 'explore the mutual meanings emerging within the research relationship' (p. 215), for example, with the producers of the video and other participants? In particular, informed by the work of Sartre (1969), Finlay cautions us that this form of reflexivity goes beyond reflection and instead, 'radical self-reflective consciousness is sought where the self-in-relation-to-others becomes both the aim and object of focus' (p. 216).

Third, linked to the notion of participants in participatory visual research as co-researchers and therefore as capable of reflexivity, like Finlay, we might then engage in reflexivity as mutual collaboration, involving participants in continuous dialogue about their productions, from planning, creating and speaking back to their videos. Fourth, in most of the literature, reflexivity is seen as a tool for acknowledging and indeed confronting the unequal power imbalances between researchers and participants, and to some extent, between participants and external audiences such as policy makers. Finlay suggests that this form of reflexivity functions as social critique, where unequal power relations concerning such identity markers as social class, gender, and race and others, can be acknowledged, confronted, and addressed throughout the research process. For example, what role does our positionality as middle-class university professors doing research with young people in a poor rural community play in influencing the research process and the content of what is produced in the form of videos such as the one described above? How might we take the reflexivity and dialogue to the community and to policy makers?

Community Engagement

Emerging from the interaction among the three elements discussed above – audience engagement, political listening, and reflexivity – is community engagement and dialogue which enhance opportunities for social change. The term community engagement might conjure up heart-warming images of community elders sitting in a circle pondering the concerns of a group of earnest children who have just produced a photo exhibition about some aspect of social change, or a group of citizens taking action to clean a polluted pond. The reality may be quite different with angry protesters on a picket line or blocking a highway. Social change rarely comes without a struggle and without someone giving up something, re-allocating resources or ceding power. There are few participatory visual projects that we can think of that do not link directly or indirectly to social injustices, and while not all may appear, at least on the surface, to be life-and-death situations, they are inevitably about changing something in the lives of individuals and groups in communities. Few participatory visual studies deal with issues that are supposedly solved simply by carrying out a photovoice project or having a group of people make a video. Rather, they call for buy-in, mobilization, and all the various activities and strategies that might lead to change, and through various community members – the school community, health-care personnel, the municipality or town council. For some researchers working in the area of engagement, this work is about resistance, and we see, for example, in the work of Tuck and Yang (2014a), the significance of youth resistance research and theories of change. For others it is about 'learning from the ground up' (Choudry & Kapoor, 2010, p. 1) with the idea that knowledge-production at a grassroots level is at the centre of change.

Linked to the fact that most of our work focuses on participatory visual research, which privileges the meaningful participation of community members most affected by the phenomenon under study, it is important for us to consider the significance of community-based participatory research (CBPR) in this work. In a scoping study focusing on ethical issues in community-based participatory research, the Durham Community Research Team (2011) defines CBPR first in terms of community-based research which refers to investigations that focus on 'issues relevant to people belonging to, or with interests in, a community of place, interest or identity...' (p. 4). Thus CBPR involves researchers and the community (largely through the participants) most affected by the phenomenon being studied as partners in the research process, often with a focus on identifying and/or developing strategies for change (Horowitz, Robinson, & Seifer, 2009). This way, the community has ownership, in relation to identifying the research issue, developing the research approach, and co-constructing knowledge, usually with researchers from outside the community (Durham Community Research Team, 2011). We see participatory visual research methods, including photovoice, drawing, participatory video, cellphilms, and digital story-telling as key to putting CBPR into action.

While CBPR is often regarded by many as inherently 'ethically good' compared to 'traditional' research, like any research, it is prone to the influence of unequal power relations, particularly resulting in 'ethical challenges relating to developing/maintaining partnerships, difficulties in maintaining anonymity and blurred boundaries between researcher and researched (e.g. community researchers researching their own communities)' (Durham Community Research Team, 2011, p. 6). For example, what would it mean, ethically, for the young people who produced the rape video described above to screen it at their school or to their community, including their parents and other adult community members? How would they (and us) respond to the likely negative responses of the various audiences to the production?

OVERVIEW OF THE BOOK

This book is concerned with the role of participatory visual research in deepening our understanding of social issues, as well as in facilitating community and policy dialogue around the issues and possible strategies for social change. Our aim is to provide both theoretical and practice-based work that offers researchers and practitioners ways of seeing how the very compelling data coming out of participatory visual research can influence social change (new conversations and dialogue, altered perspectives of participants to take action, policy debates, and actual policy development). The book frames social change within the use of participatory visual methodologies such as photovoice, participatory video, and digital story-telling in relation to such policy areas as gender violence, safety and security in housing, food security, gender and agriculture, water and sanitation, environmental issues, teacher education, bullying, and HIV and AIDS.

Chapter 1 has provided a context for the focus of the book, both in relation to the historical and the political, and as such will be a useful reference point for scholars working in the area of participatory visual research who want to understand fully the question 'Why participation in relation to social change?' It builds on Luc Pauwels' (2002) observation that visual research has the potential to draw more effectively on the use of the visual *at all levels* of the research, from research design through to the research process and communication. The chapter offers a framework for going 'beyond engagement' to include community and policy dialogue, in the context of research that seeks to contribute to social change. Within this context, the chapter explores the notion of critical community engagement and dialogue, and political listening as key elements of participatory visual research for social change.

Chapter 2 sub-titled *Beginning with the End in Mind*, focuses on what participatory visual research design might look like when right from the beginning the aim is not only to understand the issues, but is also about influencing social change. What would happen if our decision-making as researchers is informed by a concern not only for community participation in the research itself, but also for how that research might be used to engage the community, and beyond it, the policy makers in dialogue? The chapter explores the features of the various participatory visual methods, including drawing, photovoice, participatory video, and digital story-telling, and how each might be used to engage communities and policy makers in dialogue towards social change. In the chapter we offer a case study based on our work over a three-year period with a group of young women on a South African university campus who are addressing sexual violence.

At the heart of the book are tools and strategies for engaging participants as audiences, along with various community members. Chapter 3 asks how visual researchers might provide opportunities for research participants to engage in speaking back to, or critiquing their own productions (including photographs, participatory videos, cellphilms, digital stories. Even though many visual researchers would probably say reflection is an inherent feature of the various methods and their resultant productions it is in the process of working with the productions 'over and over' that we have found that participants get the opportunity to critique and revise their productions.

Chapter 4, *Pictures at an Exhibition: Taking Visual Images into Public Setting* focuses on the politics of and procedures for mounting exhibitions, using photovoice and other visual methods to illustrate how these kinds of productions can be made public and reach different audiences in a variety of community and policy contexts through exhibitions. We are interested in how exhibitions offer opportunities for learning, including deepening the audiences' understanding of the issues, as well as of potential strategies for addressing them. The chapter explores questions such as: What are the ethical issues in relation to the question 'who should see this exhibition'? What are some examples of how audiences have engaged with the visual material and what have been the policy outcomes?

Chapter 5, *On the Pedagogy of Screenings* responds most directly to work with participatory video (including cellphilms) and digital story-telling. Building on work in media studies, communication, participatory visual research and edutainment, the chapter takes what often appears to be the simple act of screening a video before a live audience into the realm of the pedagogy of celebration and the pedagogy of discomfort. It seeks to explore the ways in which the design, implementation, and follow-up to a screening can be its own form of participatory community dialogue.

Chapter 6 focuses on the creation and use of visual artefacts to build stakeholders' (including participants and community members) understanding of the issues, as well as to stimulate dialogue that seeks solutions to the identified issues. The chapter highlights and contributes to the emerging body of literature and practices that makes the production process (and not just the actual production) and the screening of such productions the focus. At the heart of the chapter is a consideration of the development and use of various 'digital dialogue tools' as we term them, short digital productions (combining sound and image) that draw together and organize visual data for the purposes of engaging participants and various audiences (communities, policy makers).

Chapter 7, *Engaging Policy Makers* explores the various approaches participatory visual researchers have used to engage policy makers. Often, policy-making and the role of policy makers as audiences of research are left to the end and even then, their role is reduced to some fleeting musings about what they might learn from the research. The chapter addresses questions of what impact our participatory visual research might have on policy dialogue, what policy it might lead to, and which policy makers it should target.

In the final chapter, *What Difference Does this Make?* we draw on a variety of approaches to addressing change. How might we frame our work within theories of change, but also what kinds of tools might we use to document change? We conclude the book with a consideration of interpretative and ethnographic approaches.

Taken as a whole, the book will be, we hope, a useful resource to the broad community of researchers interested in participatory visual research, working across such areas as Education, Sociology, Social Work, and Public Health. At the same time, the book is also meant to frame what we see as a next step (for our own research and the work of others) in advancing the study of participatory visual research in relation to Critical Audience Engagement.

KEY POINTS OF THE CHAPTER

- It is critical to consider the significance and methods for exploring the question of what difference participatory research makes.
- Policy and community dialogue are important in thinking about impact.
- Audience research offers an important link to deepening an understanding of community and policy dialogue.
- It is useful to have a framework for studying Critical Audience Engagement in participatory visual research.
- Political listening offers a new angle on working with communities and policy makers.
- A strength of participatory visual methodologies is their support for reflexivity of (producers, audiences and researchers).

2

PROJECT DESIGN: BEGINNING WITH THE END IN MIND

━ CHAPTER CONTENTS ━━━━━━━━━━━━━━━━━━━━━━━━━━

INTRODUCTION

In 1942, T. S. Eliot, in *Little Gidding* drew attention to the significance of our understanding the end before we begin. We see this, in our work, as needing to be aware of the impact and results of reaching audiences in contributing to community and policy dialogue, but to which audiences, and which dialogues, and which results do we refer? In a global context in which social injustices abound, social science researchers are not lacking problems that need to be researched. Understanding an issue is clearly necessary, but how might the research process have an impact on society? Is it not the social scientist's responsibility to 'not just...examine the social reality of the country, but to try to remedy the grave injustices' that they expose (Gott, 2008, para. 2)? Should social science research not be about making a difference (Flyvbjerg, 2001; Schratz & Walker, 1995)? Should social science researchers not be research activists contributing to change (De Lange, 2012; Hale, 2001)? While this might be disputed by some, we have, over the years, tried out participatory visual methodologies in various contexts to explore and simultaneously address a variety of issues. Numerous authors have hailed the value of participatory visual research in making a difference in the lives of the participants and communities, yet others have cautioned against the exuberant tone said to be used in describing the difference participatory visual research is said to make (see Low et al., 2012; Milne, Mitchell, & De Lange, 2012). In spite of this warning against exuberance, we think that participatory visual research holds potential to bring about change. We draw on Caroline Wang's (1999) ground-breaking work with rural women farm workers whose visual productions were used to engage policy makers. She seemed to have started with the end in mind: to generate a collection of photographs – produced by the women themselves – to be used to engage and persuade policy makers to improve and change the women's working conditions.

But how does this sort of change happen? We acknowledge that sometimes change is entirely serendipitous; someone is somewhere just at the right time, but we do see that research that starts with the end in mind – the kinds of dialogues that need to take place – is critical. While this chapter is not meant to be an exhaustive study of research design, what it does set out to do is offer a sense of what design in participatory visual research might look like when community and policy dialogue are key features of the work. We begin by considering how research for social change can be designed. We then look at four commonly used methods in participatory visual research: drawing; photovoice; participatory video; and digital story-telling. While each is a separate and unique method, they have common features such as participation, the use of the visual, the creation of a product, digital production, and the potential for widespread dissemination through exhibitions and screenings. We therefore highlight the ways in which thinking through the process of doing, the nature of the final productions (drawings, videos, photo exhibitions, digital stories) as well as who will make up the various audiences are all crucial to having the end in mind before we begin. Finally, as a way to contextualize this work – particularly because community and policy dialogue is typically about a particular community and a particular policy framework – we then go on to include a case study of a project in South Africa that addresses sexual violence on a university campus.

RESEARCH DESIGN FOR SOCIAL CHANGE

Essential to any qualitative research project is a rigorous design which fits the identified research problem and the research questions formulated about the problem. Given our 'from the ground up' approach to effecting social change, we have found Reed's (2007) *Appreciative Inquiry: Research for Change,* useful in informing our research design. While focusing on inclusivity and researching in a collaborative way to generate and analyse data with participants and drawing on their strengths, it also demands an understanding of power before, during, and after the research, as well as the importance of voice, audience, and dissemination. Reed's work however, points to the importance of the principle of 'simultaneity' (p. 26) that drives research such as ours which is simultaneously empirical and theoretical, and that also has a built-in, as it were, orientation towards intervention. The qualitative participatory visual research then works as research-as-intervention or research-as-social-change located in a critical paradigm and focused on addressing a social problem or 'identifying and transforming socially unjust social structures, policies, beliefs and practices' according to Taylor and Medina (2013, p. 6). Donna Mertens (2009) sees such work as located in what she aptly refers to as a transformative paradigm.

Several approaches such as participatory action research (Hughes & Seymour-Rolls, 2000), community-based participatory research (O'Fallon, Tyson, & Dearry, 2000) and participatory visual methodology (Mitchell, 2008) all fit coherently within a critical and transformative paradigm. We have argued elsewhere that when we are working with marginalized communities or with sensitive topics, a participatory visual methodology is more suitable since it allows ease in participants' expressing ideas around an issue that is difficult to articulate or that falls into the area of subjects that are deemed inappropriate for discussion. In several chapters of this book we also show how the visual data is used with the participants, in the community, and with other stakeholders such as policy makers, to leverage action towards bringing about social change. While this idea is developed more in the area of research in health and well-being than in the social sciences, as D'Amico et al. (2016) point out, it is a useful framework in which to discuss design. As Haalboom, Robinson, Elliott, Cameron, and Eyles (2006) note, 'Research as intervention entails purposefully using aspects of a research process and results feedback to contribute to desired changes in knowledge and practice of research participants and stakeholders' (p. 292). This kind of research is not just a data-gathering activity. D'Amico et al. (2016) focus on the ways in which arts-based research that draws on the visual is particularly appropriate as intervention. For Barndt (2009), 'The researcher/artist may structure processes to engage participants in creative inquiry, but if the process is to draw on the knowledge, skills and visions of community members, there must be space for this [research-as-intervention] to happen' (p. 360). In this context 'research using the arts can facilitate change while at the same time provide evidence of such changes' (D'Amico et al., 2016, p. 360).

Who might the initiator(s) of social change be? And how might researchers participate in enabling engagement which could contribute to layers of positive social change? Participatory research is a critical methodology in relation to social change in that it extends the range of who participates in the process of knowledge production, and, perhaps most importantly, it draws in marginalized voices along with new voices. To achieve this we have often relied on using more than one visual method in a project and thus ensuring the generation of rich data from many voices to enable crystallization – or internal validity – as Merriam (1998) puts it. While the co-produced knowledge is critical to the context in which social injustices occur, the knowledge produced needs to be shared widely not only to enable social action, but also to promote critical consciousness, and overcome internalized oppression (Gaventa & Cornwall, 2001), and oppressive systems. The knowledge produced can then be disseminated and used to direct social change. As Knowles and Cole (2008) argue, participatory visual methodologies position participants not only as knowledge producers, but also as key to spreading the knowledge to a wider audience.

Potential for Sustainability

As we have pointed out above, social science research can contribute to knowledge that recognizes unjust social structures in society and, therefore, to social change (Gaventa & Cornwall, 2001; Mertens, 2009; Mitchell, 2006a; Schratz & Walker, 1995). We acknowledge that the contexts in which social science research is done in itself exert a powerful influence on the potential for change. However, the participants in the research are enabled to push back and to position themselves not as victims, but as able to take action, even if it is in small ways. The potential for social change is thus in the hands of the research participants and their community since they have the necessary strengths and resources, and in the researchers establishing a relationship of trust to deepen their engagement in the community so as to carry out research alongside its members. We have found that the use of participatory visual methods, with its potential to enable engagement, reflection, and taking action 'ensures a sense of ownership and enhances the potential for sustainability once the research team withdraws at the end of the project' (De Lange & Combrinck, 2011, p. 236). We are interested in what happens when we're gone (Mitchell & De Lange, 2011). We have considered whether a project we started together would continue, whether the participants changed their understanding of the social issues we addressed together, and whether such change in understanding would enable them to do things differently in their own lives and in that of their community. We were also interested in what we could (or should) leave behind when we left the field. For example, in our participatory visual work with a rural community that generated a collection of videos about issues that affect their lives and what they envisaged doing about these issues, we, the researchers, created a composite video of their videos, to be left in the community when we left, and which could be used to sustain the momentum of change (Mitchell & De Lange, 2011).

Gubrium and Harper (2013) refer to an early example of a participatory visual research of Paulo Freire in which he used photography in a literacy project to ask the participants (street children) to say what they thought exploitation is. They had to respond by taking photographs of how they saw their own exploitation. The photographs revealed examples of institutional exploitation and this enabled them to talk about ways they deemed suitable to addressing the exploitation. In participatory visual research such as this, a space is created for 'empowerment, engagement, ownership, and agency', as Mitchell et al. (2011, p. 22) point out, which could linger in the lives of the participants as an afterlife to the research.

PARTICIPATORY VISUAL METHODS

There are numerous participatory visual research methods that can be used with participants in their local contexts to co-construct knowledge for social change, ranging from digital platforms to photovoice, and from digital story-telling and participatory video to what might be regarded as low-tech approaches (body mapping and, sometimes, drawing). As the themed issue of *Global Public Health* on participatory visual methods highlights, this is a dynamic area as a result of new technologies such as GIS (Geographic Information System) mapping and the design of new apps, but it is also dynamic in the sense that methods and tools that have been used in one context have been adapted for use with other populations or in other social contexts (Mitchell & Sommer, 2016). When we found ourselves in a research context in our work with girls with disabilities in Vietnam, for example, it was an on-the-spot decision for us to combine photovoice and drawing so that the girls could produce policy posters. As we explore in Chapter 7, they very clearly had an audience in mind since they had just met with a group of policy makers at a forum, and there was high motivation to create something meaningful and concrete (Nguyen, Mitchell, De Lange, & Fritsch, 2015).

These participatory approaches serve to move towards making research democratic and also to move away from the idea that research is for a 'highly selected group of specialists' (Schratz & Walker, 1995, p. 14). As Reavey and Johnson (2012) observe, participatory visual methods 'hand over agency to the participants rather than requiring them to answer researcher-defined questions' (p. 174). They also work as a 'springboard for more talking, listening and reflecting' (Clark & Moss, 2011, p. 8). Van der Riet and Boettiger (2009) point to this shift in research dynamics in participatory research, highlighting that by addressing the issue of power in such research, the participants' participation is increased; multiple knowledges from the research context are voiced. This enables participants who are implicated but often marginalized to address their own problems, express their knowledge, reflect on their knowledge, and offer an analysis of how to contribute to taking action and bringing about change. The purpose of such work is 'not to tell truths about the world but to open up spaces that allow us all to think about how our worlds may be changed' (Cotton, 2007, p. 41). As Wallerstein and Duran (2008) highlight, participatory research is not a simple linear process, so it is important for participants and researchers to engage with the knowledge in reflexive ways to develop their understanding and learning.

Reflexivity is a defining feature of participatory research and should thus be a constant part of the researcher's work (Holliday, 2007; Pillow, 2002) in making transparent the research processes and the epistemological stances (Ruby, 2000). In participatory visual work reflexivity is also central to participants; they should be enabled to be reflexive about their own lived experiences, as Pink (2001) suggests. Yang argues that 'researchers have come to acknowledge the intricate relationship between researcher and researched, and [should] critically reflect on the methods they choose, the roles they play, and the power relationships they create in research settings.' (Yang, 2012, p. 100).

We go on, now, to describe briefly the basics of four participatory visual methods that we explore further throughout the book. By referring to basics we are not implying that using such methods are without challenges and so we point them out as we go along (see also Buckingham, 2009; Guillemin & Drew, 2010).

Drawing

Claudia, with the research team in Nairobi, Kenya (Mitchell, Chege, Maina & Rothman, 2016), started with the end in mind, wanting to engage with the housing policy makers and getting them to see the conditions the children were living in and for them to improve the safety and security of the children in the Nairobi slum areas. Drawing was seen as an appropriate method for working with the young children and the drawings were intended to be included in the digital production to be shown to the policy makers (see Chapters 6 and 7).

Drawing, whether done with pen and paper, or digitally using software and a computer, is a simple method of data generation that has been used across a wide range of social research areas. Theron, Mitchell, Smith, and Stuart (2011) in their edited book, *Picturing Research, Drawing as Visual Methodology*, frame the use of drawing as a participatory method for use with children, youth, and adults particularly in contexts in which partic- ipants have difficulty expressing themselves in language, or because of the nature of the topics under discussion. While adult participants and even young people past a certain age may often feel daunted by the idea of drawing because they think that an aesthetically pleasing masterpiece is required, it is in the process of drawing that their thoughts might become crystallized and clarified so that they produce an artefact that can be drawn on to ease them into a discussion of their viewpoint. Drawing as a method can facilitate the expression of and engagement with one's own ideas and understandings of the issue under study, and can also enable engagement with each other's work thus leading to

Figure 2.1 Drawing, depicting safe and unsafe spaces in Nairobi slum areas

Drawing from *More than Bricks and Mortar: Housing, the way children see it*

improved mutual understanding. The simplicity of expressing ideas through drawing and generating something tangible as findings not only gives the participants immediate access to these ideas but also helps them to think about taking action and thus acquire and/or exercise agency which leads to giving them a sense of empowerment.

MacEntee and Mitchell (2011) address the thorny issue of analysis, pointing out how the drawings might be analysed, first by the participants through their writing captions and explaining their own drawings, but also collectively and in a participatory way in collaboration with the researcher. This allays the fears of the researcher community of subjective analyses during which the researcher reads into the drawings what she wants to see, as Theron points out (Mitchell, Theron, Smith, & Stuart, 2011). Using drawings in publications, toolkits (Khan, 2015) and also in various forms of dissemination such as exhibitions and catalogues and videos (Mitchell, Chege, Maina, & Rothman, 2016) to engage relevant audiences is extremely valuable in, for example, reaching stakeholders and policy makers as can be seen in our work with children (see Figure 2.1) in slum areas in Nairobi, Kenya (Chege, Maina, Mitchell, & Rothman, 2014).

Photovoice

We worked together on our first research project, *Learning Together*, in South Africa, in a rural community ravaged by the HIV and AIDS epidemic. While in this project we wanted to understand how people in the community were affected by the epidemic in a time when

Figure 2.2   Photograph, showing an exhibition in the *Learning Together* project

Photograph taken by Naydene de Lange

HIV-related stigma prevented people in the community from disclosing their status and accessing treatment, we also wanted to contribute to opening up a space for the community to openly talk about HIV and AIDS. We understood that interviewing the participants on such a sensitive topic might not be easy, and knowing that working with the visual eases expression of difficult and sensitive issues, and that if we could work around the ethics of the visual, the participants might generate photographs, from their perspectives, which could be displayed in strategic places in the community, such as in the community health clinic and schools, and so open up spaces for talking (Mitchell & De Lange, 2008). With this in mind we set out to generate photovoice data, as we explain here, which might be used in an exhibition in the community (see Figure 2.2).

Photovoice, putting cameras in the hands of marginalized groups and working with the photographs in various ways, requires participants, for example, to access meanings that they attach to situations of injustice and to explore whether and how these social conditions could be changed. Caroline Wang (1999) coined the term photovoice. She worked with Chinese peasant women who toiled in rice paddies and asked them to take photographs of their unsatisfactory working conditions. These were then shown to policy makers who had the power to improve their working conditions. In this example, photovoice created a democratic space in which these women could tell their stories, and, by having them framed in terms of human rights, be given power. Lykes and Crosby's (2013) work, like Wang's, situates photovoice work in the feminist tradition. De Lange, Mitchell, and Stuart (2007) in *Putting People in the Picture, Visual Methodologies for Social Change*, draw together examples of how photovoice has been used with various groups of participants and in different contexts in South Africa to engage communities about conditions that require change. As we have already said, it is often difficult issues that need to be addressed and in our photovoice work with girls and young women in Vietnam, for example (Mitchell, De Lange, & Nguyen, 2016) we could see that taking photos made it less difficult for them to talk about the sensitive issue of being excluded (see also Aldridge, 2007). As Coffey, Budgeon, and Cahill (2016, p. 15) put it, we, too, were impressed by the 'performative, playful, staged and situated nature of the photos'.

Photovoice involves the use of any type of camera (disposable, point-and-shoot, digital, cellphone) available to the researcher and participants.[1] While there is not any orthodoxy to photovoice, participants typically work with a prompt like, for an example, 'Take photographs of challenges and solutions to addressing HIV and AIDS in your community.' Once the technicalities of the camera or device and how to take photographs have been explained, the participants work individually or in groups to take a small collection of photographs in response to the prompt. It is necessary that the participants understand visual ethics; they must make sure not to take photographs of people without their permission, or take photographs of themselves which might compromise them in some way, or take photographs that show faces, and so on (see Mitchell, 2011). When the photographs have been printed, the participants typically write captions and also explain what they intended to show in their photos (see Figure 2.3), and this is then followed by a discussion. This serves as a participatory analysis and prevents the researcher from imposing her own interpretation on the images. Dissemination could take the form of exhibiting the collection of images in the community and to policymakers.

Participatory Video (and Cellphilming)

In our early participatory video work in the *Learning Together* project in a rural community in South Africa, we wanted to further understand the challenges in the community in the context of HIV and AIDS, through the making of participatory videos. We soon realized that if we set out with the idea of screening the videos in different community contexts, we needed to ensure that what was being shown did most good and least harm, and so we

---

[1]We note that the practices of finding photographs, often on the internet, is also sometimes regarded as a type of photovoice, and indeed in one of the projects that we refer to in Chapters 4 and 7, many of the participants found photographs on the internet as representative of what they saw as change, rather than taking photographs with a camera themselves. The participants did create their own captions and these eventually led to discussions about change so in some respects this could be regarded as photovoice. Most researchers, however, follow the practice of participants actually producing photographs.

Figure 2.3   Photo poster, created by teachers to depict the challenges in the context of HIV and AIDS

Photograph taken by Naydene de Lange

set out with the end in mind, to generate participatory videos (and later cellphilms) which could be used in the community to enable discussion about addressing HIV and AIDS (Moletsane, Mitchell, De Lange, Stuart, Buthelezi, & Taylor, 2009).

Participatory video (and cellphilming), a method for working with communities has been used to explore issues troubling them. This approach allows participants to engage with an issue/topic through collaboratively planning, filming, and, sometimes, showing the video. This process includes generating solutions to the issues, as Choudry and Kapoor (2010) put it, in learning from the ground up. The criticism that the research team arrives with the video cameras and, when they leave they take the equipment back with them thus rendering the community unable to continue similar work, falls away given the ubiquity of cellphones with good video camera functions. Dockney and Tomaselli (2009) coined the term cellphilm to denote a film made with a cellphone. This has changed the dynamic of our participatory video work. This resolved the access to equipment dilemma that we describe elsewhere (Milne, Mitchell, & De Lange, 2012). As we point out in the *Handbook of Participatory Video*, while participatory video 'often aims to reveal hidden social relations and provoke collective action' (p. 1) it enables a deeper engagement with communities and allows and promotes agency while also offering opportunity for reflexivity on the lived experiences and how these might be changed. In this regard Milne et al. (2012) point out the value of participatory video in terms of creating high-impact materials and its usefulness in contributing to policy outcomes. Participatory video is also central in getting the point across to as many people as possible in a way that is real, local, and, therefore, relevant to the community.

The video-making process like photovoice, typically involves lead-in time, engaging the participants with the purpose of the work (Mitchell & De Lange, 2011). Operating in a participatory frame we ask the participants to work in groups and to brainstorm all the issues or challenges in their community and then to vote on these to pinpoint the most pressing one. We then facilitate a discussion on whether the topic is the most pressing and whether it could become the subject of a video. The groups then plan out and create a storyboard and film the story. Before filming, we provide, if video cameras are being used, a brief overview of how they work. No particular genre of getting the point across is stipulated, but we have found in our work in South Africa that many participants draw on performance and melodrama to stage their story. We have used a No-Editing-Required (NER) process: the shots are filmed one by one, by the participants pausing the camera, and then continuing to film the next shot. This means that the video is filmed right there and then and that the participants can view their video immediately after the filming (see Figure 2.4).

With the advent of our use of cellphones, we have followed the same process as we did with video cameras, and have found that the participants often spontaneously use a one-shot-shoot (OSS) (Mitchell, De Lange, & Moletsane, 2016) process, filming all the planned

Figure 2.4 Participatory video, *Poverty*, showing teachers working in a vegetable garden at school
Screenshot of *Poverty*, a video made by teachers in the Learning Together project
Learning Together (Producer).(2006). *Poverty* [Participatory Video]. Durban: University KwaZulu-Natal.

shots on the storyboard as one shot, without pausing the filming. This filming without editing immediately provides further opportunity for discussion and reflection on the issues being captured. Such participatory videos or cellphilms made by the community, in the community, and for the community are materials for getting the ideas across in a visceral way to the broader community, other communities, and the policy makers. As we highlight in Chapter 5, the screening of the videos or cellphilms is key to getting the message across (MacEntee, Burkholder & Schwab-Cartas, 2016; MacEntee & Mandrona, 2015; Mitchell, 2015b).

Digital Story-telling

A digital story-telling project, *Taking Action* II with 18 Indigenous young people from various regions of Canada began with the idea that each of these participants would be involved in a week-long digital story-telling workshop in Toronto, and would then go back to their communities as youth leaders to screen their productions related to HIV prevention activism (Flicker et al., in press). In such a 'beginning with the end' approach, the messages produced by the participants highlighted much more of the themes that youth themselves saw as critical (addressing Indigeneity and decolonization) as opposed to conventional public health messaging focusing on individual harm reduction strategies.

Digital story-telling, in similar ways to research methods such as drawing, photovoice, and participatory video, also enables participants to reflect back and to look forward to how things might change. Gubrium (2009), who uses digital story-telling in health promotion research, describes digital stories as '3- to 5-min visual narratives that synthesize images, video, audio recordings of voice and music, and text to create compelling accounts of experience.' (p. 186) (see Figure 2.5). The power of these short digital stories in making hidden stories heard, and then acted upon and repurposed to inform social policy, should not be overlooked. In their *Participatory visual and digital methods,* Gubrium and Harper (2013) point out how the digitally produced stories can be used for advocacy purposes and to mobilize the community. Locating the use of digital story-telling in community-based participatory research, according to Gubrium (2009, p. 186), enables 'new knowledge to emerge that is mediated by Indigenous perspectives and returns this knowledge to communities as indigenously informed'.

As Gubrium highlights, the process of making digital stories entails having participants work in groups in story circles to tell their stories in a safe space. The stories might be about difficult issues, and, as with focus group discussions, the participants are required to keep the stories they hear confidential. Within the circles the participants listen to and do not interrupt each other but they are given the opportunity to make affirming comments and suggestions, keeping in mind that each story is owned by the participant. According to Lambert (2006) there are seven elements important to digital story-telling. These include point of view, dramatic question, emotional content, voice, soundtrack/music, economy, and pacing all of which have to be kept in mind when one is creating a digital story. The story is thus written and rewritten several times to ensure

I am a tortoise. I chose this animal because I wish I could just hide in the presence of people I know. I was born with HIV and I have recently started ARVs. It is hard for me to go to the clinic and get my ARVs because I always hear people - adults, even those with HIV - gossiping about me when I am in the clinic to get my treatment. They do not know that I was born with it [HIV]. They say *"izingane zishesha ziqale ucasi"* ["nowadays children have an early sex debut"] because they think I contracted it through sex. My friend's mother works in the same clinic and helps me with my needs such as the ARVs and the food that we get from the clinic. I always throw it [food] away in fear of bringing it to the school since I start at the clinic then to [go] school. The other students call me names and judge me because of my status. I fear carrying the food parcel because it is known that it is donated to the HIV-positive people. I need the food, this affects me at school. Even my school work has declined. My mother passed away two years ago and it has been hard for me as a teenager, growing with no one to talk to or no one who cares about me. I wish people can come to a better understanding about HIV and stop stigmatising so that I can feel accepted, especially [because I am orphaned] orphans. I chose a tortoise because I am trying to live with a purpose, but when someone offends me I crawl back into my dark, cold and lonely shell. After that I have to come out again and rebuild my character by trying to be optimistic ...

Figure 2.5   Digital story, *Tortoise's Story*

Tortoise's Story, a digital story made by one of Thoko's participants

Mnisi, T. (2014).

that it adheres to these elements and then it is turned into a digital story, using the voice of the owner of the story, and, sometimes, a selection of multimedia content. Gubrium (2009) argues that in the discussion of participants' stories, 'a unity of mission develops, forming a sense of collaborative accomplishment' (p. 186), which could be turned into taking action. She adds that the story circles can also offer a sense of healing to those who have experienced difficulties.

Cross-cutting Features of Participatory Visual Methods

These methods draw on the centrality of both the process and on the visual/artistic productions. Both imply the intense engagement of the participants, thus ensuring optimal participation, developing the understanding of the issue under study, and creating opportunities for taking the issue forward. We offer some cross-cutting features of using participatory visual methods that are particularly powerful in the context of community and policy dialogue.

Digital Production

First, the use of the visual opens up a variety of possibilities for exploration and digital production. While it is argued that the internet creates an egalitarian space, Schradie (2011) warns that a digital production gap remains that leaves the vast majority of people with little possibility for digital production. Using research methods that draw on digital production then can enable those on the other side of the digital divide to participate in production and to acquire new skills. Geldenhuys (2016), for example, explored rural school children's understanding of gender-based violence in their community by using digital drawing, a digital archive, and digital story-telling, all of which enabled them to participate as digital consumers and digital producers, through remixing content for use in engaging other school children in a dialogue about addressing gender-based violence. Although Schradie (2011, p. 145) suggests that 'elite voices still dominate in the new digital commons', participatory visual research methods seem to enable access for those who are most often marginalized, and whose voices are not heard, in particular in relation to policy-making. Through digital production, their collectively produced knowledge can be disseminated on digital platforms, thus enabling a wider reach of audience.

Participation and Co-production

A second point is that participation is seen to be key when we are using visual methods, making the co-production of knowledge possible. Power, however, is linked to participation and hence participation may vary at different stages of the research process (Van der Riet & Boetigger, 2009), depending on how power is shared. Ensuring meaningful participation is challenging. We refer to how several authors have conceptualized participation, and focus on the end they had in mind. While the end each one suggests is commendable, reaching it is no mean feat and is not without challenges, requiring the researchers and participants to negotiate relationships as well as the realities of contexts. In Arnstein's (1969) ladder of participation, for example, the highest level of participation is participant control; in Hart's (1992) ladder it is youth-initiated, shared decision-making with adults; in Pretty's (1995) ladder it is self-mobilization; in White's typology (1996) it is transformative participation; and in Treseder's (1997) it is child-initiated and directed participation. Getting participants to participate at these levels means that power shifts away from the researcher to the participants. Clearly, when there is meaningful participation at such level participant autonomy is enhanced, thus paving the way for sustainability of agency and social change.

Participant Use

It is important to recognize that the creation of a production enables the exploration of the issue under study but also leaves the research participants and community with the actual productions to return to, to reflect upon, and to use individually or collectively. As Flicker et al. (2014) highlight in their work with Indigenous youth in Canada, the productions are, in and of themselves artful. These productions include drawings, photographs and photo posters, participatory videos and cellphilms, and digital stories. The drawings could be low-tech paper and pencil/pen/charcoal/crayon individual productions or high-tech digital drawings, each with a caption created by the producer. In photovoice the products can be printed photographs with captions added by the participant or photo posters containing printed photographs and clarifying text. However, we have also found that some participants preferred to create PowerPoint slides with their images, so the materiality of images is not necessarily a given. The participatory videos made using a video camera or a cellphone could be short two-to-three-minute films made in groups, with title, subtitles, and credits. These short videos could be assembled into a composite video that draws together the participatory visual work done and that consists of contextualizing footage and the collection of short videos, ending with a section that raises further issues or asks the audience members to consider how they might contribute to resolving the issue (see Chapter 6). The digital story-telling process enables the production of short digital stories which could again be used to elicit dialogue.

Dissemination and Knowledge Mobilization

Finally, all these approaches offer the potential for widespread dissemination through exhibitions, catalogues, and screenings, extending the individual or group knowledge and learning to a wider audience. A particularly compelling feature that we build into both the training that we do on participatory visual research and in our work directly with participants is the idea of what we have come to call 'over and over and over again'.[2] While we sometimes refer to it lightly in relation to the refrain of the vintage 1960s pop song by the Dave Clark Five, 'Over and over and over again' we offer it as a serious point: a set of photographs or drawings, a set of cellphilms, participatory videos or digital stories have high currency for being exhibited or screened many times over.

Farrington, Bebbington, Wellard, and Lewis (1993) talk of narrow inclusion when the participatory research is undertaken with a small group of participants but we see that it could be extended to wide participation through screenings and exhibitions. For example, in our participatory research with a group of girls and young women with disabilities in Vietnam, they produced drawings of how they see themselves in their community. The collection of drawings with participant-produced captions were exhibited to an audience consisting of the participants themselves, community members, NGOs, and policy makers (De Lange, Nguyen & Nghiem, 2016) and engagement and comment was invited. A second example is the collaborative video production of Eberts and Cotton (2008), *Where the water*

---

[2]At a Higher Education AIDS Education Community of Practice training session we introduced the idea of using and showing the visual productions many times by chanting 'over and over again'.

meets the sky, made with a small group of rural women in a remote area of Zambia to explore gender violence and HIV and AIDS, but which was disseminated to the whole community with the women themselves presenting their video, engaging the community, and raising awareness of the issue with the goal of bringing about change.

Which Mode?

We are often asked questions about each of these modes of representation and whether they work similarly? Are there certain themes and issues that are best addressed through one mode versus another? In the broad area of visual representation these are of course broad questions that are also framed by the study of drawing, photography, and video production, each of which has its own bodies of literature and conventions. In some cases there will even be convergences as we see in the use of visual art in creating a drawing and the use of drawing in creating a storyboard as part of the participatory video process. Figure 2.6 is a drawing created by one of the children in a project on safety and security in an informal settlement in Kenya. Participants highlight the storying process represented in the drawing.

Figure 2.6 Drawing, depicting home as an unsafe space in Nairobi slum areas

Drawing from *More than Bricks and Mortar: Housing, the way children see it*

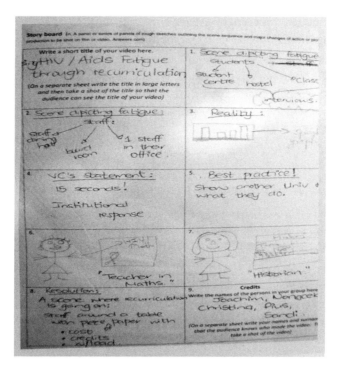

Figure 2.7 Storyboard, *Integrating the Disintegrated*, created by teacher educators

Storyboard created in the HIV and AIDS Education Community of Practice

HIV&AIDS Education Community of Practice (2011). *Using a different lens for HIV and AIDS Education*. Port Elizabeth: HIV and AIDS Education Research Chair, Nelson Mandela Metropolitan University.

Figure 2.7, a storyboard produced by a group of teacher educators in a workshop addressing HIV and AIDS similarly draws attention to the use of drawing and writing in mapping out the story. At the same time, when located within the area of participatory research the questions are perhaps more contained since, as we highlight above, it is the narratives of the producers and the emerging dialogue that is so critical.

While this is clearly an area that warrants further study, we can point to some work that has begun to explore these questions. Digital storytelling as applied to work in the area of identity is often carried out as an individual activity (see for example St John Ward, 2015), also in the area of HIV-related stigma (see for example Mnisi, 2014), although MacEntee (2016b) offers examples of how young people have worked in small groups to develop digital stories about HIV and AIDS and sexuality. Mitchell, Walsh, and Moletsane (2006) consider the ways in which gender violence might be taken up differently in projects involving young people, depending on whether the work involves drawing, photovoice or participatory video. Drawing is more likely to be an individual activity. Picture taking in photovoice can be either an individual activity or a group activity although typically, as we note above, the analysis is done by the groups. Participatory video, because it is typically done in small groups 'can create a strong collective response that includes both producers and viewers – although this could overshadow the individual' (p. 111). To examine further meaning-making through digital representations of gender violence, Weber and Mitchell (2007) offer an analysis of a video, *Rape*, produced by a group of secondary school boys in KwaZulu-Natal. In their analysis they detail the various ways that participatory video contributes to creating a collective response, highlighting the significance of such features as constructedness, collectivity, embodiment, and reflexivity and negotiation (see also De Lange, Olivier, & Wood, 2008).

Which Device? Which Technologies?

We would be remiss if we did not say something about technology given the focus on digital production in this chapter and in the rest of the book. When we first started doing participatory visual work using photovoice in 2003, the technology debate for us was primarily between using simple point-and-shoot self-loading cameras or single-use disposable cameras although we were also inspired by the more artistic focus that Wendy Ewald (2000) describes in *Secret Games: Collaborative Work with Children, 1969–1999* and her numerous other publications that highlight her work with children. As for using participatory video with communities in 2006, the main technology was some type of a camcorder, although again we have also been inspired by the work of Sadie Bening and her innovative use of a Fisher Price pixel camera she received as a gift when she was 16 from her father (Mitchell & Reid-Walsh, 2002). Although initially angered about receiving a child's camera, she turned its use into an artistic mode of expression. With the advent of digital cameras, especially those with a good video function, we of course found that it was possible to do photovoice and participatory video on a single device. Around 2010 thanks to the ubiquity of mobile phones, especially in our work in rural South Africa, the idea of the cellphilm emerged and the cellphone camera ensured that participatory visual research could easily be done. However, with the proliferation of tablets with similar functionality for video and photo production, the questions are now more related to cost, access, fashion, opportunities for dissemination through a variety of social media platforms, and the principle of building on the media making practices and technologies that already exist in a community. We highlight this point as a way to maximize local engagement and to minimize the control of the equipment primarily in the hands of researchers. New debates of course emerge: Is a digital production created on a tablet still called a cellphilm? Does the 'everdayness' of a particular technology or device minimize its significance? What is gained and what is lost through various technologies? What are the limitations? We have discovered for example that although everyone in a group might have a cellphone that is appropriate for cellphilm production, participants might not have enough memory left on their device to produce a film. Some adaptations also require more sophisticated knowledge than was required for making a simple N-E-R video using a camcorder or a 2010 entry-level cellphone, and require additional editing knowledge and skills unless the participants opt for a one-shot-shoot film. Time may also be a feature then, something that is particularly important in a workshop format where it is key that participants get to screen their productions during the session.

At the same time we have known participatory visual researchers to opt in 2017 for single-use disposable cameras as a way to 'liberate' the process or as one of our colleagues commented 'to capture the moment', something that is perhaps not that different from the popular practice of having disposable cameras available for guests at a wedding to capture the moment. As Mitchell McLarnon observed in relation to a project with Montreal youth:

We discussed how with cellphones and digital cameras, we were constantly looking for the perfect shot and spent more time editing shots and images and less time in the moment. We started with one camera to be shared amongst 5 participants but soon they each asked to have their own disposable camera so that they could concurrently document their home lives … . The project continued over the entire summer with some youth carrying the cameras around on shoestrings, snapping moments throughout the day and others taking photographs while they were partying. We eventually did digitize the photos to upload them to online platforms they engage with. Interestingly, one youth even scanned the printed copies to preserve the 'original graininess.' I call the disposable camera aesthetic 'the original Instragram filter'. (Mitchell McLarnon, personal communication, March 20, 2017)

We might think of this disposable camera aesthetic as aligning nicely with the work with Bening's Fisher Price aesthetic, or with the pin-hole camera, or even photobooth photography as a precursor to the selfie and perhaps the foundation of participant-led visual research. As Hines (2002) observed of photobooth photography; 'It doesn't matter whether you are in a train station, on a busy street, or in the middle of an amusement park … . What matters is that you are both photographer and subject. Alone in the booth, you forgo the behaviours and attitudes expected when a camera is forced upon you. You cannot be coaxed into position; you cannot be commandeered to smile … . In the photobooth picture, unlike any other portrait or photograph, truth and fiction easily commingle. In a photobooth we choose the moment and the way we represent ourselves. We choose the truth' (n.p.). As for polaroid aesthetics, very well-known photographers such as Robert Mapplethorpe and Andy Warhol used polaroids in the 1970s, and various artistic practices with polaroids continued until 2007. There is an emerging new interest in this earlier technology. Claudia worked with Super8 film in a participatory way with ninth graders in a small fishing village in Nova Scotia in the 1970s (see Mitchell, 2011). We however see a renewed interest in these earlier technologies and what the medium itself might portray. More than anything though, this discussion on choice of technology should be a reminder of the need for continuous reflection and re-assessment on the part of the research team in close consultation with community members and participants.

A CASE STUDY: ADDRESSING CAMPUS-BASED SEXUAL VIOLENCE

When other researchers ask questions about the design and findings of a participatory visual research project, we find that it is often difficult to actually answer the question 'How did you get here?' especially when one gives a 20-minute presentation at a conference. We so often want to show the cellphilm or photo exhibition, *and* talk about the participants, *and* talk about the policy context, *and* talk about all the dialogues *and* talk about how we came to be doing the work in the first place, *and* where the project is now. Projects sometimes go on for a long time, and, as we highlight in another publication, long after the research team leaves the field, or long after the original participants have left (De Lange & Mitchell, 2012b). Often there is not a clear beginning, middle, and end, especially if one works in the same community over a period of years while drawing on different funding sources. We even challenged ourselves to try to produce a visual essay of a project as a journal article as a way of addressing some of the challenges of representation (De Lange, Moletsane, & Mitchell, 2015). In order to show the beginning with the end in sight, we offer a case study of our work on addressing sexual violence on a university campus in South Africa, a problem that is becoming worldwide (Bennett, 2009; Phipps & Smith, 2012; Schaffer, 2016). The focus is on the use of participatory visual methodology to influence broader policy processes in relation to addressing sexual violence at a university.

Beginning at the Beginning

To situate the case study, we start first with the policy context. This does not have to be the first step in any study but it is an important area to consider early on and throughout the study. What are the participants seeking to change? What is it about the visual that is important? Who needs to hear or see what they have to say? In this case study the broad policy context is sexual violence, and the very specific policy context is campus-based sexual violence.

In South Africa violence affects every sphere of life (Dartnall & Gevers, 2015). It is a country with one of the highest rates of sexual assault in the world (Abrahams et al., 2009). Sexual violence within as well as outside sexual relationships requires being addressed continually (De Lange et al., 2015; Jewkes, 2010; Wood, Lambert, & Jewkes, 2007) because it has far-reaching public health and human rights implications. This broader context of sexual violence in South Africa provides the frame for understanding what is happening in the higher education sector since university campuses are no strangers to sexual and gendered violence (Phipps & Smith, 2012; Schaffer, 2016). Research, for example, points to coercive sexual practices and gender-based violence (Clowes, Shefer, Fouten, Vergnani, & Jacobs, 2009); to transactional sex (Shefer, Clowes, & Vergnani, 2012); as well as institutional violence (Dowler, Cuomo, & Laliberte, 2014) in South African universities. More recently the South African news media reported on the rape culture in place at some universities, the protest demonstrations by young women demanding proper investigations into cases of rape at universities (Mail & Guardian, 2016), as well as how university policies are set aside when it comes to reporting rape.

The Constitution of South Africa protects the rights of all South Africans, and commits the state to addressing discrimination and inequality, including gender-based violence, while Acts such as the Protection from Harassment Act 2010 (No. 17 of 2011) and the Criminal Law (sexual offences and related matters) Amendment Act 32 of 2007 focus specifically on gender-based violence. It is within this policy framework that universities are required to formulate their own sexual harassment policies to prevent gender-based violence and sexual violence on campus. While the university policies might be meaningful, they do not seem to be able to halt the gender injustices on campus. There are several reasons for this; relevant policy is not implemented; sexual violence is normalized; and ensuring gender equality at universities is not prioritized. Bennett (2009), in an article entitled, *Policies and sexual harassment in higher education: Two steps forward and three steps somewhere else* therefore argues that 'feminist activism in South Africa needs once more to theorize and challenge overt and covert forms of sexual violence facing higher education communities' (p. 7).

Positioning

Although we have engaged in participatory visual research in many different settings, the case study we discuss here is one that is particularly close to the work we do of conducting research and teaching in a university setting, and, at the same time, it reflects a key theme in much of the research we have carried out together in rural settings. We started thinking about the vulnerability of first-year women students entering the university, especially young women who come from rural areas, because of our work in such areas where sexual violence is already a huge problem (De Lange, Mitchell, & Bhana, 2012; Moletsane, Mitchell, & Lewin, 2015). We know of the challenges that young women often face just to graduate from high school and to get accepted into university. In some of the settings where we have worked, it has been hard, if not impossible, to reach policy makers, perhaps because we ourselves had to try to figure out who the policy makers might be. But we have been working in university settings for decades and we saw that we could bring to bear some of our insider knowledge on what from the ground up or grassroots policy-making could look like. From our previous experiences of using participatory visual methodology we also knew how powerful working with the visual could be – powerful in raising consciousness and in enabling agency, but also powerful in persuading (Burns, 2011) those who might view the visual productions, in this instance the university policy makers. So beginning with the end in mind we worked with 14 young women to consider how best we might get our voices across to the university policy makers.

We chose to engage with the purposively selected first-year women students in a safe space away from campus and where we could work and stay together for two days over a weekend. Such a retreat approach (Mitchell, DeLange, & Moletsane, 2014) provides a conducive space for working on a sensitive issue such as sexual violence on campus. We engaged the 14 women students in introductory activities to first get to know each other, and also to introduce the work. With all the necessary preliminary work done, talking about ethics, and visual ethics, and about how we would handle any discomfort or upset they might experience, we began exploring their understanding of sexual violence on campus.

We used participatory video as a research method to engage with the issue and to have the participants represent their understanding of sexual violence on campus by exploring the prompt, *feeling safe and feeling unsafe* on campus. The young women worked in four groups and used cellphones to produce four videos (see Figure 2.8). The videos themselves were illuminating and diverse in relation to the themes and issues they raise. *Careless Securities* highlights how the failure of security personnel to fulfil their task professionally leads to unsafe situations for girls in the residences. *Getting into Res[idence]*, as the title suggests, talks about how personnel at some off-campus residences coerce the new women students to have sex with them in exchange for a placement. *The Game* shows the vulnerability of young women students when members of the public come onto campus to sports events, and *Xanadu Square* depicts how girls are sexually harassed by their male peers when passing a particular square in front of the male residence. In those early sessions we viewed these productions together and discussed the messages contained in each of the videos.

The cellphilms evoked a great deal of discussion in the group especially about the idea of getting the message out about the issues that had been raised. The idea of audience, however, also came into play, and while the cellphilms were, of course, available for screening, there were some limitations (screening space and time, and interpretation of the messages), so the idea of producing a simple and clear message that a poster might convey seemed like a useful plan. With this in mind, we worked with the young women to make

Figure 2.8 Cellphilms, *Getting into Res, Xanadu Square, Careless Securities, The Game*

Screenshots of *Getting into Res, Xanadu Square, Careless Securities, The Game*, cellphilms made by Girls Leading Change

Girls Leading Change (Producer) (2015). *Getting into Res, Xanadu Square, Careless Securities, The Game* [Cellphilms]. Port Elizabeth: Nelson Mandela Metropolitan University.

policy posters. As we describe in greater detail in Chapter 7, policy posters consist of a photograph or a drawing to represent the issue, along with a message. Here, too, the process of participation deepened and six policy posters (two new issues that emerged during the process were added), with the following messages were produced.

My body your toy? No such luck; Safety in our home away from home, we need to feel protected and safe in our residences; My right to privacy, your responsibility to respect it! Male visitors to women's residences compromise the privacy of women students when using the bathrooms; Unsafe in my space; Sexual harassment, we are victims of our protectors! Who should we trust? and Date rape, it is still rape! Report it!

Working with the cellphilms and the policy posters, the young women considered what needed to be done. What could they do by themselves and what did the relevant policy makers at university need to do to address sexual violence on campus? We introduced the idea of writing action briefs, which explained the particular situation on campus, outlined the problem, and then listed several carefully thought through actions which could be taken (see Chapter 7 for Policy/Action briefs). In total, six action briefs were produced which were linked to the policy posters, which were developed from the cellphilms.

While the participatory video process was, as always, quite open-ended and informed by decisions the young women took throughout the participatory research process, we, as researchers, worked to insert an approach based on beginning with the end in mind (see Figure 2.9). We conveyed that idea as a strategy to them since we thought about what would be needed to facilitate campus-wide discussion about policy, and with which policy makers. The set of productions (four cellphilms, six policy posters, and six action briefs) were to be used in the meetings we were able to set up with a number of different university policy makers (see De Lange, Moletsane, & Mitchell, 2015), representing the various facets of the university community such as top management, residence, campus security, and institutional transformation. While we, as researchers, facilitated setting up the meetings, the young women took ownership of the presentations. They wanted T-shirts with their activist group name, Girls Leading Change, printed on them to ensure a united look but also to reflect their goal. Together we composed a PowerPoint slideshow and each young woman prepared to present a section or two. The young women responded to the questions coming from the audience. Following Jessica Taft (2010), these in themselves were powerful in strengthening the young women's sense of agency and political activism to ensure their own safety and well-being.

It is important to ask what difference this has made in bringing about change so far. We have seen the change the engagement has brought about in three areas; the young women's agency, political engagement, and in the university context. Their agency can be seen,

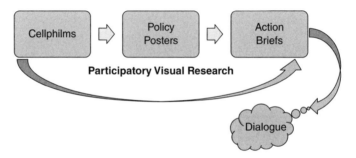

Figure 2.9 Participatory visual research methodology design of *Girls Leading Change* study
Diagram developed by Naydene de Lange

for example, in taking up invitations to address audiences on issues of sexual violence, as well as initiating their own activist activities in the university (participating in the #bringbackourgirls campaign against Boko Haram's abduction of young girls in Nigeria) but also in their communities (addressing school youth in their rural home towns on safety and well-being). Their political engagement – and the idea of political listening that we introduced in Chapter 1 – is seen for example, in their talking with policy makers at the university to make the issue of sexual violence a priority; putting forward what should be done; and participating on a national level in the *Agenda* Feminist Dialogues.[3] Material change in the university context, as a result of their work, was monitored and tracked when the young women visually documented changes they saw as a result of their engagement with the university policy makers. Using their cellphones, they took photographs of the improved lighting for security purposes and the clearing of overgrown areas to eliminate possible hiding places for attackers to ensure the safety of personnel and students according to the requirements of the university Occupational Health and Safety Policy. They also took photographs of clearly displayed codes of conduct in the residences that adhere to the House Rules and Procedures Policy. The Higher Education Act also requires an Institutional Forum which, inter alia, has to address issues of gender. While the university does have a Gender Equity Policy, a very significant change was the university's steps to initiate the establishment of a Gender Forum. Some of the Girls Leading Change members were invited to participate in the initial meetings.

Some Challenges Encountered

Participatory visual research can throw up several technical and conceptual challenges. While the current era is said to be a digital one, not all participants in the case study of the Girls Leading Change, especially those who are marginalized, share and participate

---

[3]Agenda and Feminist dialogues, http://radiodut.co.za/the-agenda-feminist-hosts-dialogue-talk/

online. They do not necessarily fit the profile of what Howe and Strauss (2000) refer to as the Y generation or Millennials. This can make digital production a tedious process since we as researchers have to ensure that the participants gain the necessary skills to enable them to do the participatory visual work, as in the case of using digital software to make a drawing, or using a video camera or cellphone to make a video, or using digital tools to create a digital story. In our work with the young women, one challenge we experienced in making the participatory videos using cellphones was getting the participants to understand how the camera works so that the images in the end product are not upside down or sideways. Not all cellphone cameras have a pause button, so we sometimes needed to do a one-shot-shoot to film the story. The cellphones we used, however, had a pause button, and so pausing to stop the filming between the shots of the storyboard, often left them with a cellphilm consisting of the participants talking about how the shot should be filmed, instead of the shot itself.[4]

Doing participatory visual work is also time consuming since the process of producing the visual product is important in enabling the agency of the participants. In each of the methods we refer to, the process takes time; the participants have to think about and engage with the issue under study; learn how to use the equipment to express their thinking; learn how to work within the particular visual method; and then follow a participatory process of data production; explaining their production; getting feedback; and even considering how to adjust the production to make the point they want to put across clearer. Throughout the process there needs to be lots of time for discussion among the participants and with the research team. Dissemination also requires preparation; scheduling the meetings; preparing the presentation or the exhibition; and then of course engaging with the policy makers.

Authors such as Thomas and Britton (2012, p. 209) write about the aesthetics in artistic collaboration, referring to the 'quality of the art' in relation to social and cultural practices. They point out that what is considered aesthetically pleasing in one culture might not be considered so in another culture. For us, this raises the issue of whether the visual production should be improved or left as it is to reveal the original work of the participants. We have grappled with this and even though we have digitized the productions, we have not tampered with the original composition of the representations. As viewers ourselves, we might try to fix sound, but we have learned that the flavour of the local and the real is appropriate and appealing when we are showing the cellphilms in the community and to the relevant policy makers. The policy posters, too, might have benefited from an artist's

---

[4]We acknowledge the range of digital media available, the changing landscape of apps that could be used for cellphilming, and how these various apps might influence the productions. Snapchat and Instagram, for example, offer easier ways to share cellphilms, but the time constraints on how long a particular 'shot' might last can change the type of production. The relatively simple project cellphones that we have typically used have made No-Editing-Required and one-shot-shoot approaches very easy to accommodate. At the same time we recognize the quality of the production and various aesthetics may change.

airbrush. We do wonder what the policy posters might have looked like had an artist been included in our research team and been part of the process of making them.

While the participatory visual research process often concludes with a collective expression of the issue under study, the research team and the participants have to carefully engage with the issue of power and ownership. Miller and Smith (2012) have written about this in relation to participatory video and the dissemination of the work, and Wheeler (2012) has written about it in relation to participatory video and engaging in policy processes. For us the dissemination should be negotiated, in terms of what format it will take; where it will happen; how the work will be exhibited and engaged with; who gets to speak; and who gets to answer questions? In the case study described above, we presented the work to the policy makers as a team of researchers and participants with each one contributing in her own way. As months went by the young women grew in confidence and took full ownership of the presentations; they responded to the questions, enabling us, the researchers, to withdraw from the presentations and wait and watch in the wings. On their own, too, the young women decided to add song, typical of their Indigenous cultures, to introduce the presentations and to conclude them. This turned the presentations into powerful ones that accentuated their indigeneity and that contextualized the work in a participatory way.

Finally, then, when does a project actually end? When do we measure and/or describe the impact? Drawing on the question of what gets left behind and the fact that participants get on with their lives, regardless of what we might see as interventions, the idea of studying what difference this makes becomes all the more complex, as we explore in Chapter 8. Working over several years, writing and presenting findings for different audiences, we know that there are clearly many different ways of talking about the impact of this work that just keeps going on and on. For example, long after the young women had presented their policy posters and action briefs to some of the policy makers on campus, it was clear that they had much more to say and indeed, perhaps reaching these policy makers was only a tiny part of what needed to happen. In a follow-up session where the 14 young women reflected on the processes thus far, it was evident that talking about sexual violence so publicly and in a collective way had also evoked a great deal of the personal for them. A follow-up writing workshop led to their writing a collection of personal narratives, *14 Times a Woman: Indigenous Stories from the Heart* (2016). This work has, in turn, been choreographed into a performed reading with the young women dressed in their Indigenous clothes reading their stories to an audience, thus sparking further dialogue about being a young African woman at university in South Africa.

CONCLUSION

We have shown how we see the value of participatory visual methodology to envisage and inform policy dialogue and return here to the idea of beginning with the end in mind. A collection of drawings or photographs, or a set of cellphilms or digital stories presented to policy makers by the participants themselves has the power to engage the audience and to evoke responses which could move them to bring about change. A policy informed by the people's from the ground up local knowledge recognizes the importance of how communities experience their realities and what changes they want and how these could be brought about. In this way, policies that are made have a better chance of being implemented and of contributing to social change.

A participatory visual research study designed with the end in mind builds in appropriate methodological opportunities to explore the social issues under study and to enable different facets to be made visible and multiple voices to be heard. It is in these methodological engagements that participants reflect on and deepen their own understanding of the social problem and begin to explore the potential of their own agency. When the participants are community members who might not necessarily have the confidence or opportunity to engage with policy makers who are tasked to ensure that policies address the issues on the ground, the self-created visual artefacts are critical resources that can be used in the process of dialogue, and to ensure that policy makers can see close up what the social realities that need to be changed, actually look like.

KEY POINTS OF THE CHAPTER

- Starting off by thinking – with the participants – what the issue is that needs to be addressed and how the results might be shared with audiences to enable community and policy dialogue to contribute to social change.
- Framing participatory visual methodology within a critical and transformative paradigm in the project design.
- Regarding the visual productions as key in enabling the participants to drive the social change when the researcher leaves the field.
- Understanding the range of participatory visual methods available (for example, drawing, photovoice, participatory video and digital story-telling) and their relative benefits and limitations.
- Considering the potential of participation and co-production, the produced artefact, and audience (disseminating and mobilizing knowledge) in the design of a participatory visual research project for social change.
- A case study as example of a participatory visual research project: Young women at a South African university contributing to change in relation to sexual violence.

3

SPEAKING BACK AS METHOD

CHAPTER CONTENTS

INTRODUCTION

One of the challenges of participatory visual research is that there is sometimes an uncritical acceptance (on the part of both researchers and participants) of the words or images produced. This is not unique to participatory visual methodologies as we know from the vast body of work on interview data, for example, and the challenges of interpretation. In some cases the researcher misinterprets what was said as we see so powerfully in Katherine Borland's (1991) chapter *'That's not What I Said': Interpretive Conflict in Oral Narrative Research* that is based on a set of oral history interviews with the author's grandmother. In other cases, even the participant, upon reflection and over time, might not agree with what he or she said or produced thus creating what we might call a *that's not what I meant to say* statement. But arriving at a critical perspective is not necessarily a straightforward process. Moletsane (2011), for example, highlights in her work on youth sexuality in rural South Africa that 'variations in the retrieved and reinterpreted cultural understandings and enactments of masculinity and femininity [in any community] contain many contradictions' (p. 203). Indeed, beyond the obvious binaries of adults/children or males/females, we might also think of other worrisome discourses such as abled/disabled, urban/rural, or non-Indigenous/Indigenous. Sometimes the group process involved in creating visual productions cause individual or group members to paint themselves into a corner through what might seem, at times, like pat answers and the reliance on stereotypes to make a point. There may be a need for participants to embark upon a process of rethinking or contesting a previous position and even a need to contradict themselves or take a different angle. To do this kind of rethinking, Desiree Lewis (2003) calls for 'innovativeness in contesting discourses, practices, and identities that police our rights, freedoms and desires' (cited in Moletsane, 2011, p. 4) and for the development of a 'capacity to go beyond what is given, to fantasize, to create new possibilities…for thought and action' (Moletsane, 2011, p. 6). In this chapter we consider the participants (or producers) as the first and perhaps the most significant audience in participatory visual research. Building on the idea of transformation, we explore the ways in which 'speaking back' in participatory visual research – regardless of whether it is done through talking, writing, or filming – can be a method or approach to re-examining, rethinking, and re-representing a position.

DEFINING SPEAKING BACK

Perhaps one of the greatest strengths of participatory visual research in which participants produce photos, videos, cellphilms, or digital stories is its resilience over time. For example, we have seen how inviting it can be to go back to the same visual texts, not only in relation to screening or exhibiting them with new audiences 'over and over and over again', but as we explore in this chapter, in reworking this material. Here we consider ways of seizing on the opportunities afforded by the pedagogy of 'over and over and over again'. We borrow from Katharine Gelber's (2002) term in the title of her book *Speaking Back: The Free Speech vs Hate Speech Debate* in which she focuses specifically on speaking back to issues of racism. While Gelber uses the term 'speaking back' to describe the processes of addressing contradictions in everyday discourses in relation to racism (typically those most marginalized speaking back to and contesting or contradicting dominant discourses), we are interested in the ways in which participants who are themselves often marginalized might engage in contesting the contradictions often evident in their own productions – the worrisome discourses. As we highlighted in Chapter 2, some kind of reflective process is already a central component of participatory visual methods. Consider the questions we ask: What did you like best? What would you like to change? If you were to do this over again what would you do differently? Who should see this? Clearly, these questions are ones that could already signal the potential for deep engagement with participants, but they are also ones that are action oriented in that they take audience into consideration. The questions here might include the following: How will the video be received? Upon reflection is there anything problematic? These are the kinds of questions that frame the idea of speaking back and of re-making and re-storying (Strong-Wilson, 2008). When we use the term speaking back, then, we are referring to practices that go beyond this level of reflection. In our speaking back activities, participants are typically engaged in creating new digital or artistic productions that seek to contest or contradict the content or messages of the previous productions, and in relation to questions such as the following: What's missing? Who's missing? What stories are not being told? What does our doing do? As we highlight in this chapter, these are not easy questions to ask and having them answered requires time. A one-day cellphilm or video production workshop, for example, may give only enough time to speak but not to speak back. We do not, however, see speaking back in participatory visual research as a unitary set of activities; rather, we use the term to highlight a range of deliberate practices that have resulted in participants revisiting their own visual productions, reflecting on their work, often changing their minds, and productively challenging and contradicting themselves.

While we might look to Freire's work on conscientization in a broad way, building on bell hooks's (1989) *Talking Back: Thinking Feminist and Thinking Black* feminist and anti-racist work, and Ashcroft, Griffiths, and Tiffins' (1989) *The Empire Writes Back: Theory and Practice in Postcolonial Literatures* takes us up to contemporary interrogations of indigenizing and decolonization (Grace, 2001). In her work on Indigenous communities in Canada's North writing back to the south, Grace draws attention to the problematics of using such terms as writing and writing back:

The discursive evidence I am exploring is not always written if by written one understands only language as written down. ... Thus I use the terms writing, writes, and written very loosely indeed to include many forms of address and activity, many semiotic codes and modes of representation from music and wall-hangings to radio, television, comic strips, festival, conferences and speeches. (p. 232)

Of particular relevance to speaking back through the visual is the work of James Hubbard (1994) and Lana Wong (2000) on the idea of *shooting back* in which marginalized young people from reservations in the United States and from the slums of Nairobi respectively were given cameras to shoot back to mainstream photo images of how they are typically represented.[1] We see this work that has taken place in a variety of settings, as a critical advancement in our own participatory visual research. While speaking back can have variations, depending on the context and the issue explored, this chapter as a whole contributes to deepening an understanding of how participatory visual work might contribute to participant-led and participant-driven critique in the context of policy dialogue. The central questions for us are: How can participants speak back to their own work? What tools and methods support speaking back?

ON USING SPEAKING BACK AS METHOD

Here we offer two detailed examples, one from the Global South related to speaking back to and through cellphilms, and one from the Global North, focusing on speaking back to and through curating albums. In the examples we discuss how we developed a speaking back approach that served to challenge the discourse underpinning the visual productions, and to contribute to changing the discourse.

Teachers Speaking Back To and Through Cellphilms

This first example of speaking back is framed in the policy context of education in addressing HIV and AIDS in rural South Africa. Notwithstanding the robust policy context for sexuality education in the Department of Basic Education, teachers are often left out of the equation. A national study organized by Higher Education of South Africa (HESA) several years ago *Being a Teacher in the Context of the Pandemic* (HEAIDS, 2010), highlighted the significance of teachers' knowledge of local contexts of stigma, AIDS denialism, gender and sexuality, and cultural practices, all issues which are relatively under-studied in the teacher-education literature and school-based literature on prevention and sex education in sub-Saharan Africa (Boler & Archer, 2009). While the findings of the study (hereafter

---

[1]We acknowledge April Mandrona's lively exploration of '--- back' at the Gender and Circumpolarity Conference at the University of Mid-Sweden, October, 2015. Extending the work of Sherrill Grace (2001) who wrote about Indigenous people of Canada's North 'writing back' in comic strips such as *Ice Box*, Mandrona drew attention in her paper to various creative expressions with implications for participatory methodology: 'filming back' in *The Fast Runner*, 'gaming back' in *Arctic Rescue* and *Never Alone*, 'tweeting back' as can be seen in the work of film maker Alethea Arnaquq-Baril (Unikkat Studios) who created #SEALFIE, and 'you tubing back' based on a response by 17-year-old Killaq Enaraq-Strauss of Iqaluit to Ellen Degeneres's campaign against the Canadian seal hunt.

referred to as *Being a Teacher*) related to many different concerns (i.e. collegiality, care, and biomedical information), one of the main conclusions pertains to the idea that without a deeper understanding of the meanings of the specific cultural issues raised by teachers, particularly as they relate to rural young people and communities as well as on their own lives, education interventions, as they stand, are doomed to failure (see also Bhana, De Lange & Mitchell, 2009; Helleve, Flisher, Onya, Mukoma, & Klepp, 2009). The study did not suggest that educational initiatives are the definitive answer to addressing the cultural issues, but it does highlight the fact that, in rural settings at least, the school remains one of the main points of entry for working directly with young people, particularly in the context of contested sites, including virginity testing and medical male circumcision, that involve gender and youth sexuality.

Significantly the discourses of youth sexuality in sub-Saharan Africa and elsewhere increasingly point to the need for a more nuanced understanding of the politics of safe sex (Bhana, 2012), Life Skills (Buthelezi et al., 2007; Campbell & McPhail, 2002; Francis, 2010; Smith & Harrison, 2013), masculinities (Morrell, Jewkes, & Lindegger, 2012; Morrell & Makaye, 2006; Sathiparsad & Taylor, 2006), gender-based violence (De Lange, Mitchell, & Bhana, 2012; Leach & Mitchell, 2006), pleasure in relation to youth sexuality (Fine & McClelland, 2006; Francis, 2010; Ingham, 2005), youth engagement (Robbins, 2010), and, particularly relevant to this study, the context of rurality itself (Balfour, Mitchell, & Moletsane, 2008) and a place-based consciousness (Corbett, 2007). Clearly there is a challenge as far as teachers' professional engagement in South Africa (and elsewhere in sub-Saharan Africa) is concerned since teachers, and the field of Education itself, have often been sidelined. This is also evidenced by the fact that dedicated courses in the area of Sexuality and Life Skills in teacher education, or well-designed courses on integrating HIV&AIDS across the curriculum are difficult to find (Van Laren, Mitchell, Mudaly, Pithouse-Morgan, & Singh, 2012; Wood, 2012).

In responding to this challenge, we became interested in exploring the ways in which rural teachers' voices could become integrated into an analytic framework. Thus, in our project *Digital Voices of Rural Teachers: Participatory Analysis, 'Being a Teacher in the Age of AIDS' and Social Action* (hereafter referred to as *Digital voices*)[2] (Mitchell, De Lange, & Moletsane, 2011) we worked with a group of primary and secondary school teachers from two schools, one of which is a former comprehensive Catholic school in rural KwaZulu-Natal, and the other a farm school in Eastern Cape. The series of digital retreats, as we came to call the series of workshops held with the teachers, aimed to produce cellphilms or

---

[2]This project, *Digital Voices* (Mitchell, De Lange, & Moletsane, 2011) aimed at identifying ways in which the voices of rural teachers could become more central to identifying and addressing critical issues of youth sexuality in the age of AIDS. *Digital Voices* asks two key questions: 1) 'What difference can the participation of rural teachers make to deepening an understanding of youth sexuality and HIV&AIDS?' and 2) 'How can these meanings be translated into more nuanced understanding and treatment of critical social issues in community based programs and policy?'

cellphone videos on youth sexuality and sexuality education. It would be safe to say that when we first embarked on producing the cellphilms with the teachers during the digital retreats, we had not yet conceptualized the notion of speaking back. The dilemma, as we have explored in several publications (Mitchell & De Lange, 2013; Mitchell, De Lange, & Moletsane, 2015) is that it was evident in the teachers' productions that they had not really considered how much their own views about youth sexuality remained adult-centric and moralistic. For example, in a teacher-produced cellphilm entitled *HIV-AIDS Free Generation by 2020*, a teacher discusses the HIV epidemic and then proclaims that abstinence is the way to ensure not becoming infected. In *Stay Fresh Live Longer*, the teacher advocates abstinence, too, but also refers to medical male circumcision and virginity testing as ways of avoiding spreading the infection and of becoming infected. In another cellphilm, *Be Enlightened*, the teacher seizes a pedagogical moment when she discovers children playing with a used condom they had picked up on the playground, and teaches them that using condoms can prevent infection, but then she loses the weightiness of this moment since she goes on to say that condoms are not for children, but for adults. These three cellphilms in particular, we thought, contained the teachers' own viewpoints and messages to youth about safe sex with which we had to engage critically and so we came to organize our first speaking back workshop.

Speaking Back Workshop

The one-day speaking back workshop was a turning point in our work with the teachers as far as the worrisome discourses we talk about in the introduction were concerned. How do participants arrive at a point where they might critique their own work and contradict themselves? We organized the day into a series of five steps (or sessions) (see Figure 3.1) which would result in the teachers coming up with their own version of *'we've changed our minds'*.

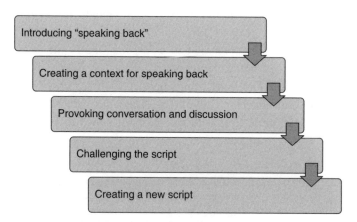

Figure 3.1 Workshop on speaking back to and through cellphilms

Diagram developed by Claudia Mitchell

Step 1: Introducing speaking back method

We started the workshop by introducing the idea of 'speaking back', drawing attention to the work of Hubbard (1994) and Wong (2000) and others who have used the speaking back/shooting back formulation to facilitate self-criticism.

Step 2: Creating a context for speaking back

In creating a context for the work, we drew on a digital archive[3] containing a collection of visual artefacts in the age of AIDS created by youth, teachers, and community health-care workers from a rural community in KwaZulu-Natal. In a PowerPoint presentation we showed a selection of the photographs depicting youth at risk of HIV infection, HIV-related stigma, gender-based violence, teenage pregnancy, and suicide, many of which we discuss in Moletsane et al. (2007). We also showed a collection of photographs created by young people and teachers from the farm school community in Eastern Cape depicting promiscuity on the school terrain, gender-based violence, HIV-related stigma that also showed youth at risk. Having them look at these images enabled a rich discussion among the teachers about the realities of the youth in rural schools and the communities in which they are located.

Step 3: Provoking conversation and discussion

The next step was to actually go back to one of the cellphilms the teachers had produced with the idea of provoking conversation and discussion. For the session we focused on *Be Enlightened* with the theme that knowledge is power. The cellphilm uses the form of a drama, with the teacher participants enacting a school-based scene. At break time two school children (played by teachers) find a used condom and play with it as if it is a balloon. At the end of break time the teacher (played by a teacher) calls the children back, but notices that two children are still not in the line. She looks for them and finds them playing behind a shrub with the condom. They all return to class and she takes this opportune moment to teach the whole class in an unemotional didactic approach to what a condom is and what it is used for. She makes them understand that using a condom can contribute to safe sex and can prevent HIV infection, but then towards the end of the cellphilm, she concludes: 'So for when you are an adult you are going to know better about AIDS. But never, never again play with condoms.'

The cellphilm is engaging and humorous, and it plays with the idea of what it means to be enlightened. In this case the cellphilm portrayed the teacher as enlightened and able to share important knowledge about using condoms to prevent HIV infection, and the children

---

[3]*Not leaving data in the dark: Participatory archiving and visual data to address HIV and AIDS* (NRF) (2012–2014) N. De Lange, C. Mitchell, R. Moletsane, J. Stuart, and M. Taylor.

are enlightened in that they are given information about condoms. The viewpoint of the teacher that condoms are only for adults, however, contradicts the content of photos taken by young people in the community that indicates that the need for sexual health instruction is high. In their photos, they highlight, for example, the stigma attached to being HIV positive. One of the most dramatic, a photo we have discussed earlier in the chapter and elsewhere (Mitchell, 2011), shows a boy preparing to hang himself because he sees no hope as a result of his HIV positive status. To open up the discussion on *Be Enlightened* we posed three questions for the teachers to respond to in their groups: What do you think was the main message of the video you just saw? Who do you think the audience for that video is? How do you think the cellphilm speaks back to the photographs that you saw? We include below some of the comments of the teachers:

Magdalene: Our message that we saw is knowledge is power, when you have got knowledge you are able to control what happens to you, you are able to control whatever situation that you are faced with. So for us for the learners to have knowledge about HIV and AIDS, those who are infected would know how to handle themselves among the others. They would not see themselves as being different from the rest of the group. So our main message is knowledge is power and when you have got knowledge you are able to control each and every situation that you are faced with.

Thabi: Our main message is directed to the teachers and parents. They should educate learners to know what's the use of a condom.

Thandi: What we were trying to show is the fact that limited knowledge is dangerous as you could see that the children were playing with the condoms so what we thought is that was dangerous because what if they found used condoms. Imagine kids blowing these condoms. Children need to be taught it in early stage about HIV and sex as well, because if you remember one of the children said, 'I normally see my dad and my mom going to the bedroom and taking this balloon with them', so it means they do have an idea of who exactly uses these things but now they need to be taught more about it so that they get the correct information.

Lindo: We also noted that little knowledge can harm someone because those learners were playing with condoms they didn't have knowledge about condoms. Also still in question one, we thought that people must break the silence because these things are real and they are happening in our houses and we ignore them and our children see us do these things and we keep quiet about them, we pretend as if they don't exist, and we pretend as if our 15-year-olds don't have boyfriends, we don't want to talk about sex to them, we don't want to talk about boyfriends as well to them. Even at school we just tend to overlook these things because we don't want to talk about it so, we must break the silence so that learners as early as young age they know about sex education and everything. We also thought it's also carelessness because those learners were playing

---

> and they found the condoms in the school yard, it's the carelessness to the adult or whoever was using the condom. Also we thought that education should begin at home as I was saying that these things start as early as home because that's where they get almost the whole knowledge, it's just that they do not know exactly what is happening, because their parents they tend to be secretive about it. They go to school they share about these things and sometimes they share wrong knowledge to each other and they end up practicing this knowledgo that they share.

Their responses clearly highlighted the dilemma the teachers were faced with in knowing that they need to teach the children from an early age about sex and safe sex, but that feeling that sex was for adults and that children and youth should not engage in having sex, and in adhering to tradition and taboo in maintaining the silence around youth and safe sex.

There are, no doubt, different ways of challenging the teachers to think critically about their productions. The questions we used helped but we also added in what might be described as *catalyst* comments. Relebohile was perhaps in the best position of the three of us to take on this role:

> Starting with the film…I thought that the film is really well made so I think on the technical side I really like the film…the sound was good, the images were good, the storyline was well developed, [but] it just didn't get to where I wanted it to get. I sat up as the teacher took the children into the classroom and I was looking forward to the teacher really educating the children about these condoms, but then the teacher did what we all do as parents. As parents we believe that knowledge is power, right? Our children need knowledge in order to be empowered, so we are going to educate them. But then we censor that education and say to them these are condoms, but these condoms are for adults. So our view is [that] children are innocent, children are not sexual and therefore our duty is to keep them away from sex and from condoms. But I know for a fact that many children are having sex and many children are getting infected. And so are we going to continue making our cellphilm comfortable … in saying that well, I'm educating my children not to have sex until they are 30. Sacrificing them into getting infected because we want to feel comfortable as parents? I'm just putting it out to all of you.

This input from Relebohile, makes it clear that the general view is that children should not be having sex and should not be educated about condoms. The reality, however, is that children are having sex and they are getting infected because they do not have enough relevant information about sex, safe sex, and sexuality and they cannot talk about any of this to their parents. So they talk to their friends and end up not necessarily getting the correct knowledge. Relebohile's response elicited a lot of discussion which enabled the group to think about how they could speak back by putting a more nuanced message – less didactic and moralistic – across in their cellphilms. We encouraged them to consider making cellphilms which could be used as effective teaching materials for all in the age of AIDS.

Step 4: Challenging the script

In this step the focus was on challenging the sexuality education script by speaking back to the dominant cultural discourses. As the teachers embarked upon producing their new speaking back cellphilms they had different thoughts and ideas about what the message was and why, and about who the audience was, and why? This activity resulted in the production of four new cellphilms – *Breaking the Silence, Breaking the Silence 2, Speak Out,* and *Teen Vibe* – that they made in their groups with the teachers tackling the issue of engaging the youth differently in understanding what the critical issues really are. In *Breaking the Silence* a mother approaches her son, who had a girl staying overnight in his room, and discusses with him the importance of using a condom if he is having sex, to ensure that it is safe sex. In *Breaking the Silence 2*, a mother first harshly admonishes and slaps her daughter after seeing her viewing pornographic material on her cellphone. She then follows through, much to the consternation of her husband, in discussing safe sex with her daughter. In *Speak Out* the mother, unlike the teacher in *Be Enlightened*, explains the use of condoms to her daughter when the latter enquires what condoms are for, and makes the point that when she is ready for sex she must use condoms to ensure that she is having safe sex. In *Teen Vibe* a mother, realizing that her daughters had snuck out – without permission – to go to a party and had then taken a ride home with a stranger, admonishes them but sits them down to discuss with them the dangers of hitching a ride with strangers given the possibility of being raped.

Step 5: Reflecting on the new script

The new productions, of course, led to new screenings within the group and new reflections on their speaking back cellphilms. Interestingly the teachers spoke very differently about the messages and audiences of their new cellphilms in response to *Speak Out*.

Thoko: We were trying to show that when you are talking to a kid, you must be flexible and calm, not like already they are doing this thing so what they are doing is wrong. Because our parents are used to shouting at us...

Lindo: And also the mother said there, there's nothing wrong with having boyfriends, there's something wrong in sex, yeah I was just laughing there; advising them that you can have boyfriends but not sex.

After viewing *Breaking the Silence 2* participants highlighted a cultural context that might be missed in more conventional discourses.

Nandipha: I like the idea of showing the child that she did something wrong and then afterwards explaining everything, even though I'm not so sure about the hitting, if that works, because I saw she was scared after being hit. And then I also saw the role of the father in the house…because we usually see that the fathers aren't so much involved in such things, and they are normally against such things.

Thoko: It's quite an interesting part but when you look at things you will never be sure whether the child will come back when she has got something terrible or something that she thinks is wrong to discuss it with the mother because she knows first she's going to hit and shout, before the solution.

Magdalene: What we actually wanted to bring out is…usually in our African homes when something like this happens the natural reaction is you get angry and you want to act, you want to [slap]. I know the European version is you don't smack, but in our African way, the first thing is we smack and then we calm down and we want to speak. So I wanted it to come out that that's where we come from.

Thoko: Where we come from, the bringing up…

Magdalene: Yes and bring out the calming down and giving the child a lesson.

Thoko: Yes, I do understand but the times are changing. Our children are no more in our community; they are exposed to the world, you see; they are exposed to everyone, to different cultures. But I like it. It gives us something to brainstorm about.

Nellie: We also wanted, remember our audience are the parents, we also wanted them to see themselves there. So that after watching it they can think about what is right that happened there and what is wrong, how can they behave, what is the better way of doing things? You see the father did not agree with the mother and it ended there. He was stubborn, whilst the mother was content that what she was doing was right, then with what we did there we were opening a debate between the parents, after watching it. And that is what we did, we actually had something to say immediately after watching it. That's the response we wanted.

Magdalene: It's speaking back!

While the speaking back cellphilms showed how the teachers approached the issue in a more nuanced way and with greater clarity about the audience, the discussion on the speaking back cellphilms further elaborated on the development of the teachers' critical engagement with their own work especially in contextualizing it within their rural and cultural experiences:

> Veronica (referring to Getting lost – Small knowledge kills):
>
> We use what's going on in our lives. When people are sick and they are dying – especially HIV – they want to go to an inyanga (traditional healer) first … they don't want to go to the clinics and make check-ups, they prefer to go to the inyanga instead… That's why we said 'Small knowledge kills'.

If we compare the earlier cellphilms and these speaking back ones, we can see important shifts in the teachers' thinking. All the new speaking back cellphilms position the adults quite differently in terms of offering information and being supportive, although it is interesting that all the groups (made up of women teachers, many of whom are mothers) shifted away from the classroom context to the home. This may suggest that the teachers were still not ready to take up issues of youth sexuality in their classrooms and instead, while they recognized the need for a shift in the approach, they assigned this role to parents.

When we embarked upon the *Digital Voices* project, we were keen to engage classroom teachers through digital media production in advancing meaningful school-based programming to address HIV and AIDS. To do this, the project adopted a form of research-as-intervention approach (see also Chapter 2). A limitation of the project was that it did not focus directly on how teachers could implement this work over time. What this kind of work highlights, however, is the complexity of the issues, but at the same time, the somewhat obvious point is that teachers need time to work concomitantly in low risk and creative ways to, first, speak about the social conditions, and then to speak back in relation to the change that is needed. This calls for a policy shift in both pre-service and in-service teacher education to recognize teachers' knowledge, something that is particularly challenging at a time when the ministries responsible for sexuality education have been moving in the opposite direction by developing scripted Life Orientation lessons (Adams Tucker, George, Reardon, & Panday, 2016).

Speaking Back To and Through Family Photographs

In this second example we shift our focus from work that is more group oriented, building as it does on the principles and practices of participatory video, to the individual and to the use of family photographs in participatory visual research. Much of this work, ranging from curating photo albums and other visual productions such as photo-collages to projects related to producing digital stories, is very much about identity. In contemporary postcolonial contexts and with a sensibility about decolonization and indigenization, this is personal and collective work that calls for tools and methods that facilitate the interrogation of contradictions. Several decades ago, Jo Spence and Joan Solomon (1995) edited a book called *What Can a Woman do with a Camera* which extended Jo Spence's generative work with her own family photographs or what she described as 'putting myself in the picture' (Spence, 1986). Spence's early work with Rosy Martin (Spence & Martin, 1988) set in motion a playfulness in staging family photos but also a way of reworking or re-storying the past that allowed for the possibility of exploring issues such as class and gender. For example, as women in their 40s, Spence and Martin revisited their schoolgirl so-called nice girl selves by photographing themselves as the bad girls they never got to be. They did not refer to this work as speaking back, but through performance and photography they were able to delve into and contest what they saw as patriarchal practices in relation to girlhood. While this practice pre-dates any type of selfie, it highlights one way in which the participatory process of working with family photographs offers an approach to speaking back.

When Spence was diagnosed with breast cancer she used these same practices of personal and political photography to challenge policies related to health. In her well-known *A Picture of Health* project, she worked with self-portraits, many of them showing her breasts and some of them including writing directly on her body. Exhibiting these photos of vulnerability in public galleries helped to draw attention to doctor-patient relationships (see Lee, 2013). Spence was an exceptional activist and artist whose work in one sense is quite beyond the everyday of community research. At the same time, however, her work serves as an inspiration for challenging the everyday, and for up-close interrogations of family photos or the proliferation of images that many of us accumulate on our cellphones. Even more than that, her work, located as it is in artful inquiry and visual practice, invites a serious and playful examination of 'what is already there' as Kuhn (1995) describes family photographs.

The idea, of course, that photographs colonize is something that many visual anthropologists have written about as we see in Lutz and Collins's (1993) *Reading the National Geographic* and Hartmann, Silvester, and Hayes's (1999) *The Colonizing Camera*. We also see representations of colonization in relation to African American identity in work by bell hooks (1994) and more recent interrogations of official portraits of residential schools (Daniels, 2013). Annette Kuhn's (1995) *Family Secrets: Acts of Memory and Imagination* offers powerful evidence of the ways in which memory-work in relation to family photos is itself a type of speaking back, something that Mitchell and Weber (1999) also write about in relation to school photographs in *Reinventing Ourselves as Teachers: Beyond Nostalgia*. Here, we consider two examples of how working with personal photos might be used to speak back to social justice issues.

Decolonizing the Family Album

The *Curating an Album* project described elsewhere (Mitchell & Allnutt, 2008; Pithouse, Mitchell, & Weber, 2009), was not originally conceived of as a speaking back activity so much as a project of personal identity and cultural production. The visual artefact produced in the album project is a small photo album, typically framed in a Dollar Store (discount shop) 10 cm by 15 cm photo album containing plastic sleeves. The format is simple: a title page, a typed up or hand-written curatorial statement fitting into one plastic sleeve; each photo fitting into a plastic sleeve on one side of the album and the caption for that photo in the plastic sleeve directly facing it, typically a process explanation in a plastic sleeve near the end, sometimes an author's statement and something about the author/artist.

In the words of one of the first participants, a rural teacher in South Africa, it was a case of 'doing my own work' (see Mitchell et al., 2009). In that study carried out in 2004, Tembinkosi, a young teacher who participated in a curated album documentary project, created a photo album that offers an account of his sister's death as result of complications associated with streptomeningitis and AIDS. As we reflect now on that project as a type of speaking back, we think of Tembinkosi's words in the video *Our Photos, Our Videos, Our Stories* when he talks about his curated album that 'tells a story that we never heard.' The policy implications in relation to the silencing and the stigma related to HIV and AIDS are key.

In another album project Smith (2012) describes the work she carried out in the context of heteronormativity and assimilationist politics. As she writes:

My initial impetus was an investigation into the ways in which my assimilation into the dominant discourse of heteronormativity can be seen particularly in photographs until the emergence of my self-identification as a lesbian, with its oppositional politics to such heteronormativity. Then as I put together a photo album, the actual process served to shift my emphasis away from this aspect of self-identification towards that of a feminist teacher. (p. 57) (See also Mitchell & Pithouse, 2014)

The album project became even more explicitly a speaking back project when it was transformed from an individual project to a participatory workshop activity. A group of 14 Canadian teachers completing a Master's degree and doctoral students working in education came together to engage in this curating activity as part of a course based on visual and social change that Claudia was teaching at a university in Western Canada. The protocol for the activity was as follows:

- Find (not take) 5–7 photographs dealing with social change.
- Bring copies of your photos to the workshop. Share and discuss your photos, in small groups. Help each other put the photos in an order that will show the issue of social change you have chosen. Discuss possible titles for the album in the group.
- On your own, arrange your photos in the order you feel best works for you.
- Write a curatorial statement of 100–150 words. Your curatorial statement is an opportunity to help guide the way audiences perceive your exhibition. It's a chance to communicate directly with viewers, help them understand your point of view, and get them excited and curious about the work they're about to experience.

- Create a title for your album.
- Write a caption for each image. Each caption should be 2–3 sentences long and about the theme. Captions are brief summaries of what the images mean and why they were chosen.
- Add in an artist's statement (optional): How did this album link to your larger project? Were there any other insights in working with the photos or creating the album?
- About the artist (optional).
- Present (and exhibit) your final album to the rest of the group, and to other audiences.
- Reflect in writing on the process of making the album and working with different audiences.

Using this protocol, it is necessary to remove the photos from their everyday place(s), and then reposition them in a newly constructed album and sometimes even re-photograph them as Smith (2012) describes in her essay on working with family portraits that are hanging on the wall.

In the original versions of creating a curated album in the projects described above, the main group process activity was at the very end when the artist would present his or her work in a group (Pithouse, Mitchell, & Weber, 2009). The adaptation for this group of university participants was the participatory workshop (Figure 3.2) which led participants to engage in reflexive writing about the process.

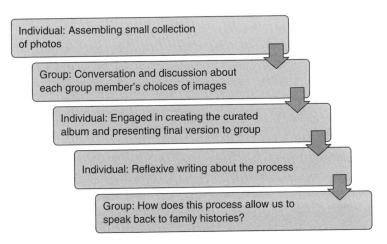

Figure 3.2 Workshop on speaking back to and through family photographs

Diagram developed by Claudia Mitchell

In two examples, Bronson Chau's and Patti Allison's, both teachers in schools in British Columbia, we see different ways in which participants reflect in writing on the album project and the ways in which they were able to speak back to social justice and social change issues.

Bronson

Claudia, as the observer of the workshop session offers a brief reflective account adapted from her fieldnotes in relation to Bronson:

Bronson's process is a fascinating one in relation to participatory visual methods. He arrives at the workshop with very few photographs other than several graduation photos, one from his high school graduation and graduation from a B Ed teacher-education program, and the worry that he really cannot think of anything and that there has been no real idea of social change that he can think of in his life. I am aware as I circulate among the groups that the talk suddenly changes in his group and I find myself moving closer. It seems that the group itself has hit upon Bronson's story as he begins to talk about the fact that his mother was one of the boat people who left Vietnam in the late 1970s. It is of course a dramatic story that reflects the long and dangerous journey that so many people, including Bronson's mother, endured to escape from North Vietnam. There is a certain irony in Bronson's remembering to tell this amazing story only with some prodding from the group. But it is also understandable that when he came to the workshop with the idea of using pictures that he actually owns or is able to download, this significant piece of history would be absent. He highlights the fact that of course there are no photographs of his mother's journey. Prodded on by his group he realizes that he can go and interview his mother, and that her story, like his own, is about the theme of taking up opportunities. The group hits on the idea of including what they now call non photos in the album so that the dramatic escape of his mother and the rest of the family can be included. (Claudia, Reflective Field Notes, August, 2015)

The inclusion of the idea of a missing photograph with a caption attached to an otherwise blank page in the album is reminiscent of bell hooks' (1994) essay on a missing photograph she remembers from her childhood. In Bronson's case the photo was never taken; it does not exist. The very act of identifying photos that were never taken is itself an act of speaking back. As Bronson writes in a reflexive account:

Although the initial creation of the album felt daunting, by the end of the process, I had a better idea of my own thoughts and beliefs. The hardest part of the creation process was coming up with a common theme. Despite having a broad overarching idea of 'social change', pinpointing my idea of 'taking opportunities' took some time to come up with. I had never curated an album before, so explaining the meaning behind each photo was challenging. I thought that the initial non-photo of my mother was a good starting point because it helped guide the rest of the album. Through researching the photo with my mother, I found out a lot about my family's history. I came to understand the sacrifices she made to get to Canada and the opportunities she gained from making the decision to leave Vietnam. The other images with me were easier to work with because it was my own story. (Bronson, Reflective Journal)

He also wrote about presenting the album to peers and the role of audiencing:

Initially, I was worried about sharing personal stories with my peers. I think many others felt the same way. In the end, however, being able to share my mother's journey to Canada was worthwhile. (Bronson, Reflective Journal)

For Bronson there is a speaking back to a significant part of his family's history but clearly something that he does not often talk about. At the same time, it is a story that provokes a great deal of discussion in the group about what material traces of childhood and ancestry exist (or disappear) because of migration and especially during the kind of refugee conditions that people like Bronson's mother endured. This work with an adult participant is a reminder of Glynis Clacherty & Diane Welvering's (2006) *The Suitcase Stories* with refugee children in Johannesburg. But it also evokes questions about the hidden curriculum not only of schools but public galleries and museums: In a multicultural society, whose narratives and images are dominant?

Patti

Where Bronson deals with absent photos and even creates a non-photo for his album, another teacher, Patti, queries the presence – the abundance – of images in her album. Like Bronson, Patti starts off in her reflexive writing with the concern she had about what she could possibly explore in her album project.

I felt drawn to this project as soon as I realized we would have the opportunity to explore our own photographs and family ideas. I did feel a bit overwhelmed about finding the 'right' photos because I have many, many print photos and digital photos. Additionally, I had some doubts about my ability to find a 'social change' theme. What did that have to do with my family photos? I began looking at the idea of decolonizing or colonialism which then helped me to whittle down the photos to 20–30 choices...I was tempted to ask my sister for help with the project because she can be a great resource at times. However, I decided to let myself be guided by the photos. (Patti, Reflective Journal)

Reflecting, as well, on a history of migration in her family, she embarks in her writing on a type of re-storying of the family album based on the experiences of her grandparents who come as settlers to Western Canada from Scotland. For her, though, it is the idea that these are images of white privilege. Speaking back through family photographs for Patti links to what Tuck and Yang (2012, p. 5) refer to as 'settled colonialism' or about the oppressor and not the oppressed as is more typically seen in participatory visual research. As they observe:

Settler colonialism is different from other forms of colonialism in that settlers come with the intention of making a new home on the land, a homemaking that insists on settler sovereignty over all things in their new domain. Thus, relying solely on postcolonial literatures or theories of coloniality that ignore settler colonialism will not help to envision the shape that decolonization must take in settler colonial contexts. Within settler colonialism, the most important concern is land/water/air/ subterranean earth (land, for shorthand, in this article.) Land is what is most valuable, contested, required. This is both because the settlers make Indigenous land their new home and source of capital, and also because the disruption of Indigenous relationships to land represents a profound epistemic, ontological, cosmological violence. (p. 5)

In writing about her album Patti highlights the settler colonialism that she finds in the photographs:

My family is fortunate to have a wealth of photographs starting with my great-great grandparents. Both of my parents' families immigrated to Canada in the early 1900s from Scotland and their path can be traced through the photos so I always enjoy going through the photos. However, this time, I began looking with a more critical eye as to what social change can be found in the images. According to family stories, our families left Scotland in order to find a better, more prosperous life. Although, the photographs show struggle and success which can be seen as positive from a family point of view, I have begun to look more critically at what these images do not tell, which is the underlying story of Canada. My goal is to decolonize myself and this activity is another step in that direction. (Patti, Reflective Journal)

One of the features of the album project is its materiality and its low-tech quality. Given the ubiquity of cellphones and the everydayness of digital technology, there are, of course, other ways to explore processes of speaking back through personal photography. As more and more people rely primarily on iPhones and other mobile devices for taking pictures, fewer people are likely to have the kinds of bountiful historical photos and family albums that Patti has. At the same time, with the new greater ease of sharing images, participants might actually find this sort of project much easier. Unlike album projects of the past where participants might live far from where their photos are, participants will often actively engage parents and other family members in sending the images digitally. Alongside these reflections, we consider that there is a rich body of work on digital story-telling and other work with digital media that meshes well with Patti's idea of decolonizing through speaking to and speaking back.

The dialogue and written accounts coming out of just one of the groups in the workshop, offers a rich example of how speaking back can have both personal and social dimensions. Given that all the participants were educators or education researchers, it was not surprising that discussions evoked by the personal linked to policy were typically about schools and education. While not all participants in the workshop chose to 'decolonize themselves' as Patti termed it, everyone used the opportunity to speak back in some way to images that they now questioned – photos that were never taken, conversations that they would now like to have and so on. The most obvious one from the two examples of albums above relates to the 'Call to action' of the Truth and Reconciliation Commission (TRC)[4] and the implications for schooling in Canada both in relation to Indigenous and non-Indigenous teachers, something that Patti highlighted in her observations at the end of the workshop. This clearly has implications for teacher-education programs across the country. Currently only some teacher-education programs in Canada have a required course in Indigenous education. What provision can be made for pre-service teachers in various workshops and courses to follow this notion of decolonizing the self?

A promising example of such provision can be seen in the work of Ashley DeMartini, a doctoral candidate with whom Claudia has been working, who has embarked upon the idea of integrating digital story-telling and cellphilm production in relation to decolonization in her teacher-education classes. How do non-Indigenous teachers represent and address their relationships with land within Canada's settler-colonial past, its ongoing implications in the present, and the future? She is interested in ways of deepening intercultural understandings and developing a sense of responsibility to the shared stories that Indigenous and non-Indigenous peoples to North America have with land in Canada. In particular, she is committed to fostering a critical land literacy – a critical consciousness that understands how socio-political and economic narratives shapes peoples' experience with land in a settler colonial context. She is also interested in tracing how participants' forms of consciousness change as they create their digital stories. How has their thinking about land changed through their multimodal representations? As she observes:

I asked pre-service teachers to create cellphilms that examined the role of reconciliation (as outlined by the TRC) in their own lives, to determine what such a process looks like. Many of their stories revealed students struggling with dominant narratives about who they are in relation to the past and present. In another assignment, I asked students to create digital stories that examined their

---

[4]The Truth and Reconciliation Commission (TRC) in Canada is very much about a 'call to action' for addressing the legacy of the Indian Residential Schools.

relationships/connections with land. (This assignment became the foundation of my doctoral project). For both assignments, the visual and oral narratives revealed how students struggled to come to terms with their own investments in Canada's foundational myths in relation to their connections with land, or failed to do so. What I find interesting is how students' stories about Canadian/Indigenous relations varied in their scope, structure, and content as a result of the different modes of story-telling in participatory visual methodologies. Each mode reveals a different way of seeing unique to each genre's production parameters (cellphilm 60–90 seconds/ digital story-telling 3–5 minutes). (Personal communication, DeMartini, 2016)

FEATURES OF SPEAKING BACK AS METHOD

As we note in the introductory section to this chapter, speaking back is not about one unitary activity but is, rather, a set of practices. In some ways, most participatory visual work, including photovoice, cellphilming, participatory video, and digital story-telling, is already speaking back to something (for example, the absence of images from the perspective of the marginalized, the abundance of dominant images and so on). Notwithstanding the idea of cultural production, we frame this work very much as a conscious rethinking and repositioning – which we think can be identified as key features and practices. In this final section we highlight cross-cutting features of this work.

Participants as Audience

An under-studied area in audience study is the idea of the producers (participants) as audience. This may be self-evident in small group work, and especially as we noted in Chapter 2 and in our various publications on photovoice and participatory video workshops (Mitchell, 2011; Mitchell & De Lange, 2011). However, how participants look at their own work, and how they might revisit their own work in order to change it implies a more expansive idea of audience in visual research, and indeed one that might resemble work in performance as in the case of Forum Theatre.

Deliberate Working and Reworking

A key feature speaking back is its deliberateness in the reworking of material that has been previously produced by the participants. We borrow from the extensive body of literature on memory-work and especially Patricia Hampl's (1996) idea of first draft and second draft writing based on deliberate looking back and working with memories (see also Mitchell,

Strong-Wilson, Pithouse, & Allnutt, 2011; Mitchell & Weber, 1999). Our examples of speaking back highlight the significance of the process of going back over and over a piece of work in the context of personal and social critique. Most forms of organized protest and resistance rely on carefully studying what is missing as is evident in a range of work on politics of change in social movements as we see in Taft's (2010) work with girls and young women, and Choudry's (2015) work on *Learning Activism*. Engaging participants in doing this same kind of deliberate resistance to what they have already produced is the defining point of speaking back as opposed to only what the oppressors (or those whom they might have perceived to have been the oppressors) have produced.

Opportunities for Dialogic Engagement

Dialogic engagement draws on the notion of having a dialogue with another in order to understand each other and each other's viewpoint. For Bohm (1990) this is 'a stream of meaning flowing among us and through us and between us – a flow of meaning in the whole group, out of which will emerge some new understanding, something creative' (p. 1). When everybody is sensitive to all the nuances, and not merely to what is happening in their own mind, there forms a meaning which is shared. And in that way we can talk together coherently and think together. Moving away from superficial discussion in research to dialogic engagement through a speaking back approach, for example, is how participatory visual research can be done, and the way in which the visual productions could be used to ensure dialogic engagement. At each step of conceptualizing, co-constructing, and disseminating the work, opportunity for meaningful dialogic engagement among the participants and between the researchers and participants is created. In this way each participant gets the opportunity to share her views, but also to engage with and critique her own views and the views of others, and so to move forward to some new understanding. The interaction between Thoko, Magdalene, and Nellie around how children are raised in an African family demonstrates a moment of dialogic engagement that disrupted but also deepened their understanding of gaining some new understanding. Dialogic engagement is linked to the notion of cultivating criticality – the skill to judge the merit of the truth proffered. In the examples provided we have demonstrated how speaking back can be used to cultivate critical awareness of one's culturally ingrained ideas (as in the teachers' cellphilms) or to reposition one's own story (as in the family albums).

Catalysing

How do people come to challenge their own biases about race, class, gender, sexuality, age, disability, and so on? We acknowledge the vast range of work in critical pedagogy that seeks to disrupt, and the value of terms such as 'troubling' (Kumashiro, 2002, p. 202) to signal that there is some provocation for change. In the album workshop, the actions were peer-led. We saw, for example, the ways in which Bronson's group allowed him to arrive at a way to solve the problem raised by the absence of photos. Speaking as both an insider (isiZulu speaking, black, and a frequent visitor to the community) and an outsider (and provocateur) during the cellphilm project, Relebohile offered commentary and posed provoking questions during the speaking back in ways that that Claudia (a white Canadian) and Naydene (though South African, also a white woman) could not do so easily. She does not take a neutral stance or one that is affirming no matter what. Rather, she lays out in clear terms why she thinks the cellphilm *Being Enlightened* is problematic.

Repositioning

Not all speaking back activities necessarily result in dramatic shifts in perspective. Perhaps the most important point is that through reflection participants arrive at an awareness that they have altered their position in some way. We are not quite sure what to call the environmental factors that are so central to speaking back (and even changing one's mind), other than to say there needs to be an environment for critical engagement that does the very opposite of entrenching people in positions where there is no movement or possibility for change. As we have argued in this chapter, one of the strengths of the visual (photos, videos) is the fact that the images can be used over and over and over again. However, this can also be a limitation, since, for example, situations might change or the message might become dated in some way. The speaking back cellphilm work took place after the teachers were comfortable working together, and when there was no likelihood at that point of anyone outside the group seeing what they had produced. Timing is everything and in our experience, as we highlight in Chapter 2, when participants first produce a video, we might aim for a celebratory mode. However, we have also realized from our work with various groups that after a video has been produced there should be time for a reflexive mode: What did you like best? If you were to do it over again what would you do differently? Often, there are, of course, opportunities for critique, but in some instances it may be too early to speak back. That is why it was so important that the teachers worked on their speaking back videos after a period of time when they could come back to the work with fresh eyes. In the album project, in some ways the timing was higher risk as the workshop participants had not worked together for very long. However, the setting was low risk in that people could say as little or as much as they wanted about their photos.

A missing feature but something that we have begun to consider is the notion of theorizing back, the term Tuck (2009) and Guishard and Tuck (2014) use in their work on youth resistance research to describe the process of going beyond speaking back or engaging in what they refer to as 'confronting the proposition that theory flows down the royal lineage of grand narratives and (ag)grand(ized) theory' (p. 191). We think this is an important concept for expanding the participatory potential of this work. Resisting the idea that the only way to progress is to bring along all the history of the past, the authors call for mechanisms for confronting the present. Tuck writes that theorizing back 'contains a critique of the ways in which whitestream voices are considered rigorous, logical, reasoned and valid, while voices outside of the whitestream are considered experiential and emotional, representing devalued ways of knowing…' (Tuck, cited in Guishard & Tuck, 2014, p. 192). Kindon, Hume-Cooke, and Woods (2012) also draw on this idea of theorizing back following six screenings of a film made by members of an Indigenous group in New Zealand, Ngáti Hauiti. Having screened it to various academic audiences (with mixed responses), the research team reported on the responses to the 12 members of Ngáti Hauiti. As the authors note: '…project participants shed light on our research relationship, highlighted the potentially fraught nature of bicultural research, and acknowledged the risks for Kiwi members traveling to present with audiovisual products' (p. 352). We see this work as not only compatible with the examples noted above, but also expansive. There is already a vast body of work on practitioner knowledge, ranging from Schön's (1983) notion of the reflective practitioner in work with professionals from a variety of disciplines, to Connelly and Clandinin's (1992) work with teachers' personal and practical knowledge. However, this work still needs to challenge and confront existing bodies of knowledge from above, as it were, so that even if teachers in the cellphilm project, for example, speak back, there is still the challenge of considering the question of whose knowledge is valid. Perhaps there is no one set of answers except to allow for the complexity and messiness of this work. As Guishard and Tuck (2014) conclude, 'The goal of theorizing back is not resolving the sour notes or mending the divergence between what parts of an idea survive reflective analyses and resonate in particular contexts' (p. 192).

CONCLUSION

In this chapter we have focused on how participatory visual research can be used to facilitate a speaking back approach. The possibilities for this type of speaking back are vast, and while we have offered two instances of speaking back, one through talking and filming and one through writing and the use of photos, in relation to participant-led media production (cellphilms and curated photo albums), we can see other variations. One would be to have participants engage in speaking back by first carrying out some type of critical media analysis (of films or public service announcements) resulting in an analytic text, and, based on that work, produce cellphilms, photos, or digital stories. Work with multidirectional digital methods as described by Strong-Wilson, Mitchell, and Ingersoll (2016) might also involve participants speaking back to their own productions and to productive dialogue within a group setting. Overall, we have highlighted the significant role of participants as their own audience and as the ones who are best suited to repositioning the arguments in response to their own productions.

KEY POINTS OF THE CHAPTER

- Participants as producers in participatory visual research should be the first audiences for the productions, and as such positioned to re-think for themselves the issues that need to be challenged.
- Speaking back offers a method or approach for researchers and facilitators to engage participants in reworking and rethinking their productions.
- A case study on the speaking back through and to cellphilms provides the framework for a 5-step process:

  o   Being introduced to the idea of speaking back
  o   Reviewing the context for the 'why' of speaking back
  o   Engaging in provoking discussion
  o   Challenging the cellphilm script
  o   Creating and reflecting on the new cellphilm script.

- A case study on speaking back through and to family photographs provides a framework for a participatory workshop:

  o   Assembling family photographs
  o   Group conversation about the images
  o   Creating the curated album and presenting to the rest of the group
  o   Engaging in reflective writing about the process
  o   Participating in a group discussion about how speaking back to and through family photographs.

- Identifying the key features of speaking back as method allows for thinking through how the method itself can help to extend the value of participatory visual research in transformations and social change.

4

PICTURES AT AN EXHIBITION

━━ **CHAPTER CONTENTS** ━━━━━━━━━━━━━━━━━━━━━━━━━━━

INTRODUCTION

In the previous chapter, it is the participants themselves who are the audiences for their own work. In this chapter we consider audience through the idea of display and exhibition. The notion of display-as-inquiry, as an idea that was introduced by Mitchell (2011) captures the interplay of the technical aspects of exhibiting, participatory processes, images, and audience. This chapter as a whole responds most directly to photovoice and related forms of visual production where either virtual or physical/material exhibiting is central to reaching audiences. As Mitchell highlights in the final chapter of *Doing Visual Research* (Mitchell, 2011) the idea of mounting an exhibition has come to be regarded as an essential component of photovoice projects. We would go so far as to say that the mounting of an exhibition has become *de rigeur* in photovoice projects because in this way the photos that are typically produced to voice a concern reach those who need to know; this is crucial. But we see this as an area that is perhaps more complex than the simple observation that we had an exhibition and the whole community came. What are some of the critical issues that need to be considered? To what extent is the idea of a community exhibition a very Western notion or one that is primarily a middle-class practice associated with the leisure time occupation of going to museums and art galleries? The chapter begins with a consideration of the politics of exhibiting, drawing in particular on exhibitions in a variety of community contexts. We are particularly interested in the idea of production in relation to multimodality as a way of beginning to frame the notion of exhibiting as part of display as inquiry. Building on the work of Zuromskis (2013) and others on vernacular photography, we then go on to consider the idea of circulating the vernacular, and, in so doing, map out a range of strategies for capturing the learning attached to exhibiting.

COMMUNITY-BASED EXHIBITIONS

If one scours the literature for something called the politics of exhibiting in community-based photography, the findings are likely to be scant, though there is, of course, a vast body of work on curation and exhibiting in such areas as Art History and Museum Studies where the politics of representation is critical (see Butler & Lehrer, 2016). This work can have implications for exhibiting and co-curation in community-based research in everything from the technical aspects of mounting and framing photos, through to creating captions and curatorial statements. Various studies have focused on specific exhibitions of photos taken by ordinary people and exhibited in museums and galleries with Edward Steichen's *Family of Man* being one of the best known (Ribalta, 2008; Sandeen, 1995). In her book *Snapshot Photography: The Lives of Images* Zuromskis (2013) draws on the work of Geoffrey Batchen and others to study several of these well-known international exhibitions made up of snapshots, including the *Family of Man* exhibition of the 1950s which toured for 8 years in 63 countries, and the more recent *Pictures That Matter* exhibition mounted after the attack on the World Trade Center in New York in 2001. She terms this work 'aestheticizing the vernacular' highlighting the 'contentious relationship between photography's vernacular culture [the snapshot] and the aestheticizing function of the museum [public display]' (p. 119).

However, as Delgado (2015), Reinikainenand and Zetterström-Dahlqvist (2016) and others working in participatory visual research are acknowledging, exhibiting community-based research regardless of whether it is in a gallery or a community hall brings with it many complexities. Here we embark on a brief reflexive journey on exhibiting photovoice projects over a period of 14 years. Our exhibiting work dates back to our first participatory visual research project. This took place with a rural community in South Africa struggling with high levels of HIV infection. Coming out of our first photovoice project together was an exhibition entitled, *Seeing for Ourselves: Photo-voice in Addressing HIV and AIDS* (hereafter referred to as *Seeing for Ourselves*). This consisted of 12 black-and-white photographs with captions created by teachers and community health workers, and a curatorial statement. As of 2017, the exhibition is still displayed in the entrance of the clinic in this rural community, and another version of it is still displayed in one of the corridors of the University of KwaZulu-Natal. This same exhibition was also exhibited in a rural community on Pensioner Day so that it would reach as many people as possible in the community, and later it was transformed into laminated poster-sized images to be used as visual aids in the classroom.

When we co-curated *Seeing for Ourselves* we knew very little about exhibiting other than to make sure that the pictures stayed up long enough to be seen, and that they did not curl, and, ultimately, that removing them did not remove the paint from the walls on which they were mounted. We learned about captions and how to display them, but also to consider the absence of captions as Edwards (2002) recommends if the point of the exhibition is to highlight the viewing and meaning-making of the audience. We considered questions like: How many images should be exhibited? Who makes the final decision on which ones? We learned to consider when and where it was most effective to have the captions in the language and original spelling of the participants, and in their own handwriting, and when they were better edited and in typed format. We came to think about framing (and what type of frame to use) and mounting on poster board, and the significance of enlarging photos or exhibiting them as small-sized snapshots and even in small albums. We have spent long hours thinking about and experimenting with different ways to mount an exhibition, including considering using wire and magnets, and clothes lines and clothes pegs. We have tested out various ways of creating titles and curatorial statements, again drawing as much as possible on the perspectives of the participants. We have typically exhibited each photo separately, but we have also tested out the production of large-sized posters, some containing four to five photos and captions printed on the poster. In one exhibition we had a huge poster (the size of a door) that was made up of 35 or more images. We have also experimented with different products on which to print photos: heavy poster board, glossy or matte finish photo paper with and without borders, fabric, and postcards.

Collectively we have probably been involved in one way or another (curating, co-curating, advising, supporting) in approximately 100 photovoice exhibitions. In some ways every exhibition we have ever curated or co-curated has been a precursor to the next one.

Now we can look at this history and realize that we were on a journey as choice makers as Jewitt (2013) and Kress (2008) in their work on multimodality term the practices we were exploring in relation to design. As Jewitt explains, multimodality offers:

...methods and a framework for the collection and analysis of visual, aural, embodied and spatial aspects of interaction and environments ... Multimodality emphasizes situated action. This refers to the importance of the social context and the resources available for meaning making, with attention being paid to people's situated choice of resources, rather than emphasizing the system of available resources. Thus it opens up possibilities for recognizing, analyzing, and theorizing the different ways in which people make meaning and how those meanings are interrelated. (p. 250)

This work on multimodality has been applied to a variety of digital production sites involving young people, including digital story-telling (St John Ward, 2015), and social change oriented vlogs produced by Canadian young people (Caron, Raby, Mitchell, Thewissen-Leblanc, & Prioletta, 2016). Taking into consideration the significance of semiotics in exhibition practices, our decision-making has been informed by practicalities (an available wall, safety and security, the portability of the images, costs, and weather), aesthetics, and the perspective of both the participants and the audience. While some of these concerns no doubt appear in some version of a course on exhibiting 101 that might take place in a Fine Arts or Design department, they expand into the specifics of community-based research, and as such might differ significantly from Zuromskis's 'aesthetics of the vernacular'. We highlight several here, taking into consideration some of the features that are likely to have an impact on choice-making.

Images and Intentions

We start with the intention of the photographers. Unlike the image-makers of many family snapshots including the ones that are exhibited in the *Family of Man,* for example, the participants in photovoice projects are, typically, interrogating a social issue (for example, safety and security, health, environmental issues, stigma, sexual violence) that is critical to their well-being and about which they wish to speak in relation to various community actors. The images are typically provocative and are meant to disrupt. These may be very different from Steichen's *Family of Man* exhibition which, as Sandeen (1995) observes, is 'a compendium of beautiful but unchallenging photographs to be paged through as a relief from a world of harsher realities' (p. 180). Moreover, unlike Steichen's exhibition in which he, as the curator, explored the 'universal language' of photographs, presenting a world he observes 'as a global community, a "family" united by the supposedly fundamental experiences of birth, death, work, play, war, marriage, procreation and the like' (Zuromskis, 2013, p. 124), in a participatory visual project it is typically the image-makers whose images inform the perspective or point of the exhibition. Ideally, in participatory visual research it is the image-makers who will also participate in the exhibiting by choosing the images, deciding on venues and audience (where the exhibition should be mounted and who should see it). We recognize, of course, that sometimes this is not always possible.

Expected Outcomes

The image-makers in participatory visual research because they have embarked upon the idea of identifying challenges particularly around social issues may expect something to happen, or something to come out of their exhibition besides appreciation and a pat on the back for a job well done. This may be very different from exhibitions where exhibiting an aesthetic production is the whole point.

Audience Familiarity

Unlike the audiences of non-local people of many of the exhibitions that Zuromskis describes, in community-based research, the anticipated audience members (especially local policy makers) are likely to be known. Typically, the image-makers will be present at the exhibition and this may have an effect on what can be exhibited.

Location

Even the spaces themselves may be problematic. Where do community audiences go to look at exhibitions? Art galleries? School halls? The lobby of the Ministry of Agriculture? A petrol station? The middle of the village on Pensioner Day? As described elsewhere (Mitchell, 2011), these community locations bring new issues in terms of managing public spaces and the technology of display in relation to such factors as safety (no glass), durability (exhibiting outside and under various weather conditions), portability (exhibiting over and over again), along with such obvious factors as cost (avoiding ostentatious display in an under-resourced community centre).

Local Viewing Practices

Tied to location, viewing practices themselves are not to be taken-for-granted. What does it mean to look at a collection of photos, especially as part of a community or social group? We know from museum practices that the idea of this kind of leisure looking is often linked to class and other social factors. As we describe in more detail later in this chapter, in an exhibition in an informal settlement in Nairobi many participants chose to view the exhibition catalogue as opposed to looking at the exhibition.

PROCESSES IN CURATING

To date there have been few examples in the social sciences of what happens behind the scenes of curating exhibitions, although there are several notable exceptions, ranging from Church's (2008) detailed description of setting up and curating an art exhibition featuring her mother's work as a dress-maker of wedding dresses in rural Alberta in Western Canada, through to Reinikainen and Zetterström-Dahlqvist's (2016) essay that uses an autoethnographic analysis of an exhibition that they developed at Mid-Sweden University as part of a project they carried out with Claudia on curating the types of personal albums described in Chapter 3. In their exhibition *Social Change: Individual Lives Mirror Social Change – Curating Albums as an Autobiographical Genre,* they worked with six curated albums (their own plus the albums of four other colleagues at the university), something that brings with it a concern for representation. While the photos in the exhibition all came from family collections of photos rather than from photovoice images, the process of creating the albums is a visual method that is not that different from photovoice itself (see Mitchell & Allnutt, 2008; Mitchell, Weber, & Pithouse, 2009), and curating the full exhibition brought with it extensive choice-making, as they discuss in their essay. For example, location was a concern and although they considered a community venue, they realized that exhibiting at the university would make a stronger statement about personal connections to research. At the same time this brought other concerns. The authors include in their essay a particularly evocative section called 'Walking through the halls':

As we began to really see our familiar everyday campus halls, we also started to become more aware of the fact that once the exhibition was up, the curated albums project would be visible to others at campus in a way that none of us in the group had been before. Showing pictures from our personal photo albums and displaying our curatorial statement connected to the album for the first time, we would actually expose ourselves in a way we were not used to. (pp. 76)

They also considered the display medium and in the end chose a large poster format (7- X 100) for each album.

Central to their chapter is its focus on three different aspects of reflexivity. As they observe:

One temporal dimension related to the past, that is, the actual curating of the albums as an emotional journey to be considered in the curation of the exhibition process. Another time dimension relates to the present – the curation (or the doing) of the exhibition and, finally, the third related to the future – how will we write about it? However, our point of departure was in the present, that is, in the actual process of producing the exhibition while, *at the same time* [emphasis added] reflecting back to the past and into the future. (p. 75)

There are even fewer detailed accounts of co-curation involving researchers and participants, or exhibitions entirely curated by participants although accounts increasingly do refer to consultation with participants about which images, which location, and, sometimes, which audiences. A remarkable exception is the work of Melissa Proietti, a member of the Urban Arts Project team at McGill University, who, with a group of students from James Lyng High School, an inner city school in Montreal, established the UpNext Art Gallery in the school (Low, Carter, Wood, Mitchell, Proietti, & Friedman, 2016; Proietti, 2016). Building the gallery required some physical modifications to a space in the school, but otherwise all aspects of the gallery, from selecting the artistic works to exhibiting decisions, to overall curation is managed by the students themselves. Since the opening of the gallery the students have curated two exhibitions, one on Black History month which included submissions from artists from several high schools in Montreal. The other exhibition focused on DIY skateboards. What these examples of curation-in-the-making remind us of is the rich potential for these types of interventions to become more central to our work.

STUDYING EXHIBITING

Building on Zuromskis's idea of naming what it is that we are doing in exhibiting in relation to audiences, we are proposing that as a community of scholars we consider attempting to name our work officially, and study it in relation to audiences and exhibitions in participatory visual research aimed at social change. The term *circulating the vernacular* (as opposed to aestheticizing the vernacular) may be a start in its highlighting, first, the ways in which the images produced by participants (as opposed to professional artists) are still the vernacular, but second, that if they are to have an impact, they need to circulate, to be seen 'over and over and over again'. Circulating may take place at different sites, and to many different audiences. But the circulating can also take place through different modalities. For example, images and captions may be re-formatted and packaged into an exhibition catalogue or a digital exhibition as we explore later in this chapter. They may also become integrated into digital dialogue tools or digital media productions which incorporate the images and captions and which, typically, are then screened for various audiences and followed by discussion (see Chapter 6).

ONE SET OF PHOTOS, MULTIPLE SHOWINGS[1]

In this section we include Claudia's field notes of impressions and reflections on conversations related to the exhibiting of *Our Photos, Our Learning, Our Well-being* in several different

---

[1]Much of this section 'One set of photos, multiple showings' draws from an article first published by Mitchell (2015) in *Educational Research for Social Change*.

sites and over several months. The images in the exhibition were produced by 80 young people in Ethiopia enrolled in Agricultural Technical Vocational Education Training (ATVET) at four ATVET Colleges. As part of a Canadian funded study,[2] the four colleges were participating in a needs-assessment exercise. Given that young people are the main clients of the colleges it was critical to get their perspectives on what it meant to be 'a male or female student attending an ATVET college'. Working in small photovoice groups of three or four the participants first took photos and then had a chance to explain their images to the rest of the larger group, and to consider what their photos might mean in relation to changes at their college. At the time of the needs-assessment, the research team working with each of the colleges drew on the themes in the photos to deepen an understanding of the gender contexts for teaching and learning, and to build into the follow-up programming ideas that could respond to the concerns raised by the photographers. However, it became clear that the collection of photos could have uses beyond the initial needs-assessment, ranging from giving a face, as it were, to the project at the time of a

Figure 4.1   Exhibition poster: *Our Photos, Our Learning, Our Well-being*

Poster developed by Fatima Khan and Claudia Mitchell
Mitchell, C. (2015b).

---

[2]The project Agricultural Transformation Through Strong Vocational Education (ATTSVE) is a project funded by Global Affairs Canada (2014–2019), led by Dalhousie University and involving as partners McGill University, Jimma University, and the Mennonite Economic Development Association.

public launch in Canada, to becoming a tool for self-study for the institutions themselves. To address this dual focus, team members working on the project designed an exhibition, drawing together a number of key themes found in the images – the significance of surroundings (with many photos highlighting issues of water and sanitation), knowledge being gained in such areas as environmental science, issues of health and well-being (including sexual violence), and barriers to learning (inadequate technology, lack of teacher support). The images and captions were represented on large posters (27 inches/68cm by 40 inches/1.02m). See Figure 4.1.

METHOD: STUDYING AUDIENCE ENGAGEMENT

Exhibition Site 1

The first exhibition of *Our Photos, Our Learning, Our Well-being* took place in conjunction with the launch of the project in Canada, at which at least four faculty members from each ATVET from Ethiopia were in attendance. Because the faculty members were otherwise going to be seeing the images for the first time at the launch event, it was important for them to see for themselves how their students regarded their learning. This was particularly important because some of the images were very critical of the various colleges, concerned about the food insecurity in relation to living in residence, sexual violence, and absentee instructors of a specific ATVET (even though no names were used). In fact even before the exhibition was unveiled to the team of deans, the research team met and decided to leave out a set of two posters that dealt entirely with images of dirty and inadequate toilets and lack of water. The concern was that perhaps these images simply reinforced the dominant negative images of Ethiopia, and as such reinforced an othering of 'over there in Africa'. Together the team also wondered how the ATVET faculty themselves would feel about having these particular photos exhibited. As Claudia observed:

My first thought is '…but the students took these photos. Is it fair to now not show them?' But then I think that they were taking the photos for a needs assessment. They had been asked to be honest and take pictures of their concerns. X is right. Are these images really appropriate for this audience? Is this some type of National Geographic portrayal? Why didn't I notice the cumulative effect of 15 images of dirty toilets when we put that set of posters together? Maybe the 15 images spread out would be different, but all together on two large posters they seem larger than life. (Claudia's Reflective Field Notes, January, 2015)

When the various faculty members viewed the images they expressed a sense of being pleasantly surprised about the photography skills of the students but also their surprise about how much their students knew about topics such as climate change and other environmental concerns. At the same time, they were concerned about some of the pictures. One photo in particular was particularly controversial in its showing an image of a chair with a half empty plate of food on it.

Three of the Deans, one from each of three colleges, are clustered around the image. One is adamant that it should be taken down. For one thing, he says, the student who took the picture should not be showing a picture of a plate on a chair. He thinks it should be removed and that the girl should just clean up the mess. It is not clear what good removing the picture will be other than that it doesn't appropriately represent what it should and whether it is a bad reflection on the college or not is not the point – it just shouldn't be. Another Dean steps in and assures him that actually this is how things are and we should all be open to looking at the truth. It is a back and forth dispute that goes on for 20 to 30 minutes or more and as an outsider I stay out of it, but in my heart I am hoping that they will agree to leave the image in the exhibition. It is what the students wanted to say. It is only the next day at the time of the launch that I learn the outcome. The person who is most adamant about removing the picture asks if he can say something to the assembled group of dignitaries and makes a comment that although many of the images of the colleges are very negative in that they show problems with sanitation and the conditions of the cafeterias, and it is too bad the students had to take them, but that perhaps at the end of the six years of the project they will be taking different pictures. It will be a test of the success of the project. (Claudia's Reflective Field Notes, 2015)

The intense back and forth over that one picture of a half empty plate on a chair in a cafeteria is reminiscent of the method that Moletsane and Mitchell (2007) describe in 'Working with a single photograph' and of the more recent work of Batchen et al. (2012) *Picturing Atrocity* regarding the ways that individual photos have over time and in history played such powerful roles in shaping perspectives. The photograph the deans chose to focus on was so much more than just a photograph of a half-eaten dinner on a chair. For the students who created the image, it was in all likelihood what might be referred to as a staged photo (Mitchell, 2011a). This is not to say that an image of a plate of half-eaten food on a plate in an ATVET cafeteria is impossible to find, but rather that the students wanted to set it apart and make sure that the inadequacy of the food was apparent. This is an issue that the research team learned about from many different sources when we visited the various ATVETS. Students in most cases are very poor and the colleges are under-funded. They genuinely wanted to make the point that the lack of food and/or the poor quality of the food were issues that had an impact on their learning and on their well-being more generally. For the policy makers, especially the dean who was so adamant that the young women whom he referred to as a girl should clean up the mess, the intended message from the students is missed, and in spite of the fact that the students are acknowledged as being good photographers and as being knowledgeable in terms of environmental issues, this photograph counters these positive

Figure 4.2 *Our Photos, Our Learning, Our Well-being* launch of exhibition in Canada

Photograph by Claudia Mitchell

Mitchell, C. (2015b).

points. If there had ever been a question about respecting the voices of students, this image has shattered that possibility. It is also worth noting that although any identifying features of the photographers (such as age, sex, location) are left out, the dean attributes the responsibility for cleaning up to a female student, again undermining the agency that the students have attempted to demonstrate through their photographs. Thus, it is at this point more about what the students need to do and not what the college administration needs to do (see Figure 4.2).

Exhibition Site 2

The second time *Our Photos, Our Learning, Our Well-being* (Figure 4.3) was exhibited was at an at an event in Ethiopia where all the deans come together for a week-long training session, again along with approximately eight staff members from each of the four ATVETS. This time all of the posters are set up.

This is a completely different showing. The faculty members who went to Canada are back looking at their photos but this time they themselves are part of the history of the exhibition. They have seen it before and we even have images of them looking at the exhibition when it was set up in Canada. Although there is no identifying information in any of the posters as to which ATVET is involved, in this exhibition it is clear that everyone wants to find his or her college. It is not so much how it is represented but that it is represented. (Claudia's Reflective Field Notes, April, 2015)

Figure 4.3 *Our Photos, Our Learning, Our Well-being* launch of exhibition in Ethiopia

Photograph by Claudia Mitchell

Mitchell, C. (2015b).

Exhibition Site 3 and Beyond (Travelling Exhibition)

During the course of the training session attached to Exhibition 2, the group decide to turn the exhibition into a travelling exhibition and have it travel to each of the ATVETS where the students who produced the images, along with other students and faculty members, can view them. They agree that it will be useful for each ATVET (Figure 4.4) to document the process, and as a group we come up with a common set of questions:

1 Where is the exhibition held?
2 Who attended? (Males? Females? Lecturer? Management? Students?)
3 How long did you leave the exhibition up?
4 Did you hold any special event(s) to coincide with putting up the exhibition?
5 What was the overall response to the exhibition?
6 Which photos did the people choose to focus on and talk about?
7 What did the audiences think of the photographers students were saying through their photos?
8 What actions did people suggest were necessary to address the concerns of the photographers?

Figure 4.4 Exhibition of *Our Photos, Our Learning, Our Well-being* at an ATVET

Photograph by Biyene

Mitchell, C. (2015b).

Claudia comments on the power of the travelling exhibition to promote dialogue:

Although I have only had a chance to see the exhibition set up at two of the colleges. I have been interested in some of the results. If we are to take seriously the idea of impact in relation to audiences, and especially the idea of engaging policy makers, it is important to look at actions and what has changed as a result of the students voicing their concerns through image making and the policy makers viewing the images. Just a little over a year after Exhibition One, I had occasion to visit the ATVET College of the Dean who objected to the photograph. The travelling exhibition had just arrived at the college and was being viewed by students, staff, and trainees from the other college. The Dean sought me out and pointed to an image in the exhibition of a desolate space on campus bereft of any vegetation. The students had taken the picture a year earlier to draw attention to the ways in which the campus itself was neglected. The Dean very proudly noted that one can no longer see that image since the college, as part of its environmental strategy developed within the project as a whole, had embarked upon a project of cleaning up the campus, planting trees and flowers and generally making the place a much more attractive [one] for both teaching and learning. This initiative relied on the work of the Environment Club, a staff and student organization, but also the leadership of senior management. The point is that engaging policy makers also involves some accountability for doing something. (Claudia's Reflective Field Notes, April, 2016)

STUDYING AUDIENCES THROUGH EXHIBITING

In this section we draw attention to the various levels reflexivity that might be attached to multiple showings of the same exhibition.

Researcher Reflexivity

As we have demonstrated in the previous section, as a starting point in this work we can begin with ourselves and our own reflections as researchers. What can we learn by looking inward and how can we contribute to a cumulative body of knowledge about audience engagement through our own first person reflexive accounts? This is an obvious area of study although as Rose (2012) notes, it is work that is rare in audience studies.

Participant Reflections

While it is not so apparent in the fieldwork from Ethiopia described above, except in the sense that the faculty members (who were not the image-makers) from the various colleges had the opportunity to set up and reflect on the exhibition *Our Photos, Our Learning, Our Well-being*, elsewhere we have documented the reflections of the image-makers in another study screening or exhibiting their productions. As an important component of the *Taking Action 2* project, for example, a study with Indigenous youth from across Canada producing their own digital stories about taking leadership in the area of HIV and AIDS, young people had an opportunity to screen their digital stories in their own communities. In such work we have an opportunity to learn from the participants about what it felt like presenting their work to local communities, and their own engagement with those local audiences (Flicker et al., 2014).

Studying Audiences Directly

Clearly we need to document directly, where possible, what audiences have to say. We can use a variety of tools to do this, including visitor books where audiences members note their responses, more objective post-viewing questionnaires and face-to-face interviews, along with self-administered tools. Several years ago, for example, Ardra Cole and Maura McIntyre (2006) set up an exhibition based on their work with caregivers of patients with Alzheimers. As audience members, especially caregivers, circulated through the exhibition there were opportunities for them to stop and record their own reflections or experiences. A similar opportunity is provided in the Canadian Museum for Human Rights where a small recording booth is set up in the Canadian Journey's gallery so that museum goers can record what they regard as a story or issue that is missing from the museum. The use of mobile technology to record responses is also possible. Along with these approaches to audience in more general ways, there is also the case of studying audiences such as policy makers in a more targeted way. Responses might be gauged through observation, but they might also be interviewed directly. How do they regard the images? Which images have an impact on them and why? How do they feel about the images and the image-making? Are there certain images that offer new perspectives? And, critically, of course, what do they intend to do (if anything) as a result of seeing an exhibition? The example of the dean who drew attention to the way a scene in a photograph had changed as a result of establishing an Environmental Club is an example of this (see also Chapter 7).

EXHIBITION CATALOGUES

But exhibitions do not have to be limited to the materiality of only one type of display. A significant import from Museum Studies is the idea of an exhibition catalogue or a book version of the original exhibition. While these catalogues vary in how they are organized, they typically include one or more essays or other writings about the images and, of course, the images themselves. The persuasiveness of the visual (Burns, 2011) clearly draws an audience to gaze, and is a strength when we are disseminating the findings and wanting the viewers to engage with what they see. But how, we ask, might the exhibition be extended beyond the space it occupies in the clinic, schools and university? How might the work co-created by the participants actually go home, in a manner of speaking, into the communities with the participants? How might the exhibition be owned by the participants and be used in ways they themselves choose to employ? Thinking of how to disseminate the visual and the findings in ways other than in a report of the exhibition, drew us to using a catalogue, in ways similar to that of an art exhibition.

Seeing, Believing, and Acting for Change (South Africa)

Our first catalogue, which was meant to extend a co-curated exhibition produced with our colleagues, all members of the HIV and AIDS Education Community of Practice,[3] came out of a photovoice activity in which all the members, representing faculties of education across South Africa documented visually what was happening in their universities.[4] The

[3]This Community of Practice is supported by HEAIDS as a division within the National Department of Higher Education South Africa.

[4]As noted in Chapter 2 the actual activity was framed as photovoice where we anticipated that all participants would take photographs. In the end some opted to download images from the internet. All however produced captions.

original exhibition, *Seeing, Believing and Acting for Change: Integrating HIV and AIDS in Higher Education Curricula* was displayed at a conference in Durban, while a pull-up banner version of the exhibition was produced and circulated to almost every education faculty in public universities all over South Africa. The small catalogue, formatted on both sides of an A4 page and more like a flyer, contained the title of the exhibition, the curatorial statement, and the whole collection of photographs with captions, as well as a list of acknowledgements. In this way the catalogue became an entry point for opening up further dialogue, as the excerpt from the curatorial statement shows.

> The photographs in the collection, numbering more than 40, individually and collectively serve as visual narratives of integrating HIV and AIDS into the curriculum, of reflecting on teaching sexuality education, of considering our collective responsibility, and learning from each other within the Community of Practice in teacher education. We see photographs of the vulnerability of children and youth, the importance of transferring knowledge, the need to keep on rethinking our strategies, the challenging demands placed on teacher educators, but also the imperatives to continue with the work. More than anything they highlight the idea that our work in this critical area goes far beyond the walls of our classrooms. The curriculum is everywhere!

This work – the exhibition and the catalogue (along with a website presence)[5] – as a whole throws light on social life, on the teacher educators' profession, and on a culture of caring in a time of HIV and AIDS in South Africa. With the catalogue in hand any of the members of the Community of Practice or others working in the area of HIV and AIDS education can initiate a dialogue about integrating HIV and AIDS in curricula (see also Chapter 8).

Our Voices, Our Hopes (Vietnam)

Another catalogue, *Our Voices, Our Hopes: Girls with Disabilities and Participatory Visual Methodologies* (De Lange, Nguyen, Mitchell, & Nguyen, 2014) was co-produced with a group of girls and young women with disabilities in Vietnam. The visual artefacts, drawings, photographs, and policy posters produced by the participants in reflecting on their own situation and what could be done, were turned into an exhibition with an accompanying catalogue (Figure 4.5). An excerpt from the curatorial statement follows:

---

[5]http://heaids.org.za/site/assets/files/1233/exhibition_poster_low_res.pdf

Our Voices, Our Hopes aims to showcase the collective work produced by 21 girls with disabilities in Tu Liem district in Hanoi, February 2014. It aims to: 1) highlight the productive work of girls with disabilities in participatory workshops; 2) present the ways in which participatory visual methodologies can be used to monitor rights for girls with disabilities; 3) raise awareness of the need to build on the perspectives of girls with disabilities (and with differing abilities) to foster more inclusive communities; and 4) connect girls with disabilities and their communities. We invite local communities, schools, teachers, parents, and policy makers to listen to the voices and perspectives of girls with disabilities in Tu Liem on why, how, and for whom we need to cultivate such transnational activism. The outcomes of this project, we hope, will set a stage for more inclusive policy-making to foster inclusion and social justice in Vietnam and the global South.

Figure 68: "Education for all"

Another facilitator (F) in group 6 discussed with the participants (P) their recommendations for school and the community. The girls decided they wanted to make a poster about everyone going to school and education for all.

P1: I want teachers to teach me how to draw. I will draw more beautifully.
P2: I want to socialize with all my classmates. Teachers need to care and help students with disabilities ...There should be no discrimination against people with disabilties.
P3: I want community leaders to help me.
P2: ... to create a favourable environment for people with disabilties to mobilize easily.

P1: Em muốn giáo viên dạy vẽ cho mình. Em sẽ vẽ đẹp và vẽ chăm chỉ hơn.
P2: muốn hòa đồng với tất cả các bạn. Giáo viên cần quan tâm, giúp đỡ các học sinh khuyết tật... Không phân biệt đối xử với người khuyết tật.
P3: Em muốn các chú lãnh đạo xã phường giúp đỡ em.
P2: ... tạo điều kiện cho người khuyết tật đi lại dễ dàng, tạo điều kiện thuận lợi.

Figure 4.5   Exhibition catalogue: *Our Voices, Our Hopes*

Poster produced by workshop participants

De Lange, Nguyen, X.T., Mitchell, C., Nguyen, L.A. (2015).

This catalogue is more extensive than the previously described one, formatted as a 79-page book, printed in colour on glossy paper. It begins with a foreword by the Vice-Director General of the Vietnamese Institute of Educational Sciences in the Ministry of Education and Training. Having her at the exhibition and getting her to contribute a foreword places the work of the girls and women more prominently in the policy-making arena. The catalogue also provides an overview of the project, *Monitoring Educational Rights for Girls with Disabilities in Vietnam: A Journey to Inclusion* followed by the curatorial statement: Through the Eyes of Girls with Disabilities: Using participatory visual methodologies, and an overview of the process of the girls and young women co-producing the visual artefacts. The central component of the catalogue is a systematic arrangement of the drawings (*Me and My Community*), the photographs (*Feeling Included and not Included*) and the policy posters (*Recommendation for Change*). The catalogue offers a conclusion, and ends with acknowledgements and references. It was important to us to consider the accessibility of the catalogue in terms of language, and, so as to increase the accessibility, the catalogue was translated into Vietnamese. It also has an ISBN number. As part of the knowledge mobilization plan of the project, 1,000 copies of the catalogue were printed and distributed throughout Vietnam to the girls and women in the group, and to schools, community partners, the ministry of education, and UNICEF.

Given the potential for exhibition catalogues to extend the life of a participatory visual project, we have tried to track the use of the catalogue by contacting various stakeholders about this. A comment by one of the fieldworkers highlights the significance of the catalogue to the girls themselves:

In the morning, the book [catalogue] *Our Voice, Our Hope* is introduced to the GwD [Girls With Disabilities]. They are so delighted. Some of them exclaim happily when they are allowed to take the book home. X is more talkative today. She actively talks with friends. The book discussion is really exciting since all GwDs participate enthusiastically. (Dai Mo primary school, February 2015)

What is significant for us is that each girl now owns a catalogue to revisit and share as she sees fit, thereby extending the co-produced knowledge of their social reality and the dialogue into the community and further afield.

Another stakeholder working with an NGO comments on using the catalogue wrote in an email:

Yes, our organization (DPO Bac Tu Liem) received copies. We are showing at the bookshelf in our office. Recently, we have organized a training for our members and there are some students who come as volunteers for our training. Those students looked at the catalogues and they were very interested in it. They asked if they could have some for their study reference. You know, they are studying social work and they find that book very interesting and useful for their study. They could not believe how women and girls with disabilities could do a great job: drawing pictures with meaningful messages! We sometimes welcome visitors to our office. Most of them expressed their feelings to the participants who joined the project when they see the catalogue. They admired women and girls with disabilities for their effort and they hoped to have chance to support them. (Personal communication, June 6, 2016)

Through the Eyes of Mothers (Kenya)

Building on what we learned in the two previous projects, we developed a catalogue to accompany the exhibition *Through the Eyes of Mothers*, based on a photovoice component of a larger project on access to childcare in relation to women's economic empowerment. Forty-eight women living in various sections of one informal settlement in Nairobi document visually the challenges of childcare, and some solutions. The images have now been exhibited several times, first in conjunction with a stakeholders' forum which took place at the African Population Health Research Centre in June, 2016, and then in the community hall of the informal settlement a few days later. The catalogue, a 36-page book, contains a short description of the project, a curatorial statement, several process photos, and 27 of the images from the original collection along with the captions (Figure 4.6).

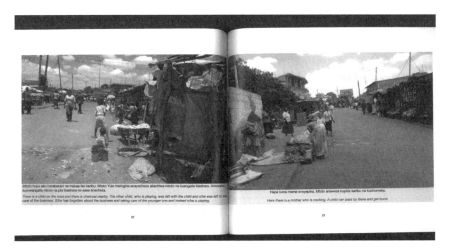

Figure 4.6   Inside exhibition catalogue

Scan taken by Claudia Mitchell

Mitchell, C., DeMartini, A., & Murthuri, S. (2016).

The text is in both Swahili and English as can be seen on the catalogue cover (Figure 4.7):

Figure 4.7   Exhibition catalogue: *Through the Eyes of Mothers*

Scan taken by Claudia Mitchell

Mitchell, C., DeMartini, A., & Murthuri, S. (2016).

In addition to a short introduction, noteworthy is the fact that our team embarked on a self-publishing plan, using online book-making resources that in North America, at least, are typically used for producing wedding albums or for commemorating other family celebrations. The catalogue is also available online.[6] As noted earlier, we have found the fascination that participants and others have had for going through the catalogue illuminating even though the much larger images were available to be seen on site, and we have numerous process photos of small groups clustered around the book as visual evidence of this fascination.

CREATING AN EXHIBITION CATALOGUE

Based on what we have learned in putting together the three catalogues, we enthusiastically endorse the idea of catalogue production as a way of addressing the ephemerality,

---

[6]http://aphrc.org/wp-content/upload

generally speaking, of an exhibition, and thus as a way of extending the life of the visual material. We also see that the catalogue serves other uses with the ownership aspects for participants being key, but also the potential for agency that participants could have over their own work. As with our discussion earlier in this chapter on the multimodal considerations of producing an exhibition, there is clearly a great deal of choice-making that takes (and could take) place including the colour of the visual artefacts (full colour, black-and-white, or sepia) which should, if possible, be negotiated with the participants, and accessibility in terms of language which should be as inclusive as possible. A tension we have seen in the preparation for some exhibitions that carries over to the production of a catalogue relates to ensuring the authenticity of the artefacts and captions. Should visual work ever be altered in any way through Photoshop or other digital programs? Should captions ever be altered to make them more aesthetically or linguistically pleasing? Under what circumstances should alterations take place and who should decide? Clearly a catalogue might have multiple purposes, but as a team we need to consider what those might be: a visual record; a statement of ownership for the participants; and/or a tool for initiating dialogue with communities and policy makers or, more broadly, a dissemination tool.

Linda Liebenberg, a colleague at Dalhousie University and who headed up *The Spaces & Places*, participatory visual project with Indigenous young people on the East Coast of Canada developed what the team called a photobook (*Spaces & Places Dissemination Photobook*),[7] capturing information and findings and the highly visual work from the various research sites. While the book was used as a gift for keynote and plenary speakers at an international conference focused on resilience in 2015, she notes that all the young participants and service provider collaborators from the project also received a copy. As she observes:

In total, 60 copies of the book were printed. Feedback from youth and service providers was extremely positive and appears to have provided youth with a strong sense of affirmation regarding their other efforts on the project. In one site, the Director of Mental Health Services has also requested a few additional copies (we had spares) to share with others. Two instances are worth noting. First, a new RCMP officer had recently come to the community. While meeting with the Director he noticed the book and started looking at it. He became really excited and explained that he had worked in the other two communities as well, and knew several of the youth across all three sites. Naturally she shared a copy of the book with him and he was thrilled. Second, the community is part of a national project focused on adolescent mental health (ACCESS-Open Minds). The Director shared the book with the team as she felt it provided a clear reflection of youth needs relating to prevention and meaningful support in terms of mental health as well as meaningful approaches to responding to these needs. (Personal communication, 25 October 2017)

---

[7] L. Liebenberg, J. Reich, B. Mott, and Participants of the Spaces and Places project (2015). Spaces & Places Dissemination Photobook. Halifax Nova Scotia, Dalhousie University.

The cost of producing the catalogue (formatting, printing, and circulating) is of course an issue to be addressed. Who will get copies of the catalogue? As we have seen in this work, the production of the catalogue can also take on a further life through digital curation. Indeed, in some contexts where there might be limited funds, digital curation might be a practical solution to extending the life of the material exhibition. *Seeing, Believing, Acting* exists in a digital form[8] as does *Through the Eyes of Mothers*.[9] We raise the issue of cost because the bulk of the research we describe here and that done by most of our colleagues working in participatory visual research brings with it issues of budgets and questions about the best use of available funds. On the one hand, we are committed to community participation. On the other, what are the trade-offs and how will a community regard a costly exhibition when most participants have limited resources? Might someone ask what the participants are getting out of this, and observe that they cannot eat an exhibition or a catalogue? Is our interest more in satisfying funders by providing them with a glossy catalogue, or do we see that this kind of dissemination can provide visually verifiable results as alternatives to costly surveys the results of which may reach no participants directly?

In a related way we raise the issue of the cultural relevance of the exhibition itself and the resulting catalogue. As we noted in the Introduction to this chapter the exhibition has become *de rigeur* for photovoice projects, but this is also the case with many other art-making projects involving drawing or collage as participatory visual tools. To date, there is relatively little in the research literature addressing cultural relevance. Is an exhibition simply a Western imposition and, if so, do we not need to think about different ways of working with images?

Finally, there remain numerous ethical issues in making the visual public (Mitchell, 2011; Nguyen, Mitchell, De Lange, & Fritsch, 2015; Mitchell, De Lange & Nguyen, 2016). Delgado has also highlighted the significance of this work in relation to the voice of young people. As he notes, how do we make sure that an exhibition is not boycotted because it contains images that some audiences might find offensive? What steps should the researcher take to make sure that this does not happen? The example of our making sure that the college deans see the exhibition before it is exhibited to a large international audience is one strategy. This does not address totally the concern of ownership or the idea that the students who produced the images should have the final say, but it does acknowledge that if community and policy dialogue is a critical part of the work, there may be instances of many different types of dialogues going on, ranging from dialogue with the participants in curating an exhibition through to dialogue with stakeholders. If the point is 'learning from the ground up' (Choudry & Kapoor, 2010) then it is these dialogues from which we are likely to learn the most.

---

[8] http://heaids.org.za/site/assets/files/1233/exhibition_poster_low_res.pdf

[9] http://aphrc.org/wp-content/upload

DRAWINGS: COLLECTIONS AND CATALOGUES

As we highlighted in Chapter 1, research on circulating and disseminating participatory visual images within community-based research is an emerging area of study. The ideas and examples that we have mapped out here on circulating photovoice images take us one step further in this work. We have focused primarily on photographs as part of photovoice projects, but acknowledge the vast area on drawings, especially, though not exclusively, children's drawings, which offer a rich area of study. As the various essays in *Picturing Research: Drawing as Visual Methodology* (Theron, Mitchell, Smith, & Stuart, 2011) suggest, this is an area that brings with it its own politics of reception and circulation. Bober's (2011) essay in this collection draws attention to the ways in which the messages and content of children's drawings are often dismissed by adult audiences, and at the same time under-valued both in relation to the rights of the producers and to ownership issues (see also Akesson, Denov, D'Amico, Khan, Linds, & Mitchell, 2014). She writes extensively on the ways in which children's drawings from various conflict zones such as Darfur are taken as evidence of human rights abuses. Many of these images are exhibited in public venues such as art galleries and museums in North America. Citing the work of Bal (1996), she observes:

Given that the children who drew these pictures are living in precarious circumstances, what does it mean to place their drawings on display? There are many questions to consider regarding sites of representation and access to them, as well as the politics of display. Exhibitions are not simply a collection of images framed in particular ways with a sequence to follow, eliciting (and evoking) particular interpretations. (As cited in Bober, 2011, p. 71)

She talks about the fact that many of these images ended up in coffee table books and goes on to cite the work of Szorenyi (2006) who observes: 'The very existence of such books in which the suffering of others is made into an aesthetic object, seems to invite questions about the politics and ethics of collecting and consuming images' (as quoted in Bober, p. 71).

As was highlighted at a symposium on exhibiting children's drawings several years ago at Concordia University in Montreal, 'Children's Art from the Past and Present',[10] the significance of ownership is critical, and yet probably one of the most common acts in the field is still for a researcher to arrive at a site, ask participants (children) to draw x or y and then leave with the data. At that symposium Walsh (2014) offered a powerful presentation on the art produced by Indigenous children living in residential schools in British Columbia prior to the 1970s. The art teacher had kept the images which ended up in an archive at the University of Victoria. It was only many years later that there was

---

[10]http://cerev.org/interpretingsca/?page id=1?, accessed 23 October 2016

any suggestion of returning them to their producers. For many of the artists, now adults, these drawings and other art works are among the few material traces of their childhood. The images have now been exhibited in the relevant communities accompanied by appropriate cultural ceremonies of healing. The artists were given the choice of having the original image returned to them, or having a reproduction given to them with the original art piece remaining in the university archive.

CONCLUSION

In this chapter we have focused on exhibitions with an eye to studying the engagement of audiences, primarily in relation to photo exhibitions but with some attention given to drawings. To do so we have offered a multimodal reading of choice-making in producing exhibitions, and some description of the behind-the-scenes processes in preparing and curating exhibitions. We conclude that such strategies as multimodal readings could contribute to expanding a repertoire of tools for studying the critical engagement of audiences. In introducing the idea of circulating the vernacular we recognize that it is possible to begin to study the circulation of images in community research by posing new questions. What does it mean to circulate images in and through various communities? Which modalities work best? Which approaches to studying audiences work most effectively? How can we build in reflexivity at different points in the process? Through a nuanced understanding of those making the images and those engaging with them we offer an even richer picture for visioning and re-visioning research for social change.

KEY POINTS OF THE CHAPTER

- Curation and processes of exhibiting are typically studied in Fine Arts and Museum Studies but we also need to study more what these processes mean in community-based photography projects.
- Participants can be co-curators as part of participatory research.
- Studying the responses of audiences provides rich data sources for visual researchers.
- Disseminating visual images such as photos and drawings through researcher-developed exhibition catalogues can extend the life of exhibition and reach more audiences.
- Documenting and studying the logistical and ethical challenges in mounting exhibitions and developing exhibition catalogues contribute to deepening an understanding of the image, the producer, and the audience.

5

THE PEDAGOGY OF SCREENINGS

▬ CHAPTER CONTENTS ▬

> **'Movie Night'**
>
> These digital stories provide a great resource for hosting a movie night in your community. You could show the digital stories and talk about them over popcorn! Have the audience point out the key themes of leadership in the digital stories, and relate it to leadership qualities that they have themselves. You could also show a digital story or two before the screening of another film (i.e. as a mini-preview) as a simple way of raising awareness in the community. (TakingAction4)

INTRODUCTION

This movie night description noted above is part of a project that involves Indigenous youth in Canada being encouraged to take leadership in the area of HIV and AIDS through creating their own digital stories. As a project activity it focuses on the ways in which the productions arising from the participatory visual project might reach local communities. Funding was built in from the beginning to support the possibility of each participant leading one or more of these movie nights (Flicker et al., in press). Along with movie nights, cellphilm festivals, community workshops, and online postings, there are numerous ways that we might plan for the circulation and distribution of such productions. But how might these activities also expand the possibilities for deepening an understanding of participatory research, and especially the use of the visual? Given the increased attention to participant ownership in participatory visual research, what does it mean for producers to screen their own work especially to local communities and to peers in their own institutions, as well as internationally? How does this work on audience complement and expand the process-work of producing texts? How does it add to what counts as data in participatory visual research? What methods and tools are appropriate for studying screening events?

As a way to begin to situate and problematize what screenings of participatory productions such as cellphilms, participatory video, and digital stories might mean in participatory visual research we use the idea of a pedagogy of screenings. In doing this we want to highlight the learning space related to preparing for a screening, carrying it out, and reflecting on it, alongside the cumulative effect of screening the same video or digital story to different audiences. While it might seem to be an obvious intervention point in participatory visual research, it remains an aspect that is under-studied. We extend this idea of a pedagogy of screenings by adding, first, what we term a pedagogy of celebration; this is based on the emotional attachment associated with both completing a video, cellphilm, or digital story-telling production and screening it. We recognize that celebration is not inevitable and also that the emotion attached to the production might shift. The second addition, as it were, is linked to what Zembylas and Boler (2002) refer to as a pedagogy of discomfort. MacEntee and Mandrona (2015) introduce the idea of a pedagogy of discomfort in relation to cellphilm screenings in a project involving

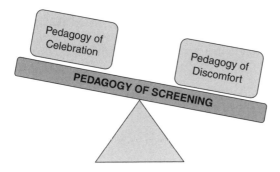

Figure 5.1 Framework: Pedagogy of screening

Diagram developed by Claudia Mitchell and Naydene de Lange

teachers' screening, to the students in their school, their own productions that deal with sexuality. While they use the idea primarily as a way to frame the discomfort associated with addressing a difficult issue during a screening, we see a pedagogy of discomfort as also offering a productive way to talk about some of the tensions of screenings before live (and online) and potentially critical audiences.

In positioning the screenings of participatory visual work as a lever balanced on a pivot point (see Figure 5.1), we attempt to show the importance of having both a pedagogy of celebration and a pedagogy of discomfort that they are both needed to leverage social change. We suggest that the screening of participatory visual work may well act to prompt audiences to engage with social change. To begin with, we want to underscore the often taken-for-grantedness of what happens before, during, and after screenings. Drawing on work in media studies, communication, participatory research, and edutainment, the chapter extends what often appears to be the simple act of screening a video before a live audience into the realm of studying what Fiske (1987) refers to as producer and audience texts.

We acknowledge that there is a growing body of work on the reception of participatory videos, especially by researchers. In this work the productions are typically being screened outside the original community setting (in universities and academic conferences). This work is important because it highlights the significance of a reflexive stance within the research community but the extent to which such screenings contribute to empowerment for the participants, and the extent to which they promote a pedagogy of discomfort, in this case, for the audience members and the researchers themselves, is of concern. As Choudry (2015) points out, reflexivity sometimes results in researchers talking to each other, but not engaging directly with the communities most affected so as to capture what is happening where change is most needed. If we are to take seriously the notion of ownership, then clearly participants need to be talking to each other as well as to communities about the work they are producing. It is thus critical to see what screening might mean from the perspective of all stakeholders – the researchers, the various audiences (communities, policy makers, and practitioners), and the participants themselves.

WHY A PEDAGOGY OF SCREENINGS?

Doing research using participatory visual methods such as participatory videos, cell-philms, and digital stories is often hailed for its recognition of the importance of the participation of those most affected by the issues being investigated. Putting cameras and other digital devices in the hands of the community members mostly affected by the challenges we target, is seen to be an effective strategy for deepening understanding of the issues and identifying possible strategies for addressing them from the perspectives of the communities themselves (Moletsane et al., 2009). Taking the visual texts to the wider community and external audiences, through, for example, exhibitions (in the case of photographs and drawings) as we discuss in Chapter 4 and screenings (in the case of participatory videos, cellphilms, and digital stories) as we discuss here, is often identified as the most effective way of making the participants' lived experiences public, particu-larly to those audiences who have the power and resources to effect social change. As Low, Brushwood Rose, Salvio, and Palacios (2012) note, for example, participatory video is implicitly understood as enabling 'a quality of participation not previously available' (p. 50), in that, following the work of Paulo Freire, it develops 'the ability to name the world and to change it' (p. 51). As Strangelove (2009) observes, the ubiquity of digital tools across various spaces and communities, as well as access to digital productions, serves to democratize the digital space. Such digital tools enable previously excluded groups to access and participate in various digital spaces. Our own work with young peo-ple, teachers, and community health workers in rural South Africa has often celebrated the power of visual participatory research in contributing to the engagement, reflexivity, and agency of both our participants and ourselves as researchers interested in doing research for social change (De Lange, Mitchell, & Moletsane, 2015).

However, scholars have cautioned against the tendency of participatory visual research-ers to celebrate their work uncritically and to see the visual productions, in particular, they or their participants develop and disseminate as liberating or empowering to the partici-pants and as contributing to social change. Instead, what is needed is constant reflection '…on how the audiovisual products of participatory video and PVR processes travel and are intercepted and consumed outside of the spaces within which they were initially produced. We need to know how their reception in external-to-project spaces may inform, or poten-tially undermine, social change outcomes for those involved. The empowerment of presenters in these spaces can no longer be assumed' (Kindon et al., 2012, p. 362).

At the same time, as we highlight in our balancing act diagram above, we think it is critical not to overlook the significance of celebration. The actual production of a video, digital story or cellphilm, with all the participant choice-making of storyline, title, music in some cases, credits and so on are aesthetic decisions or ones based on making a par-ticular statement or point. As Jewitt (2013) and others have noted, producers typically make choices with some end product in mind. As we know from the literature on multi-modalities introduced in Chapter 4, and especially the idea of producers as choice makers

(Kress, 2008) in creating digital stories, vlogs, and videos, the process is typically very involved and very engaging regardless of the overall final effect. This is something that is also recognized by Pithouse and Mitchell (2007) in their article *Looking into change: Studying participant engagement in photovoice projects*, which draws on the work of psychologists such as Csikszentmihalyi (1990) who talk about flow in relation to engagement, alongside the work of Maxine Greene (1994) and Eliot Eisner (2005) on creative engagement. The work to date really only hints at what celebration might look like, and we recognize that this celebratory mode may be transient, may shift over time, and that it may change according to the viewers.

Perhaps celebration can best be appreciated in the context of vulnerability and for this reason we can think of it in dynamic balance with discomfort. Zembylas (2015) suggests that research (and teaching) that targets social challenges often involves a pedagogy of discomfort, with significant ethical implications both for the researchers and participants as well as for the various audiences it reaches. The author suggests that such a pedagogy involves strategies in the teaching situation (and, by implication, in research) that lead students or participants to experience 'discomfort' as well as 'pain and suffering' (p. 1). He argues that such feelings may cause the participants to experience and respond to such pedagogies in ways that may undermine or negatively affect social change. However, such feelings of discomfort can also be pedagogically useful for learning about the lived experiences of those facing challenging circumstances in their lives. Specifically in his work with Megan Boler (Boler & Zembylas, 2003; Zembylas & Boler 2002), a pedagogy of discomfort is identified as 'a teaching practice that can encourage students to move outside their "comfort zones" and question their [taken-for granted beliefs]' (Zembylas, 2015, p. 1). For them, the value of a pedagogy of discomfort lies in the belief that 'discomforting feelings are important in challenging dominant beliefs, social habits and normative practices that sustain social inequities and they create openings for individual and social transformation' (p. 1). Such transformation may replace discomfort with celebration.

METHODOLOGIES FOR SCREENING

Gillian Rose (2012) reviews an extensive body of literature in her chapter on audiencing, which looks at some of the ways in which researchers, mostly in the area of media and film studies, have studied viewings. Many techniques have been used, ranging from conventional interviews to ethnographies such as Walkerdine's (1990) living room ethnography of a family viewing *Rocky II*. The focus on the viewer, however, is only one textual component, and while not insignificant in participatory visual research, is perhaps no more important than a focus on film maker or producer of the video or digital story. Indeed, while in Walkerdine's case the viewer might see the same video several times as is the practice in home video viewing, as part of participatory visual research it is most likely the film makers and researchers who see the video many times and the audience may see it only once. Thus we are interested in the kinds of reflexive moments that might come out of multiple screenings, particularly for the person who is doing the screening – the participant or the researcher. What does it mean to see one's own video, cellphilm or digital story being viewed by different audiences? When is this cause for celebration and when is it uncomfortable? We consider various types of visual production screenings and audiences: researchers screening their own productions to academic audiences; researchers screening participant-developed productions to external audiences; and participants screening their own productions to local audiences. We use this typology as a way of understanding how visual researchers have attempted to make researcher- and participant-developed productions public, as well as how they have engaged with audiences and their responses to the productions.

RESEARCHERS SCREENING THEIR OWN PRODUCTIONS

We begin with what the phenomenologist Max Van Manen (1990) terms a starting with ourselves approach, where we reflect on our own involvement as researchers in participatory visual research and the digital texts we produce. In particular, we reflect on how researcher-generated productions enable researchers to deepen their understanding of the phenomenon being investigated. Further, we are interested in exploring how, when such productions are made public through screenings to the academic community, for example, they are received and engaged with. To do this, we describe and reflect on the screening of a researcher-generated production, a digital animation production *Take a Risk: It's as Easy as ABC,* based on research on integrating HIV and AIDS into the curriculum of Higher Education in South Africa created in a project and as described in several publications (Van Laren et al., 2015).

Take a Risk: It's as Easy as ABC

Take a Risk: It's as Easy as ABC is a three-minute digital animation created through i-movie software, 2Animate!, and is based on a storyboard or plan that uses stick figure clip art. Developed by an interdisciplinary team of teacher educators from higher education institutions in South Africa, the animation focuses on the integration of HIV and AIDS into the teacher-education curriculum. The storyline in the animation involves two teacher educators and a superhero as the main characters. It addresses the issue of AIDS fatigue, particularly the Abstain, Be Faithful, Condomize (ABC) messages that have dominated HIV prevention interventions in South Africa, and the need to focus on student teachers' interest in possible strategies for dealing with social aspects of HIV and AIDS with their learners in the schools in which they would be teaching.

In the first instance, using a combination of a PowerPoint (to introduce and contextualize the animation) and the animation itself, the team screened the video to three different higher education audiences selected on the basis of their assumed interest in the integration and HIV and AIDS into the higher education curriculum and/or digital animation as a teaching method. The three audiences included: 1) a group of academics and postgraduate students whose work focuses on self-reflexive research methodologies such as self-study of practice, autoethnography, and narrative inquiry; 2) academics attending the annual conference on higher education teaching and learning organized by the University Teaching and Learning Office at the University of KwaZulu-Natal in Durban, South Africa; and 3) a colloquium organized by the HEAIDS Community of Practice (a voluntary group made of teacher educators from South Africa's higher education institutions) whose main focus was 'to launch a digital space specifically for researching and supporting HIV and AIDS curriculum integration through an online collaborative forum'[1] (Pithouse-Morgan et al., 2015, p. 247).

After each screening, we facilitated open-ended discussions prompted by the simple question: 'Is there anything that you would like to discuss?' The authors divided the audience responses into two themes: 1) the medium and the message; and 2) pragmatic use and dissemination. First, informed by the work of Marshall McLuhan (1964) in relation to the now well-known phrase, the medium is the message, they reflected on the audiences' views regarding the use of digital animation to address integrating HIV and AIDS into higher education curricula. Our findings suggest that the audiences were generally appreciative of the animation as a medium for communicating the messages related to the integration of HIV and AIDS into the curricula. As one of their audience members explained, animation 'gets people's attention and you are engaged and you want to hear further what the message is about' (Pithouse-Morgan et al., 2015, p. 248). Others, however, were less appreciative, and pointed to the challenges they would face in using unfamiliar technology and media. The critics also viewed the dual focus on digital media and HIV and AIDS as problematic, suggesting that we should focus on one and not on both.

Second, informed by our desire to understand how developing and screening the animation might be an innovative and responsive strategy for research and teaching, we reflected on the audiences' criticism of using and screening digital animation as a method for research and teaching and learning in higher education classrooms. One of the audience responses suggested that it was not clear who the animation was targeting. Was it university instructors, university students, schools or all of them? Other audience members felt that the screening must be accompanied by an information brochure, with suggestions for how to use it, including role plays and other complementary strategies. To the team, this suggested that, taking a cue from the work of Kraidy (2003):

---

[1] http://heaids.nmmu.ac.za/

...animation on its own might not be sufficient to have the desired effect, and that it would be more effective if mediated by some additional practical discussion and materials. In this way, we were reminded that, paradoxically, the digital visualization of information aids the understanding of abstract concepts while simultaneously increasing conceptual abstraction. (As cited in Pithouse-Morgan et al., 2015, p. 250)

Of particular relevance to a pedagogy of screening is the reflexive process described in the article by Pithouse-Morgan et al. (2015) where we realize that going public was only the beginning. Using our self-determined prompt, 'What was it like to screen our own work in front of others?' we proceeded to engage in reflexive dialogue which we audio-recorded and later transcribed. Clearly, all of us in some way fit the discomfort model though there were also celebrations. As Ronicka comments at the beginning of the dialogue: 'There was a lot of trepidation and excitement.' Linda goes on to comment:

> I found it also a bit scary, especially the initial screening, which was for a group of self-reflexive researchers, who were very critical. They are used to openness and constructive criticism. Because we didn't start off informing them what we had done before, they were lacking in background. They are also not an HIV and AIDS integration group. So it was different every time. I think that the people who came to the second screening, the University Teaching and Learning Office (UTLO) presentation, were people who were really interested because they didn't have to be there. I was just sad that at that presentation the screening was cut short because the projector didn't work. At the final screening it was all the people from different universities who were already really interested in integration, which makes a difference.

Kathleen picks up on the uneasiness and observes:

> I think for me the trepidation and unease were mainly because I care about producing something that I think is polished. So, doing something in a new medium was very scary for me. I guess I'm quite a control freak. But when we had to go through an intermediary to make the animation, we didn't have control!... So the medium definitely took me out of my comfort zone.

Reflecting on the three screenings and the audience responses, the team concluded that making our work public through digital animation led to a generative engagement (of the team itself, but also of the audience members). Citing our earlier work (Van Laren et al., 2013), we identified such engagement in the audience responses that were characterized by participation, enjoyment, and discernment. From this, we concluded that screening the digital animation to other academics in higher education institutions enabled free dialogue, which was both celebratory and (uncomfortably) critical, thereby generating new ideas for improving the visual production and its use in terms of the medium and the message. Screening the digital animation deepened the audience's understanding about integrating HIV and AIDS into the curriculum, as well as our own.

In Mudaly et al. (2015) we reflect on how we went on to screen our animation with teacher-education students in an undergraduate Natural Science Method module in one of the higher education institutions. The student teachers, made up of 79 third-year men and women between the ages of 20 and 24, were provided with information about the project a week prior to the screening of the digital animation. In the 90-minute class dedicated to the screening, the students were divided into small groups and asked to reflect on the digital animation, which they had watched prior to the class, and were then involved 'in a structured concept-mapping activity to consider how digital technologies and social media might be used to address social challenges in South Africa' (p. 23). The prompt for the first activity was: *Reflect on the use of digital animation to integrate HIV and AIDS in teaching* (p. 28). This was an entry point into a larger discussion on using digital media in the teaching of science. The group discussions were audio-recorded and transcribed. An analysis of these indicates that, first, this audience regarded digital animation as an effective medium for communicating social issues such as HIV and AIDS. Some of their recorded responses included: 'animation is fun'; 'appropriate'; 'appealing and attractive'; 'creative and innovative'; 'conveys information to learners [that is] more learner centred' and 'allows students to pay attention' (Mudaly et al., 2015, p. 31). Suggesting ways in which the animation could be relevant to the needs of a Millennial audience, their recommendations for improvement included:

A better background song could have been chosen and more colour should have been used;

The animation is too quick, I couldn't read the information, it is confusing because of the format…;

The speech bubbles, the words are too long and they made me [lose] concentration; and

Audio could have been added to say what was written on the video in order to assist blind learners. (pp. 31–32)

While the audience was generally positive, highlighting such aspects as its innovativeness as a teaching strategy and its information-rich content, one audience member felt that it lacked adequate information.

Reflecting on this screening, we note that the student teachers' responses to the digital animation enabled them to think critically about the so-called digital divide and how it is often an urban-rural, rich-poor, generational and racial divide (Mudaly et al., 2015). The responses also underscored the utility of digital media in addressing issues related to access to information and communicating socially relevant information as well as effectively teaching science in diverse classrooms.

These four screenings and our reflections on them, illustrate the ways in which, on the one hand there is a type of celebration as the research team steps outside their everyday lives as academics to develop the digital animation. In screening it to audiences, including peers, we develop a sense of rich engagement in the issues (the integration of HIV and AIDS in the curriculum) and perhaps even moving together towards addressing them. However, on the other, there is also discomfort as we screen our very modest attempt at digital animation to our peers – other academics and professional colleagues working in the area of HIV and AIDS – as well as to a group of techno-savvy students. Perhaps, as Zembylas (2015) has suggested, it is this sense of discomfort – 'stepping out of our comfort zone' (p. 163) – that may lead both participants and the audience to question the status quo of the teaching of HIV and AIDS in higher education, in this instance, and to actively seek innovative strategies towards making that change.

RESEARCHERS SCREENING VIDEOS MADE BY PARTICIPANTS

In this second set of screenings, we focus on the work of researchers who have screened participatory videos, digital stories and cellphilms made by research participants, largely youth, to audiences that include academics. If we think about the idea of participant ownership, this is, of course, a somewhat contested area. Should there ever be times when participants are not present for screenings? At the same time, we also acknowledge that sometimes this is not possible. While we celebrate the creation and screening of these digital productions as contributing to highlighting issues and challenges in schools and communities from the participants' perspectives, we also recognize, as MacEntee (2016a) notes, our own discomfort in presenting on behalf of participants, often without their being present at the screenings. Moreover, the screenings can also elicit significant levels of discomfort among our audiences.

One example that illustrates the complexities of screening participatory videos made by participants to academic audiences and the audience responses to the productions is the work of Kindon et al. (2012) in New Zealand. What they term a participatory video project for research (PVR) was collaboratively developed and implemented with a group of between 4 and 15 community members from the Ngáti Hauiti in New Zealand. The community members were concerned about limitations in the video documentation that had thus far been used to record 'cultural revival activities and by their absence from the then-current, place-based tourism-promotion videos of their region' (p. 351). Thus, with a memorandum of understanding in place between the researchers and the community, the project focused primarily on mutually beneficial research and capacity building.

As part of working together, the research team met with community members to report on various presentations they had made to academic audiences, and the responses they had received from them. Together, in what they refer to as a theorizing back, informed by Tuck (2009), they analysed the various audience responses and the implications for their research and also the potential risks for members of the team who travel to present the productions to various audiences outside the research setting. To this end, in terms of audience responses to their work, the authors note that it was generally received positively. However, they high-light two negative responses from two different presentations. The first instance occurred at a lunchtime seminar that one of the authors presented to colleagues and postgraduate stu-dents in a university geography department. Even though the presenter knew the audience (and the screening was therefore an in-house one), it was still outside the community in which the participatory video was produced. Thus, to introduce the making of the video and actual production, one of the team members had developed and edited a seven-minute video documentary that described the participatory video-making process, with subtitles for the various concepts such as storyboarding to help further the understanding of the process.

As the authors report, one negative response to the videos came from one of the ten male academic members of the audience after the presentation. The man (described as a New Zealander of European descent), angry at what he called a mere 'home video and not real research', directed his comments towards the project rather than the video, essentially accusing the researchers of being duped into implementing a non-academic endeavour by the community who, according to him, were interested only in the free resources the project would provide.

A second negative response came at the New Zealand Film and History Conference in 2000 in a session during which the team presented the videos. This time, the criticism, from a Maori film maker, was that the team's approach to film-making was too Western and therefore, col-onizing; he cited the team's use of the storyboard as evidence. For Kindon et al. (2012), these negative responses to their video screenings forced them to reflect on 'the factors informing their responses; …the relationship between producers, audio visual texts, and their intended audiences' (p. 354). For example, how do visual texts produced in one sociocultural context travel to another? How do the identities (for example, the race, gender, social class) of the audience members and the producers of the texts and visual texts themselves interact to influ-ence the ways in which audiences respond to the presentation of participatory visual texts? To what extent does the expected empowerment of the producers of the texts accrue from making the visual texts public? If, as Zembylas (2015) might warn, the screenings and the discussion that follow produce discomfort (instead of celebration), to what extent and in what ways could these lead to a negative impact on the lives of the producers? Alternatively, how might such discomfort be used as a pedagogically generative entry point into increasing understanding of the issues, challenging our taken-for granted perspectives on them, and working towards social change in the affected communities? These questions need to form part of post-screening discussions between researchers and participants.

PARTICIPANTS SCREENING THEIR OWN WORK

To date there are very few accounts to be found in the research literature of participants themselves doing the screening. Here we look at the screening in the same project we refer to in Chapter 3, involving two groups of teachers from two rural schools in South Africa, one small public rural school (Grade R-9) that used to be on a private farm near Port Elizabeth in Eastern Cape, and one a comprehensive public school (Grade R-12) in the Vulindlela district of KwaZulu-Natal.[2] The latter was a former Catholic school which had been taken over by the Department of Basic Education shortly before, but whose ethos and cultural practice continued to follow Catholicism. The 19 participating teachers worked with cellphones to produce cellphilms as a type of participatory video (see Mitchell & De Lange, 2013; Mitchell, De Lange, & Moletsane, 2014).

As we highlight in Chapter 3 on speaking back, the issues that the teachers were dealing with in their cellphilms were far from straightforward. Indeed, as researchers we were confronted with the realization that some of the productions could, in fact, reinforce the very unequal gender norms and practices and HIV-related stigma we were attempting to address. This, we felt, could end up putting young people generally, and young women in particular, at risk. We facilitated a follow-up workshop in which the teachers were asked to think of the messages their cellphilms were trying to convey, as well as which audiences they thought could benefit from watching them and then to engage in a sort of speaking back to the cellphims they had created. This speaking back workshop resulted in four new cellphilms being produced: *Breaking the Silence, Breaking the Silence 2, Speak Out, and Teen Vibe*. It is primarily these speaking back cellphilms (with the exception of one) that formed part of a series of screenings the teachers undertook in their school communities.

Preparing for the Screenings

What does it mean for a group of teachers who do not identify as film makers to screen their films before live audiences? Who would they choose as their audience? What would they need by way of materials or support to carry out the screening? To prepare for the screening, we facilitated a 'Going Public with our Cellphilms' workshop with the teachers. We divided them into groups according to their respective schools, and then into pairs or groups of three to discuss the screening workshop logistics. We suggested questions that could be useful in thinking about planning their screenings or pre-screenings, as well as about reflecting and assessing them in post-screenings once they had finished.

---

[2]The larger study in which this project was implemented was titled 'Digital Voices: Rural Teachers in the Age of AIDS and Social Action'.

Pre-screening

- *Which cellphilms would you like to show? To whom? Why? Who will the audience be?*
- *Do you need to advertise the event? How?*
- *How long will it last?*
- *Where will it take place? When?*
- *What do you need to have a successful event?*

Post-screening

- *How did it go?*
- *What would you do differently?*
- *What did you learn?*
- *What do you want to do next time?*

We were influenced by the assertion that screenings in communities enable members of the wider community to engage in dialogue about the issues identified in the participant-produced videos (Mitchell, 2011). However, Kindon et al. (2012) caution that we need to reflect on the factors that might influence how audiences respond to visual texts such as cellphilms, so this was also of concern. We asked the participants to think carefully about which of the cellphilms they would not like to share with audiences who were not involved in the project.

Selecting the Audience and Focus of Discussion

The participants from KwaZulu-Natal, who ended up facilitating three separate screenings, approached planning for the screenings in a variety of ways but identified similar audiences. While there had been much discussion at the planning workshop about all the different audiences (parents, district officials and so on), in the end all the groups chose their own learners as their audience. One group from the KwaZulu-Natal school chose to screen their cellphilms to an audience of Grade 6 students. As the teachers said, 'We want to *inform the learners, to educate about HIV and AIDS, the use of condoms and again they are exposed to pornography...'*. A second group chose a group of high school learners organized as the Peace Club. Their purpose, they said, was 'to get learners talking about issues that affect them, for example their sexuality, HIV and AIDS, rejection'. Going outside the classroom, a third group chose a church youth group consisting of teenagers aged between 11 to 18 years as their audience and decided to focus on youth empowerment and, more especially, on awareness of abuse and teenage pregnancy.

As part of the planning workshop we had asked various group members to act as an advisory board and to critique and advise the other group on their screening plans. After each group had presented their plans, a member of the advisory board offered comments, commenting on what might or might not work and why, and what could be changed or added to make the plan work and to ensure the success of the screening. While the participants were keen to screen their productions, considering the context of the school (its Catholic orientation in particular) and the content of the cellphilms that were about young people's sexuality and HIV and AIDS, there was concern among some of them about the acceptability of the subject matter of their productions, and the discomfort that could arise among members of the school and church community.

As part of her internship at the Centre for Visual Methodologies for Social Change, at the University of KwaZulu-Natal in Durban South Africa in 2013, Katie MacEntee worked on documenting and reporting on the screening events.[3] Here we draw on her internship report (2013),[4] to explore how the participants screened their productions, and which audiences they chose for this purpose and what the audience responses were to the various texts. All the screenings took place at the participants' school.

Screening 1

The first screening event involved 110 Grade 6 learners from the Life Orientation (LO) classes (where social issues such as those covered in the cellphilms are taught). Facilitated by three of the participants (a Grade 2 female teacher, a Grade 6 female teacher and a secondary school male teacher), the screenings included two cellphilms: *Be Enlightened* and *Breaking the Silence 2*. As we noted in Chapter 3 tells the story of two girls (played by two of the participating teachers) who find a condom in their schoolyard but mistake it for a balloon. A teacher (also played by a teacher) finds the girls playing with the condom, notices that the girls are confused about what it is, and takes this opportunity to teach them what condoms are used for, but also emphasizes that they are for adults and not for children and that the children must avoid contact with them. *Breaking the Silence 2* is about two girls whose mother discovers them looking at pornography on their cellphones. At first the mother is angry, but she then decides to talk to her daughters about safer sex. Later in the cellphilm, she has to defend her decision to talk to the children about sex, a decision their father (angry when he finds out) did not support.

After the screening, the learners were divided into groups of eight to address questions prepared by their teachers: What were the films about? What were the themes of the films? What did you like about the films? What do you do when someone asks you a question about something you don't understand? Focusing on the messages in the cellphilms, the learners' responses suggested that they 'enjoyed learning about condoms and appreciated

---

[3]We are greatly indebted to Katie MacEntee for her support to this part of the fieldwork, and especially the analysis. The report was later published as a journal article (MacEntee and Mandrona, 2015).

[4]K. MacEntee (2013). Cellphones and Rural Schools: Stories of Challenges and Possibilities: Report on Internship at the Centre for Visual Methodologies for Social Change, Durban', January–March, 2013.

Figure 5.2 Grade 6 learners watching teacher-created cellphilms

Photo by Katie MacEntee

MacEntee, K. (2013).

the messages in both cellphilms about talking frankly with parents or teachers about sex in order to get accurate knowledge' (MacEntee, 2013, p. 6). Perhaps as part of the Catholic ethos, as MacEntee notes, throughout the event the teachers ensured that they emphasized abstinence before marriage. Interestingly, in response to a teacher's closing remarks, one of the audience members, a Grade 6 learner, raised his hand and asked, 'Why do teachers or adults get to have sex?' and another male learner asked, 'What if you don't have money to marry someone?' (p. 6). (This was in reference to the tradition of a man paying lobola or a bride price in order to marry a woman). MacEntee comments that the 'teachers expressed an admiration for the learners' knowledge and their ability to express themselves by asking questions'. However, they were taken by surprise by the questions. In their post-screening interview, 'they noted the importance of discussing and teaching about condoms to the learners and explained that this was why condoms were emphasized in their cellphilms' (p. 6). This thinking is in line with our assertion that a key purpose of participatory video (and cellphilms) (Figure 5.2) 'is to engage the community in exploring and "making visible" the issues about which people are silent – those issues which are "hidden" and around which community action is required' (Mitchell & De Lange, 2011, p. 179).

Screening 2

The second screening involved 34 Grade 11 and 12 learners, all members of the school's Peace Club, a group that focuses on promoting peace and peaceful conflict resolution among learners in and around the school. The event was facilitated by three female teachers, one from Life Sciences, one who teaches Life Orientation, and a Religious Studies teacher, all of whom were from the secondary school. The teachers chose to screen *Breaking the Silence 2* (described above) and *Teen Vibe*. The latter tells a story of two girls who decide to sneak out at night to go to a party while their mother sleeps. The two (and supposedly others at the party) get drunk and are driven home by a man. At first the mother is angry and she scolds them for their behaviour. However, she calms down and sits down with the girls to talk to them about safety, sex, and sexual violence. In the post-screening discussions, the learners identified such themes as the importance of listening to parents; prioritizing education and one's future before romantic relationships; and avoiding alcohol and peer pressure. *Breaking the Silence 2* was introduced by an animated discussion on adolescence, sex, and abstinence facilitated by one of the teachers. After the screening, the facilitating teacher asked the learners questions about whether their parents talk to them about sex and, if so, how they do this. The learners talked about parents as a source of information and support for youth. However, they also highlighted the need for young people's independent decision-making about healthy sexuality. For example, with both parents and teachers emphasizing abstinence before marriage, the learners felt that youth sexuality was largely ignored in conversations. Other issues the learners raised included peer pressure, love, transactional sex, and low self-esteem as contributing to early sexual debut among young people. Again, in their closing comments, teachers emphasized abstinence before marriage.

Screening 3

The third event involved 29 members of the Community Catholic Youth Group, and was facilitated by three of the participants: a Grade 4 (female) teacher, and two secondary school female teachers, one a Life Orientation teacher and the other a Social Science and IsiZulu teacher. As part of introducing the session, the teachers stressed that they wanted to hear from the learners 'about the challenges [you face as young people] and how you overcome them' (MacEntee, 2013, p. 8). To underscore this, they introduced the youngest teacher among them as being 'still a youth and [one who] is still experiencing some of these challenges as we speak' (p. 8). Three cellphilms were screened: *Breaking the Silence 2* and '*Teen Vibe*', and *Teen Pregnancy* tells a story of a girl who goes to a party and gets drunk. A few weeks later, she discovers that she is pregnant. She is scared of what her parents will say and what will happen to her. At first she tells a friend who consoles her and advises her to inform an adult about the pregnancy.

In the post-screening discussions, the teachers facilitated a question-and-answer session, from which themes such as whether or not cellphones should be allowed at schools, the use of different mobile apps, and the appropriate age at which to start dating were discussed. In particular, following the screening of *Breaking the Silence*, a learner directly asked the teacher identified as a youth what age she was when she started dating. In an interview that MacEntee conducted with her after the screening, she admitted feeling uncomfortable 'as she interpreted the learner to be asking, in a thinly veiled manner, at what age she began having sex' (p. 8). In response to the cellphilm, *Teen Vibe*, the learners initially focused on the poor sound quality of the cellphilms. The facilitators then steered the dialogue to the issue of whether parents talk to the children about sex or not and what strategies would work best for them to engage in such conversations with their parents. While they agreed that it was difficult to talk to their parents, they also identified other adults, like sisters or brothers, to whom they could talk.

Participants Reflecting on the Screenings

Of interest is the ways in which the participants themselves responded to screening their productions, both before and after the public events. To understand these responses, in their article analysing these screenings, MacEntee and Mandrona (2015) use Boler and Zembylas's (2003) pedagogy of discomfort framework. According to them, first, the teachers experienced discomfort with finding the best ways to engage learners in discussing HIV and AIDS. Seemingly projecting their own discomfort, 'some teachers worried that the audience members would not feel comfortable engaging in a discussion about sexual health and that the teachers' existing relationships with these young people might hinder dialogue' (MacEntee & Mandrona, 2015, p. 48). Second, was the teachers' discomfort with teaching children about condoms. Linked to this was a third form of discomfort the authors identified involving teaching about alternatives to abstinence only as a way of preventing the spread of HIV. Throughout the day, the teachers punctuated every screening by reminding the audience (their learners) of the importance of abstinence until marriage, a principle held dear by the Catholic Church. As a result, when a Grade 6 boy asked for alternatives to abstinence in the event that he was not willing to wait, or that for him marriage would not be possible because of his poverty and the inability to pay the bride price, the teachers were taken aback.

The ways in which the various groups, including the participants themselves responded to the cellphilms screened seem to have been influenced by factors such as the school context and ethos and the teachers' and learners' alignment with it. The learners also responded to these based on their relationships with the producers – their teachers – and the power relations that are inherent here (Kindon et al., 2012). Within this context, we note the ways in which these screenings tended to produce, on the one hand, an atmosphere of celebration, in that the teachers were addressing real problems in their own communities and schools. As we observe elsewhere,

[T]he importance of video work resides in allowing the hidden issues to be discussed and to be viewed from different perspectives, in allowing communities to open up to the possibilities of addressing HIV and AIDS, and to shift toward taking action. (Mitchell & De Lange, 2011, p. 180)

On the other, we also see how the screenings produced significant levels of discomfort among the film makers (the teachers). It is clear that this was in large part a result of the focus of the cellphilms on youth sexuality and HIV and AIDS, two related issues that are taboo as topics of discussion generally, but more especially between children or between youth and adults, including teachers. However, there may be several other issues operating.

First, all the cellphilms are melodramas, and while this is a popular format on South African television shows including those that deal with serious social issues, the actors are the teachers themselves, so the genre itself may have been an issue. What difference, to the audience (the learners) and the producers (the teachers), would it have made if they had chosen the documentary as the genre in their productions? Further, the fact that the actors and producers (who were the audience members' teachers), both directed and acted in the productions would have added an element of discomfort, especially since the audience would be seeing their teachers acting like children in the cellphilms. At the same time, we have also reflected on the significance of the teachers choosing to screen their cellphilms to their students even though they had a budget and opportunities to screen their videos to local adult groups or district officials or even to other teachers. Choosing a comfortable audience – they are, after all, teachers – may have been their way to minimize some of the potential issues that would have also been present if they had had an adult audience (melodramatic genre, teachers as film makers, teachers playing children and teachers dealing with a topic that transgresses taboos).

Clearly, it was an act of bravery on the part of the teachers to screen these cellphilms to the learners in and around the schools. Teachers in rural KwaZulu-Natal (and elsewhere in South Africa) are typically not film makers and have very little access, if any, to technology. Although they had assistance from Katie, even the process of using technology in teaching (setting up an LCD projector, speakers and laptop) is not something that many rural teachers are familiar with (DeMartini & Mitchell, 2016). In addition, several of the participants were not Life Orientation teachers, the school subject in which the issues aired in the cellphilms are usually taught. This means that even though there is a move to integrate the issues more broadly into the school curriculum, these particular teachers are typically not the ones whose responsibility it is to deal with issues of sexuality. Local scholarship also suggests that South African teachers (including LO teachers) are often reluctant or unable to teach issues related to sex, sexuality, and HIV and AIDS (Francis, 2012; Masinga, 2009; Weiler & Martin-Weiler, 2012). Thus, the screenings by this group of teachers must be seen as an opportunity to strengthen their willingness and capacity to teach about these issues, but also to stimulate dialogue between them and their audiences (their learners) and others in and around the school. We have offered some commentary on how the teachers felt, and have also speculated about some of the reasons for this but the data missing from this example is the perspective of the learners.

ONLINE PLATFORMS AND SCREENINGS

But screening is of course not just about engaging with face-to-face live audiences. As Pamela Teitelbaum (2012) observes, 'In social research, participatory practices have moved beyond a room filled with individuals as a result of the types of participatory media continually influencing connectivity' (p. 416). In making this comment, the author draws on the work of Sherry Turkle (2011) and many others who draw attention to the possibilities for viewing as a result of online platforms. As projects such as the cellphilm work described above suggest, there are increasing possibilities for setting up and using various digital online platforms. These are sometimes led by researchers or NGOs and, with the consent of participants, post digital stories and videos. Sites are sometimes taken over by participants themselves who decide what they will do with the productions and where they can be posted. In addition, cellphilms can also be shared via phone-to-phone methods. Although it is not always possible to track these personal sharings, we can see repositories that are typically led by NGOs or researchers and that feature productions created as part of participatory visual projects according to various themes and modalities. For example, *Taking Action 2*,[5] the movie night project referred to at the beginning of this chapter, is a site that hosts a series of digital stories produced by Canadian Indigenous youth on HIV and AIDS and youth leadership. As their digital stories are uploaded and viewed through YouTube, participants and non-participants alike are able to view and comment on the content of the videos. What is particularly significant about community organizations working with open-access platforms is that users can decide for themselves if they wish to make their videos public. While not specifically located on the Taking Action website, clicking on each video's YouTube link brings viewers to the main repository to see the comments on each video, the view counts, and likes or dislikes as reflecting the feelings of a private as well as a public community.

Another site featuring the works of Indigenous youth creating digital stories is Wapikoni.[6] While the site is not specifically built upon a larger third-party site as described above, it does nonetheless offer a video-on-demand service offering to directly stream independent films created in and by Indigenous communities. All the videos on Wapikoni are free to access, even those that have garnered viewings at international festivals abroad. The site also offers a unique map-centric workshop database where visitors can view films on which Indigenous youth worked closely with film professionals, and videos developed in various aboriginal nations across Canada and in other countries around the world.

North York Community House (NYCH) is a development project based out of Toronto, Ontario, that welcomes residents into the community. One of the ways in which NYCH learns about and helps to integrate its members is through the Digital Story-telling process, where groups made up of ten members, over a three- to five-day period, create digital stories in relation to telling their unique story. In the process, participants develop technology skills like digital video editing, creating PowerPoint presentations, and becoming proficient with software packages that could also be used in their workplace setting. A unique feature of NYCH is its offering emotional support to participants one to two weeks after uploading

---

[5]takingaction4youth.org/digital-stories

[6]wapikoni.ca

their curated videos to discuss issues or emotions they may have experienced. All videos are accessible on their main site,[7] which is also linked to their YouTube Channel,[8] allowing viewers outside of the North York community to subscribe to and be notified of future video uploads.

In a similar fashion, the *StoryCenter*[9] (formerly the Center for Digital Story-telling) curates and facilitates digital story-telling workshops by working with organizations in the fields of education, public service, and health and training, such as the Department for International Development (UK), the Canadian Aboriginal AIDS Network (Halifax, Nova Scotia, Canada), and the Center for Educational Technology, University of Cape Town (Cape Town, South Africa). Digital stories created through the StoryCenter, organized according to themes such as Family, Identity, Community, and Health, are uploaded to the site,[10] as well as on their own channel.[11]

InsightShare *Global Participatory Video Hub Network* is a networking site funded by Oxfam, UN Women, and many others, that supports communities by helping them curate, create, and organize participatory videos 'as a tool for self-expression, advocacy, heritage documentation and horizontal communication'.[12] Here, partners in diverse communities in Cameroon, Kenya, and South Africa, for example, locally operate each of their own participatory video projects. The site also hosts other PV and Photo story works on the InsightShare website[13] and on their YouTube Channel, while also including an extensive instructional section on using participatory video in a variety of settings and advocacy projects.

A common element in all these video-hosting websites is that the visual productions can be screened live at community gatherings, but can also be viewed by anyone, such as community members, policy makers and funders who search for them on the YouTube website. Beyond some of these video-sharing sites, there are a number of other large-scale online video repositories that more closely follow a participant-led design that offers digital stories and screenings available for public viewing. *Vimeo*,[14] for example, is a video-sharing platform similar to Google's *YouTube* service. However, where these two differ is in *Vimeo's* cleaner interface and more mature audience following because of its complete lack of interest in advertisement banners or in the 15-second pre-video commercials that are common

---

[7]nych.ca/digital-stories/#thestories

[8]nychonline

[9]storycenter.org

[10]www.storycenter.org/stories/

[11]StoryCenter

[12]Insightshare.org/hubs

[13]insightshare.org/resources/photostory/all.html

[14]vimeo.com

place on YouTube. Another unique feature of *Vimeo* allows creators to edit their previously uploaded videos without losing their analytic information, such as the number of hits the video attracted, and, like YouTube, users are able to vote (like), share, and comment on what they watch.

In some projects, as we see in Casey Burkholder's (2016) involving cellphilming and setting up a digital archive on a public YouTube site with a group of youth from Hong Kong (*We Are HK Too*), it is the researcher who has arranged to set up the site as a type of digital archive for the cellphilms, but it is the participants who decide which of their cellphilms about growing up in Hong Kong they are going to post. As Burkholder observes:

After the cellphilm-making workshops, the participants continued writing, filming, and editing their cellphilms at their leisure. When they felt that their cellphilms were ready for screening, participants uploaded them to our shared YouTube archive. As a group, we decided to keep this space public for people to access the cellphilms, but this setting may change over time. After participants uploaded their cellphilms to our digital archive, we held a screening event at a university campus in Hong Kong. At this screening, participants and audience members discussed the content of the cellphilms and, more generally, the competing notions of belonging and civic engagement that are occurring in post-Occupy Hong Kong. After the screening event, we created a Facebook page, and began to share the cellphilms across our own networks. (2016, p. 151)

At the same time, there are networked sites drawing on participatory visual methods where the work is entirely about online platforms. As Teitelbaum (2012) highlights:

The tagline – 'See it. Film it. Change it' – that brands the work of WITNESS on its websites and elsewhere is powerful and straightforward in that the message signifies not only the value of participation, but more importantly, the value of owning the process as well as the outcome. It is a kind of do-it-yourself approach to advocacy that encourages individuals and community organizations to harness available video technologies, to learn and lead the video process with the aim of protecting their own community. (p. 419)

The potential for online platforms to alter the modes of viewing is extensive. Further, online platforms as sites of sharing and viewing digital productions involve some ethical issues that remain largely under-explored in visual research. Future research that focuses on these is needed. Notwithstanding the ethical issues, almost anyone could post her or his productions. As Strangelove (2009) notes:

Amateur online video has changed who can see what (almost everyone) and what gets represented (almost everything). It has deepened our involvement in the universals of shared culture and heightened our awareness of the particularities of local culture and difference. It has also changed our status as audiences and consumers. The mass audience is moving from their old analogue position as consumers to their new digitized position as producers. Audiences are watching and interpreting YouTube videos not just as passive viewers but as active consumers and as producers of their own videos. (Strangelove, 2009, p. 158)

These various platforms for screening participatory videos and digital stories (or rather for postings which may or may not be accessed by audiences), as Strangelove highlights, have altered the relationship between producer and audience. At the same time, postings do not guarantee viewings and what may appear as a democratic space for anyone to post anything, and especially for participants in various social change projects, does not necessarily mean that they reach audiences. As many critics have observed, the commercial world of YouTube may mean that a few amateur producers become rich (and professional) and the rest extinct. To date the relationship between producer and audience remains an under-studied area of YouTube. Burkholder (2016) notes that although there is some trace of the discussions that took place at the live screening of the cellphilms produced by non-Chinese Hong Kong youth in the project, there is relatively little known about the audiences for the cellphilms in the digital archive.

There is clearly a need to track in more deliberate ways the types of conversations that are possible. As Strangelove (2009) comments, 'Amateur videos are not simply representational practices. They are communicative, dialogic, events that can provide the basis for community formation' (p. 185). Thus, we need to know more about the conversations, but we also need to know more about the silence. Given the contested space of screenings (celebration and/or discomfort), what does it mean to post videos that receive few or no hits? Is this another version of Delgado's (2015) concern that exhibitions without audiences are yet another type of voicelessness? Caron, Raby, Mitchell, Thewissen-Leblanc, and Prioletta (2016) question the ways in which social media might foster the idea of youth public voice. As the authors note,

To what extent can it be assumed that contributing to on-line spaces of communication, in whatever form and intensity, *is* voice? Is 'liking' a video a form of participation? Is it equivalent to 'sharing' a youth-generated video or commenting on someone else's video? How do we evaluate and compare these different contributions which vary in relation to content, intensity, frequency and intentionality? (p. 9)

DISCUSSION

The pedagogy of screenings is an area in participatory visual research that, in and of itself, draws attention to the rich contextual interplay between and among the producer, the text, and the viewers. The work of both Rose (2012) and Fiske (1994) highlights this interplay, and the examples that we use here help to colour in, as it were, some of the up-close features of visual practice that have received relatively little attention in participatory visual research in spite of the significance of viewing to screen studies and to arts-based inquiry.

Looking into Screening Data

Perhaps the most critical feature of this work is to make sure that we treat the screenings as a central part of the work and not an afterthought or just a celebratory nicety. We have highlighted here some of the ways in which data are apparent: visual data (images of preparations for screenings and process data from the screenings), observational data, and transcripts of before, during, and after in relation to the screenings. Such data enable us to understand how the images travel within and across contexts, as well as how the media and messages are received and responded to. The data also enhance our ability to see the relationships that exist among the researcher, the visual texts, and the audiences, and the factors that influence the ways in which the productions are received.

Out in the World: Studying the Afterlife of Postings and Viewings

In this chapter as in the previous one on exhibiting, we have drawn attention to the significance of multiple screenings and what we have termed the over and over effect. Clearly, the use of online platforms alters the notion of multiple viewings and creates different possibilities for audience-response. At the same time, this exposure raises new questions about critical reception and the responsibility of the researcher. Not all reception, for example, is positive. At other points the work may be very controversial and while appropriate within the participant group, may be less so when it travels out into the world. Who decides what and where something can be shown? Would the pedagogies of discomfort that Boler and Zembylas (2003) and Zembylas (2015) put forward help us to comprehend the anger, fear, grief, and trauma that often confront participants in communities, as well as in developing strategies for change in post-screening dialogues?

Community Dialogue

Across the examples we have highlighted is the significance of dialogue. If the purpose of research is to increase understanding of issues and challenges in communities and to use what we learn to develop strategies for addressing them, then all stakeholders must necessarily be an integral part of the research process. This chapter has illustrated how, through screening the various productions of our research in communities, including the ones where our research takes place, as well as to academic and policy communities, significant dialogue that not only enhances our understanding of the issues, but also begins to identify ways of resolving them, is possible. What this chapter has also highlighted is the significance of the participants' speaking for themselves (to each other, to their own communities and to the academic community). In other words, making the research public through screening digital productions enhances 'a dialogic, collaborative process of meaning-making that fosters a research process that is more transparent, public, and available for ongoing scrutiny [by researchers, participants and various audiences]' (Paulus, Woodside, & Ziegler, 2008, p. 240).

Power, Aesthetics, and Audiences

We have not covered all possible screening contexts in this chapter and there are many more questions about power dynamics in relation to viewing. In what ways do different audiences – participants, local communities and external audiences, academic conference delegates, practitioners and policy makers – respond to screenings of the same partici-pant-created productions? What are some of the factors that influence audience responses to the various forms of screenings? Might they respond differently when the screenings involve researcher-created productions? Some of the questions here may relate to aesthetics and technical competence. Not all productions travel well and issues of sound quality, length, quality of the story and so on may all have an impact on audience. Participants may at first be celebratory about their production but then be forced to confront some of the technical problems. These are not all necessarily about power but they may be about status and technical competence as the research team involved in making *Take a Risk: It's as Simple as ABC* acknowledge.

CONCLUSION

Participatory visual research has long acknowledged digital visual productions as instru-mental in enhancing our understanding of the issues we target in our investigations. Also, the importance of making such productions public if the research is to translate into social change and benefit for the communities being studied cannot be underestimated. Thus, in this chapter, we have studied the nature of the making-public process. Focusing on the question, what happens when researchers take the productions to external audiences, including academic peers and policy makers, this chapter has focused on screenings as pedagogy. Screening digital productions to various audiences, including communities, can provide learning spaces in which researchers and participants enhance their understanding of the issues, to make the participants' experiences public, particularly to those who have the authority and the resources to effect social change. However, it is only when we engage in critical reflection on the ways in which various audiences of our digital productions receive and respond to them that we are likely to realize their pedagogical potential in the communities we work in.

KEY POINTS OF THE CHAPTER

- Screenings, aimed at making visual productions, including participatory videos, cellphilms and digital stories accessible to local and outside communities provide learning spaces for participants and researchers.
- Screenings can happen through face-to-face events (such as movie nights, cellphilms festivals, and community workshops), as well as through online postings such as Facebook, YouTube, and others.
- Screening strategies include research participants screening their work to each other, to peers outside the research project, and to national and international audiences, as well as researchers screening their own work and participant-produced material, to communities, policy makers, and national and international audiences.
- Screenings highlight the interaction among the producer, the text, and the audience.
- A pedagogy of screening aims to position and interrogate the meaning of sharing visual productions such as cellphilms, participatory video, and digital stories with various audiences in participatory visual research.
- A pedagogy of screening involves deliberate or intentional activities: preparation (deciding what to screen, to what audience, when and how), screening to various audiences, involving the audience in dialogue or reflection on the screenings or the issues therein.
- Can involve a pedagogy of celebration (for example, on the part of the producers who have succeeded in completing a production) or a 'pedagogy of discomfort' can involve the discomfort audiences (and the producers) might feel when the production focuses on difficult or controversial issues.
- A pedagogy of discomfort might be useful in providing a productive platform for talking about some of the challenges and contradictions involved in screening productions to live audiences, online audiences, and critical audiences.
- A pedagogy of screening allows participatory researchers to study the responses of researchers and participants, as well as external groups (policy makers, community members, the academic community) as audiences to visual productions, and to consider the factors that influence the ways in which they respond.

6

DIGITAL ARTEFACTS: RESEARCHER-LED TOOLS FOR DIALOGUE

━━ **CHAPTER CONTENTS** ━━━━━━━━━━━━━

INTRODUCTION

As we highlighted in the previous chapter, the explosion of digital technologies has changed the way we might carry out participatory visual research using online platforms. It has also changed the ways that, as researchers, we might think about involving participants in participatory analysis, engaging various audiences in dialogue, or disseminating findings in communities or at conferences. Indeed, the range of digital platforms and the relative user-friendly nature of various digital technologies has meant that increasingly research teams are likely to embark upon the production of digital artefacts ourselves. This is something that we discussed in Chapter 5 where we focus on the pedagogy of screenings, drawing on the reflexive aspects of our own work in deepening our understanding of participant-led screenings. Framed in the context of digital scholarship, this work signals new possibilities for dialogue and engagement. Abby Smith Rumsey (2011, p. 2) defines digital scholarship as 'the use of digital evidence and method, digital authoring, digital publishing and preservation, and digital use and reuse of scholarship.' Clearly, as special issues of various journals such as the *McGill Journal of Education*, Vol. 49, no. 3 (Strong-Wilson, Asghar, & Yoder, 2015) and *Sociological Research Online*, Vol. 17, no. 1 (De Lange & Mitchell, 2012a) have highlighted, research and scholarship have taken on what might be termed a 'digital turn' (Mills, 2010).

While this digital turn has implications for many different types of research, we regard this work as particularly significant in the context of participatory visual methods where the digital already occupies a prominent place in participant-led production of cellphilms, digital stories, photography, the use of social media, digital archives, digital mapping and so on. As numerous researchers have highlighted, this can alter the relationship between participants and production, and especially the idea of greater autonomy on the part of participants to be already participating in digital production (Schwab-Cartas, 2012; Schwab-Cartas & Mitchell, 2014). But as we explore here this can also alter the relationship between researchers and production, alongside the idea of co-production with participants. Thus this chapter focuses on the production and use of digital dialogue tools, a digital artefact primarily produced by researchers drawing on the visual productions with the participants, to enable a variety of audiences (both the participants themselves and various stakeholders) to see the issues being raised, but also to engage in dialogue with the issue under study for the purpose of facilitating social change.

RESEARCHER-PRODUCED DIGITAL PRODUCTIONS: A BRIEF HISTORY

Our work with researcher-led production dates back to a video production that came out of Claudia's collaboration with a film maker, Monica Mak. Mak's video production entitled

Unwanted Images (2006) drew together a selection of a set of drawings of gender-based violence created by children in the province of Free State in South Africa, complementing a manual, *Opening our Eyes* (produced for and published by the Department of Education (2001) in South Africa) for teachers to address gender-based violence in schools. The video proved to be effective in training workshops with school leaders and teachers. Given the range of visual productions coming out of our later work (drawings, photographs, curated albums and drawings) we were motivated to further explore what we could do with such a tool particularly in relation to community dialogue and policy-making towards taking action and bringing about social change.

Our first digital production *Our Photos, Our Videos, Our Stories* (Mitchell, Mak, & Stuart, 2005), captured our participatory visual work in addressing HIV and AIDS and gender-based violence with a rural community in KwaZulu-Natal. We have screened this documentary dozens of times in order to contextualize our participatory visual work in seminars, workshops, conference presentations, and training sessions. Sometimes the responses have caught us off guard. We recall, for example, one of our colleagues simply stating, 'This is just very depressing. How is your work uplifting?' Others have been very moved by one scene or another. These differing reactions continue to be a reminder of the non-neutrality of data, and especially the visual.

Realizing how much easier it is to use a visual artefact to engage an audience, we have continued to consider ways of drawing the visual data such as participatory video together, and have coined the term 'composite videos' to describe a range of video productions that highlight participatory visual processes. As described by Mitchell (2011):

While there may be other terms for what a researcher-produced data-driven video text might be called, we regard the composite video as a specific genre: a research video, a research tool, a communication tool that is more than simply video data (or visual data captured on video). The composite video is a production in and of itself, with a clear beginning, middle and end. It includes a narrative (conveyed either through voice-overs, captions, subtitles or textboxes), samples of the actual visual data (photographs, participatory videos, drawings), plus the contextual data in the form of video footage taken during the research process and often a musical soundtrack in some part of the video. What is critical is producing something that allows for the various layers of work to come together as a composite. (p. 161)

The various writings by Ruby (2000), Pauwels (2002, 2006) and Rose (2001, 2012) on ethnographic representation have been very useful in thinking about the different types of productions (video, mixture of video clips, visual artefacts, the place of narration) created by researchers. Rose (2012) in particular draws attention to being an audience member at an academic conference, and how the viewing of an ethnographic text at a conference presentation informed her reading of articles and other writings to come out of a particular project. Beyond the use of these productions in conference presentations, we have used the composite videos to enable the participants to see for themselves what they as a collective have produced but also for them and others (especially community stakeholders) to use the productions as a catalyst or trigger to take action to address the issues under study.

The idea of studying researcher-led digital tools and artefacts being used in support of community dialogue builds on work across several broad areas of practice including arts-based inquiry, media making through digital and visual studies, focusing in particular on representing and re-representing data. Here we consider several different types of digital artefacts and platforms including digital dialogue tools, a term we coined to describe short composite type video productions and re-mix/reuse digital productions.

Another composite video we created was entitled *Our Stories*, which includes something of the rural context of the participants and the participatory video process, focusing on one participatory video, *Trust No One* (a video made by rural school youth about a teacher raping a schoolgirl), to make prominent the issue of sexual violence in their rural school community. A third composite video entitled *Seeing for Ourselves*, contained four videos on sexual violence (see Moletsane, Mitchell, Smith, & Chisholm, 2008). These four videos are titled, *Rape* (with a storyline about a girl who is raped by her boyfriend, who then calls his friends who also rape her); *Stop Abuse* (a story about a girl who is raped on her way to school and who becomes infected with the HI virus); *How raping got me HIV and AIDS* (a story about a young woman who is raped by a man who is infected with the HI virus and who is callous about infecting women and girls in the community) and *Protect the Children* (a story about a father who rapes his daughter while her mother is at work). We, the researchers, developed a story board for each of these two composite videos and a videographer created a rough cut which we then commented on to enable the videographer to develop the final videos.

Lassiter (2005) in Gubrium and Harper (2013), makes use of 'dialogic editing' – a technique developed by Feld (1987) – which is a process of negotiating and creating a collaborative text with participants. This he suggests can happen through a whole range of strategies:

[i]nvolving principal consultants as readers and editors; convening focus groups to review drafts; using collaborative ethnographer/consultants; holding community forums to present research findings; discussing drafts with community-based editorial boards, and co-writing texts. (p. 191)

What is important is that such collaborative editing emerges 'as a dialogue' (p. 191) between the researcher and participants and/or the community, leading to a product – or in our work here – a digital artefact which is sensitive to the participants and the community's lived realities.

The idea for developing what we call a digital dialogue tool came when working in a project in eight informal settlements (also referred to as slum areas) of Nairobi with more than 100 children involved in creating drawings and photos on feeling safe and feeling not so safe in and around their homes and neighbourhoods. The recognition of the rich corpus of data and of the idea that it was important to go back to the children who produced this data inspired the project team to develop a digital tool that would allow us to: (1) engage in member checking with the children who participated; (2) give children across the eight communities an opportunity to see their own visual productions (drawings, mappings, and photographs of feeling safe and not so safe) as well as see how other children in the other slum areas see safety; (3) provide opportunities for them to suggest solutions – from their viewpoint – to the problem of safety and security in relation to housing; and (4) engage the parents, community leaders and local NGOs working in the area of housing. The resulting digital production of the children's drawings, maps and photos of 'feeling safe and not so safe', *More Than Bricks and Mortar, Housing, The Way Children See It*, which we describe below, served as a model for later projects.

RESEARCHER-PRODUCED DIGITAL DIALOGUE TOOLS: THREE CASES

Case 1: Working with Children in Kenya: *More Than Bricks and Mortar, Housing, The Way Children See It*

Policy Context of Housing

The production of *More Than Bricks and Mortar* is located in the policy context of safety and security in relation to housing in informal settlements in Nairobi. Physiological needs (food, water, and shelter) and safety needs are two basic needs of every human being (Maslow, 1987). We wanted to see what views children growing up in the slum areas of Nairobi, Kenya, had of their safety, security, and well-being – in relation to housing. Whether children are growing up in urban, peri-urban, or rural areas, in formal housing, public housing, or informal settlements, in times of peace and war, or in extremely different neighbourhoods, they need to feel safe. Looking closely at the nature of the home and neighbourhood, if inadequate, it could expose children to health issues (Bashir, 2002); it could limit healthy outdoor play (Molnar, Gortmaker, Bull, & Buka, 2004) and physical activity (Bennett, McNeill, Wolin, Duncan, Puleo, & Emmons, 2007); it could diminish the potential to attend school (Davison, Werder, & Lawson, 2008); and it could exacerbate violence that children might experience (Ward, Martin, Theron, & Distiller, 2007).

While housing policies might contribute to an orderly development of a neighbourhood, they are not necessarily implemented in informal housing settlements (Mitchell, Chege, Maina, & Rothman, 2016). Noting the nature of the slum areas and reading about the dangers in the slum areas, the team was interested in how children see their own safety, security, and well-being in relation to their housing. More importantly, we also wanted to know how their voices could inform policy-making about housing. We envisaged that the children's safety in the area could be improved if their lived experiences were made visible to their parents, the community, and to policy makers.

The Visual Data Sets

The fieldwork was carried out by a group of postgraduate students (who were trained in participatory visual methodologies) from the School of Education of a local university. The data production yielded an abundance of visual productions. These included 100 drawings, 100 mappings, and a few hundred photographs in response to the prompt: 'feeling safe and not so safe'. Predictably, these mostly depicted feeling unsafe in terms of an unhealthy environment, the presence of dangerous gangs in the neighbourhood, being compelled to do child labour under unacceptable working conditions and not being able to attend school or complete homework, experiencing domestic violence and neglect in the family, being exposed to sexual violence in the home and neighbourhood, as well as in public toilets. A few of the images did depict feeling safe within the home, but also in places of worship.

Producing the Digital Dialogue Tool

The 7-minute-39-second-long digital dialogue tool has a simple storyline of showing how the hundred children in the eight slum areas see their housing in terms of feeling safe and feeling not so safe. A storyboard to plot a storyline and text to be narrated was created. We selected examples of the visual images, and identified what we as the team thought to be an appropriate soundtrack. We turned this over to a professional film maker and worked with her to produce a final video. The video opens with a scene of young Kenyan children playfully running along footpaths in the veld – seeming happy and carefree. A child's voice is heard singing in the background. This opening serves as a dramatic contrast to the images that the participants produce. The title frame appears with the video going on to provide information about the purposively selected group of child participants, along with still images of how they engaged with the methods – drawing and photovoice – to depict their feeling safe and feeling not so safe in the slum area in which they live. The voice-over of a male speaking in Kiswahili narrates the story with English subtitles provided. The video then reveals the seven themes – appearing in text – which emerged from the analysis of the visual productions, supported by examples of the drawings, mapping, and photographs the children had made. Six of the themes depict 'feeling not so safe' (child labour, domestic violence, sexual violence, toilet safety, environmental security, gangs), and one theme depicts 'feeling safe' (inside homes and at churches and mosques). The mood of the video, as the research team observes is very important:

Connotatively, the video is meant to be emotive. In the production of the digital dialogue tool we were seeking anything but non-neutrality and regarded audience engagement (especially the engagement of adults) as critical and deliberate. We did not want audiences to walk away without being moved by the children's visual productions. (Mitchell et al., 2016, p. 5)

Using the Digital Dialogue Tool

It was important to first have the children to view *More Than Bricks and Mortar,* the video, to see their spaces of growing up as well as their own work in a digital format and on a big screen. During the project a total of five participatory workshops were organized with more than 300 children from the participating slum areas. The child participants first viewed the video, then were given time to draw how they thought the safety and security in their homes and communities could be improved. These drawings pointed to solutions which they individually or as a group of youths collectively could take up, such as cleaning up in and around the public toilets, and how the family and the community could be educated about child labour and abuse. They also made drawings about what they wished for and what could improve their well-being, for example, good education, a beautiful house, and running water (Figure 6.1).

Four screenings were held with adult audiences. In a first workshop approximately 30 community leaders from the eight communities viewed *More Than Bricks and Mortar,* listened to a presentation on the preliminary results of the study, and then worked in small groups to generate responses to the results and video, and also to think and plan what they might do about the results. In a second workshop, senior managers/executives of the NGO responsible for the housing program through which community members received loans and support for their houses, engaged in a similar way. A third session with the postgraduate students from a local university who had participated as data collectors was held. These screenings and

Figure 6.1 *More Than Bricks and Mortar*

Screenshot produced by Noushin Nasri, Claudia Mitchell and Dorian Mitchell

Nasri, N., Mitchell, C., & Mitchell, D. (Producers). (2015). *More Than Bricks and Mortar: How Children See Housing in Kenya* [Video production]. Toronto: Rooftops Canada.

dialogues opened the eyes of the audiences as well as the researchers to the lived realities of the children and also enabled reflexivity among these groups, particularly in relation to how children could participate in housing planning. Beyond the period of funding, we have used the video with numerous international audiences (also an international NGO) while the NGO initially involved in the project also held several screenings and dialogues.

Case 2: Working with Girls in Vietnam: *Picturing Inclusion, Voices of Girls With Disabilities*

Building on the success of *More Than Bricks and Mortar, Housing, The Way Children See It*, we embarked on a similar process in a project with girls with disabilities in Vietnam where we used drawing and photovoice as research methods, to produce a digital dialogue tool.

Policy Context of Inclusive Education

This second example is framed in the policy context of inclusive education and work with girls with disabilities in Tu Liem district, Hanoi, Vietnam. The *United Nations Convention on the Rights of Persons with Disabilities* (UNCRPD) is aimed at protecting the rights of all persons with disabilities, also girls with disabilities. A lack of inclusion deepens their vulnerability to poverty, unwanted pregnancy, and other social concerns (UNICEF, 2013). The *Human Rights of Women and Children with Disabilities* (Human Rights Watch, 2012) further points to the experiences of gender-based violence of girls and women with disabilities. A Vietnamese policy which influences how girls with disabilities are treated, is the *Law on Persons with Disabilities*, which defines disability as 'a deficiency in the bodily structure that results in difficulties in work, life, and studies' (Social Republic of Vietnam, 2010, Article 2.1). Such a biomedical definition is discriminatory and puts people with disabilities, including girls, at a disadvantage. Furthermore, despite the reforms in Vietnam, there is no reference to girls with disabilities in the relevant laws and policies, which in a way perpetuates a gender hierarchy (Nguyen, Mitchell, De Lange, & Fritsch, 2015), leaving girls behind. It is within this broader policy context that we turn to education policy in particular, that is, the *Education for All* (EFA) movement of the World Education Forum in Jomtien in 1990, reconfirmed in Dakar in 2000, and recently in Incheon, Republic of Korea, in 2015. The Incheon Declaration, 'Education 2030: Towards inclusive and equitable quality education and lifelong learning for all', clearly advocates for transformation through inclusive education:

to transform lives through education, recognizing the important role of education as a main driver of development...We commit with a sense of urgency to a single, renewed education agenda that is holistic, ambitious and aspirational, leaving no one behind...We recognize education as key to achieving full employment and poverty eradication. (UNESCO, 2015, para 5)

It is within this global and local policy context, and with the understanding that girls with disabilities are still being disadvantaged and excluded from public education in Vietnam (Rydstrom, 2010), that we wanted to explore the lived experiences of girls with disabilities – in terms of being included in education – in Tu Liem, a district of Hanoi, Vietnam.

The Visual Data

We worked with 21 purposively selected girls with disabilities from the Tu Liem district, an area just outside Hanoi. The project leader, a Vietnamese woman and academic herself, initiated our working with a Vietnamese partner, the Action to Community Development Center (ACDC), which is a Disabled People's Organization (DPO) led by women with disabilities. ACDC recruited eight women to be trained as fieldworkers, who assisted in generating the data with the children. Here too, we made use of participatory visual methods, such as drawing (draw 'Me and my community' in an attempt to explore individual expressions of inclusion and exclusion in the family and community), photovoice (take photographs of 'feeling included and feeling not included in my school' to explore individual expressions of being included and excluded at school) and finally, producing policy posters (in a group 'create a "policy poster" with a message for policy makers and other community leaders)"'. From this work 21 drawings with captions were produced, 21 sets of photographs each with one photograph depicting inclusion and one depicting exclusion along with a written caption, and seven policy posters. A catalogue, *Our Voices, Our Hopes* (De Lange, Nguyen, Mitchell, & Nguyen, 2014) containing the data sets was produced – with both English and Vietnamese captions – to complement any exhibition that we held to engage policy makers and other stakeholders.

Producing the Digital Dialogue Tool

The digital dialogue tool was plotted out on a storyboard by the project team. The storyboard and footage was turned over to the videographer, a young Vietnamese man who is himself disabled, who developed a rough cut for the research team to look at and comment on, and to suggest changes. The research team decided on a soundtrack as background to the video – the production of the digital dialogue tool was intended for use first of all with the girls themselves, enabling them to see their work in a professionally produced digital format, and for us to continue with a participatory analysis of their data, and to deepen the dialogue which had been initiated. With such a tool the girls could take the dialogue back into their community.

Picturing Inclusion, Voices of Girls with Disabilities, provides an overview of the project (Monitoring Educational Rights for Girls with Disabilities), the process, and the visual productions (drawings, photographs, and the policy posters) the girls had made. The final video, *Picturing Inclusion, Voices of Girls with Disabilities,* is 15 minutes and 20 seconds long, is narrated in Vietnamese, and has subtitles in English and Vietnamese, so as not to exclude people who are deaf. The video begins with some footage of the neighbourhood where the girls with disabilities are growing up – in the Tu Liem district of Hanoi. The context of the research project and the process of doing participatory visual research with the girls with disabilities are shown. The visual data is then presented in themes, giving an analysis of the exclusion in terms of marginalization, violence, discrimination, exclusion and environmental issues. The visual data also show the hopes and dreams, family relationships, relationships in the context of education, inclusion and participation, and accessibility. The policy posters with recommendations to policy makers refer to raising societal awareness, their right to health, and right to education. The video then shows footage of the first exhibition where they view their exhibited work and where some of them talk about their work to the other girls. The video ends with the credits to acknowledge participating institutions, individual persons, but also the girls and women with disabilities who contributed to the research. The video has been uploaded on YouTube[1] (see Figure 6.2) and accessible through Facebook and is publicly available (Monitoring Educational Rights for Girls with Disabilities (MRDG) Report, 2016).

Figure 6.2 *Picturing Inclusion, Voices of Girls with Disabilities*

Screenshot produced by Claudia Mitchell, Thuy Nguyen and Nghiem Trang

Mitchell, C., Nguyen, T., & Nghiem, T. (Producers). (2015). *Picturing Inclusion, Voices of Girls with Disabilities* [Video production]. Halifax: Mount Saint Vincent University.

---

[1]www.youtube.com/watch?v=K7R2z0_DcOo

Using the Digital Dialogue Tool

The first use of the digital dialogue tool was with the girls we worked with and the women who helped generate the data. The video was shown and the girls reflected on what they liked, did not like and what they would like changed. They also created new messages for building inclusive schools and communities (MRDG Report, 2016).

Several dialogues have been facilitated with international audiences in Vietnam and also in Canada. For example, a global inclusive dialogue was held at an international institute for community development in Nova Scotia which not only opened dialogue about the inclusion of girls (it was pointed out by a member of the audience that boys and men also need to be included in the project) but also about the value of using and extending the use of participatory methodologies in contexts of the global south.

Case 3: Working with Children and Mental Health in Canada: *How We See It*

This third example of a digital dialogue tool, *How We See It*, is situated within the policy framework of the mental health of 'very young adolescents', a term used by the Population Council to refer to young people between the ages of 10 and 14. We focus here on a school-based intervention in Canada, but acknowledge the implication of this work for broader community studies as well in terms of promoting dialogue.[2]

Policy Context of Children and Mental Health

The emerging policy framework in Canada and internationally for school-based interventions that take account of gender, violence prevention and mental health is critical. Research studies indicate that up to one in five Canadian children and youth experience mental health issues that have a significant impact on their academic, social, and family life (Kutcher & McDougall, 2009). Of particular relevance is the time of the middle childhood years or 'very young adolescence' (ages 10–14). The social features of this age range pose particular challenges as children transition into their adolescence. Children and young people at this age are often faced with increasing demands and concerns related to peer and family relationships as well as in relation to such issues as sexuality, body image, eating disorders, depression, and substance use and abuse, along with increasing issues of violence (Watt, Dickey, & Grakist, 2004). The role of gender and the ways in which boys and girls differ in their experiences of being 'very young adolescent' has not been a major feature of violence prevention interventions in schools, in spite of the extensive bodies of

---

[2]This study 'Addressing a Gender Gap in School-based Mental Health Programs' was funded through a CIHR Planning Grant.

sociological and psychological literature that highlight the differing social contexts for 'growing up girl' and 'growing up boy'. The bullying literature, for example, often takes a gender-neutral position (see Gillander, 2013).

There are numerous studies that point to the links between the mental health and well-being of teachers and students (see Ross, Romer, & Horner, 2012; Spilt, Koomen, & Thijs, 2011). A recent study by Froese-Germain and Riel (2012), *Understanding Teachers' Perspectives on Student Mental Health,* highlighted the concerns of close to 3,000 teachers in relation to the mental health of students, with 79 per cent noting that stress and anxiety were key issues in the lives of their students. Another study, *Teaching the Way We Aspire to Teach: Now and in the Future,* by Freiler, Hurley, Canuel, McGahey, Froese-Germain, and Riel (2012) found that the number one aspiration of Canadian teachers was to make a differ-ence in the lives and learning of their students, and identified the importance of teacher collaboration and participation in carrying out this work. The study used focus groups and an online survey with more than 4,000 teachers. Teachers envisioned policies and processes that would enable the development of more opportunities for working together in ways that current school structures do not always allow or promote. Many expressed the desire to collaborate on cross-grade, interdisciplinary units, tasks, and projects that connected both teachers and students in new and diverse ways.

Visual Data Sets

The actual project was a first step in connecting teachers and two classes of fifth-grade students (most aged 10 or 11) from two elementary schools in Montreal. In each of the four groups (two boy groups and two girl groups), children first had the opportunity to draw individually how they saw issues of 'feeling good', followed by a photovoice session in which they worked in groups to take photos in both single-sex and mixed-sex groupings on 'feeling safe' and 'feeling not so safe'.

The children produced drawings which focused on feeling good at school, and drew pictures of friendships, improving your own work, being creatively engaged in drawing, being with someone you love, and when playing soccer with friends. They also produced photographs of feeling safe at school, where everyone is seen as unique and different, and when they are with their teacher. In their groups they used their photographs about feeling not so safe to make photo-narratives of bullying at school, being picked on for being fat, saying unkind things about each other, being in physical fights, being in violent relation-ships, being picked on, cyberbullying, unsafe in toilets, unsafe at road crossings, in deserted alleyways, and around strangers. They continued to work in their small groups to partici-pate in what was termed 'from the ground up' policy-making wherein they offered their recommendations for change to make their schools safer (see Figure 6.3).

Some of the recommendations to policy makers included employing a social counsel-lor, ensuring that nurses are at school every day, preventing bullying in schools, anger

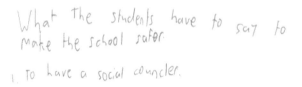

Figure 6.3   Recommendations in *How We See It*

Screenshot produced by Simone Viger and Claudia Mitchell

Viger, S., & Mitchell, C. (Producers). (2016). *How We See It!* [Video production]. Participatory Cultures Lab, Montreal: McGill University.

management training, problem solving training, relationship training, ensuring that there are more books in the school (to keep children busy), make school fun, establish a club where bullying is addressed, i.e. the 'Make a difference club', helping each other, learn to build friendships, appoint lunch-time monitors, encourage obedience, be a role model and inspire other kids, respect others, and put up a fence around the school grounds.

Producing the Digital Dialogue Tool

This video, *How We See It,* is a five minute long digital dialogue tool that was created as part of a school-based project in Montreal, Canada with fifth-grade students involved in photovoice and drawings related to mental health, particularly in relation to safety and security. Produced by the research team, the video is divided into four main parts: (1) visual and audio components on how the children were involved in creating images in the first place; (2) footage of the children in action creating photo-narratives of their work; (3) images of key issues identified by the children; and (4) the children's recommendations (for what they could do and what the school administration could do) (see Figure 6.4).

Using the Digital Dialogue Tool

The production and subsequent screening of *How We See It* to each of the classes and to groups of fifth- and sixth-grade teachers was just one of several post-production activities in this project. For the teachers it was 'an eye-opener' as they commented that they had not realized how much the children actually knew about bullying, and they were particularly impressed with the recommendations. Similarly a curriculum specialist working with the school board who had visited the project 'in progress' but had not seen all the work that the children had done, considered some of the follow-up steps that could be taken to engage children even more in 'from the ground up' policy-making.

Figure 6.4 *How We See It*

Screenshot produced by Simone Viger and Claudia Mitchell

Viger, S., & Mitchell, C. (Producers). (2016). *How We See It!* [Video production]. Participatory Cultures Lab, Montreal: McGill University.

A CO-PRODUCTION: RESEARCHERS AND TEACHERS WORKING TOGETHER ON A 'RE-MIX' VIDEO

The idea of remixing existing visual data and upcycling it and repurposing it for a different or further use draws on Jenkins, Purushotma, Weigel, Clinton, and Robison's (2006) notion of participatory cultures. This has been taken up in areas such as social media and participatory video more at a meta-level. This chapter focuses on the significance of such upcycling in education and at community level – exploring how working with the data in a public way contributes to community dialogue towards social change. Jenkins et al. (2006) and others note that there is a blurring of boundaries of the public and private when using visual images created in a research project and used in a public way, but making the private public might be necessary in a policy context where change is required.

Youth-led Community Dialogue on Sexual Violence in the Age of AIDS

We offer an example of how we worked with three teachers, who were participants in the research project, to re-mix and reuse participatory videos produced by rural school youth, to produce a 'video of videos' to address issues of gender-based violence in their schools and community (see De Lange & Mitchell, 2014). A criticism which is often levelled against participatory visual research is that while it is an exciting methodology which raises the level of participation and enables the participants to see for themselves what they can do to bring about change, it often leaves the participants without ways in which to sustain the work when the researchers leave the field. We draw on some of the conversations during the video production process which informed the way we proceeded.

Policy Context of Gender-Based Violence in Schools

The example is located in the policy context in South Africa, a country with a high prevalence of gender-based violence (Jewkes, Dunkle, Nduna, & Shai, 2010), including school-related gender-based violence (Burton & Leoschut, 2013). These realities are reflected in the small rural community in KwaZulu-Natal where the two schools we have been working with since 2004 are located. Hamilton – one of the three teachers who produced the digital dialogue tool – in referring to his community, points this out:

> Hamilton: …really, violence is prevalent. You see when I'm teaching these Grade 10–12 learners during Sunday school time, if I say draw pictures…they will draw a man with a stick and a woman with tears, showing that maybe there is a lot of violence at homes. It's terrible because sometimes you don't know what to teach after that because you are teaching…you are teaching the word of God. So it's difficult…when a child is just giving you such a picture, because this thing it's just experiencing at home.

When Naydene asked the three if they had to make another video there and then, what the focus would be, they confirmed the issue of gender-based violence as follows:

> Styles: I think it's this concept of violence, gender violence.
>
> Nonhlanhla: I think my interest would be on gender violence and also rape because currently rape again of the elderly people is very common in communities.
>
> Hamilton: …the thing that I can be able to talk about now is the rights of people.

The *Guidelines for the Prevention and Management of Sexual Violence & Harassment in Public Schools* (DoE, 2008) – a policy framework in South Africa – is an important starting point for curbing gender-based violence in public schools, and is intended to be used in the formulation of a policy particular to each school. Naydene raised the issue of the gender-based violence policy work done previously with teachers from the two schools:

Naydene: …we worked with you about two years ago on policy issues [gender-based violence and school-related gender-based violence] and then your task was … to make up a simple policy for the school. So, is there something [like that] in the school?

Styles: Yes, I think there is something like that even though it's not that detailed but it positions like the ones maybe for children caught fighting. So how were they going to be punished.

Naydene: So there is some document on – maybe it's more procedure – what to do when two people are fighting.

Styles: Yes.

Naydene: What do you do?

Styles: It's taken as a serious case that would be called and then try to talk and discuss the problem.

Naydene: So is it written down somewhere? Is there a note? Do you call it a policy? What do you call it?

Styles: Yeah, it's written down somewhere.

Nonhlanhla: Yeah, we are in the same school.

Hamilton: We do have something written like this [picking up a piece of paper] a few pages because most of the time the learners are fighting at school.

While the above does not directly speak about school-related gender-based violence the three teachers were clear that a policy of some kind existed. It was therefore important to revisit how they might produce a digital dialogue tool to also address gender-based violence and school-related gender-based violence through ensuring that each school had a policy not only on violence, but also on gender-based violence, including sexual violence.

The realities of gender-based violence (Gender Links Report, 2012) and school-related gender-based violence (Burton & Leoschut, 2013) in the rural community which the teachers have to contend with raise the significance of their roles in addressing it as well as informing relevant policy. In the light of the above it seemed meaningful to work more with the existing participatory videos on sexual violence made by the youth in 2006 so as to enable teachers to take action in school. Hamilton, one of the three teachers we were working with was adamant that they as teachers, should address gender-based violence but that one could not do it as an individual.

Hamilton: Every corner should have a person who is vigilant. Every corner because if you are just standing alone …

Styles: [completing Hamilton's sentence]…it will be difficult.

The re-mixed video, developed by teachers for teachers and focusing on gender-based violence and school-related gender-based violence could be useful in initiating a dialogue within their school and the community and to make their voices heard in terms of policy-making.

The Data Set

Earlier, when working with the school teachers, school youth, community health workers and parents and asking them to work in groups to respond to the prompt: 'What are the key issues affecting your daily lives in your community?' five of the eight participatory videos (see Chapter 3 for the process) were made by youth, all focusing on sexual violence. The titles are: *Rape at School* (a group of boys raping a girl at school); *Trust No One* (a male teacher raping a girl after school); *How Raping Got me HIV & AIDS* (a young man who is HIV infected deliberately rapes girls); *Rape* (a young man out of school raping a girl on her way to school); and *Protect the Children* (a girl raped by her father) (see Moletsane et al., 2008).

Producing the Re-mixed Video

The video, *Youth-led Community Dialogue on Sexual Violence in the Age of AIDS*, is 28 minutes long – planned and directed by teachers and framed around the five videos on sexual violence school youth from the two participating schools had made. We viewed all five participatory videos, discussed what the main issue of each one was, and decided whether it had merit to be included in the new production. The three teachers then worked on the storyboard and created the storyline for the video, considered who the target audience is, then drew on documents we had engaged with earlier in the day to source data to contextualize gender-based violence in the community and school. The documents included the *School Violence in South Africa: Results of the 2012 National School Violence Study*, by Burton and Leoschut (2013), *The War @ Home: Findings of GBV Prevalence Study in South Africa* (Gender Links, 2012), and *Opening our Eyes* (DoE, 2001).

The teachers came up with five referenced findings which we decided to put in text boxes in the video (see Figure 6.5 as an example).

They negotiated the order of the five videos and chose to end the new video by posing questions to engage the local community of parents, teachers, and youth in dialogue, such as 'What measures can we take to prevent sexual violence?', 'How can we assist victims of sexual violence?', 'What are the responsibilities of educators and community in stopping sexual violence?', 'How can youth voices be used to inform policy?' and 'What can you do?', concluding with the question, 'What can we do together?' Once the storyboard was completed they played around with titles such as *Youth-led*

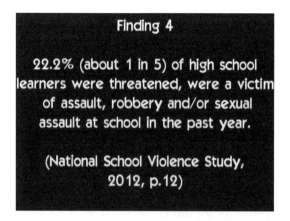

Figure 6.5 Textbox in *Youth-led Community Dialogue on Sexual Violence in the Age of AIDS*

Screenshot produced by Nonhlanhla Gasa, Hamilton Shelembe and Styles Colvel

Gasa, N., Shelembe, H., & Colvel, S. (Producers). (2015). *Youth-led Community Dialogue on Sexual Violence in the Age of AIDS* [Digital video]. Vulindlela: University KwaZulu-Natal.

Policy Dialogue on Sexual Violence, Youth-led Dialogue on Sexual Violence in the Age of AIDS, and settled on, *Youth-led Community Dialogue on Sexual Violence in the Age of AIDS*. The group wanted to add a soundtrack for the beginning and ending of their video and Nonhlanhla suggested a Xhosa gospel song, Phendula (Answer me) by Zahara, which was also acceptable to the two other teachers. Rounding off the storyboard they inserted their names and surnames as directors, and Naydene reminded them to acknowledge the funders, and the learner participants.

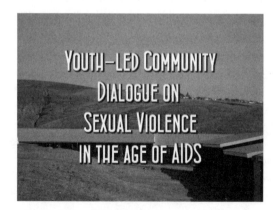

Figure 6.6 *Youth-led Community Dialogue on Sexual Violence in the Age of AIDS*

Screenshot produced by Nonhlanhla Gasa, Hamilton Shelembe and Styles Colvel

Gasa, N., Shelembe, H., & Colvel, S. (Producers). (2015). *Youth-led Community Dialogue on Sexual Violence in the Age of AIDS* [Digital video]. Vulindlela: University KwaZulu-Natal.

We turned the storyboard and the footage over to a videographer who created a rough cut for the teachers and team to view and refine. The first image in the final video, a shot over the school grounds with the mountains in the background and its title is shown in Figure 6.6.

Using the Re-mixed Video

We discussed which storage format would best suit the teachers and the resources available to them, who should see their video, and how they would use it:

Styles: So this one that we are making now, this one it's planned, so I think it would, if all the stakeholders can get involved so it will have a very big impact on the learners and even the community.

Hamilton: But make sure that if you give to schools even the principal should take part in that because the principals…sometimes it's not easy to call the learners without the permission of the principal and say all this, because these videos, if I may speak, they are very good even for the community itself. … The governing body when they call meetings can also pass it to the community themselves, to the parents.

Nonhlanhla: …it opened our eyes because it was like this is something which is happening in our communities, but it's like as communities we turn a blind eye as if nothing is happening…It was amazing for me to do this task to see to it that something can be done do develop our kids to become responsible citizens.

The teachers each were given a USB with the video, *Youth-led Community Dialogue on Sexual Violence in the Age of AIDS,* to use as they saw fit in the school and community. This resonates with what one of the participants alluded to in a previous workshop, 'That's what I like about the video. It did not end here.'

What We Have Learned in Producing these Digital Dialogue Tools

These four examples demonstrate how digital dialogue tools have been used to stimulate dialogue towards social change. Design of the tools required that we looked closely at the visual data we had generated, and indeed immersing ourselves in it in order to be able to develop productions which were sensitive to the communities and appropriate for stimulating dialogue. In this regard the interpretation process is clearly important. Going back to Susan Sontag's (2003) work highlighted in Chapter 1 on the power of images, this sensitivity also required acknowledging emotion – our own and that of potential audiences – in working with visual data and ensuring that we do most good and least harm. In screening these representations of the visual artefacts in a variety of places, we have come to recognize the 'travelling' potential for this work. The production of these digital dialogue tools can help to extend the number of dialogues that might take place in relation to any one project, and also to ensure that these dialogues are not limited to our presence as researchers. Participants themselves can use these digital dialogue tools in their communities.

DIGITAL ARTEFACTS: ISSUES TO CONSIDER

Who Gets to Produce It?

Producing a digital artefact, we believe, is an efficient way to collate the visual data produced with a clear purpose in mind – to stimulate dialogic engagement between the participants and the researchers (also as a way of enabling participatory analysis) and between participants, researchers, and other stakeholders, such as policy makers and communities. We have referred to three examples where the researchers led the production of the digital dialogue tools and one example of a re-mix video where the participants plotted and planned how to use existing visual data in a video, directing it from their insider knowledge of the community in which they work and of the children they teach, in a way which Feld (1987, cited in Gubrium & Harper, 2013, p. 190) referred to as 'dialogic editing'.

In participatory visual research we have often reflected and have asked ourselves whether we – in spite of acknowledging the value of participatory visual research enabling the voices of those not often heard – have represented the participants, their work, and their experiences 'as it is', and whether we have done justice (or not) to their lived experiences. In this regard Gubrium and Harper (2013, p. 55) refer to the participants holding 'a certain representational power' but they ask a further question:

[W]hat happens when representation of the subject matter is not 'nice' and, instead reaffirms dominant discourse supporting negative stereotypes of particular social groups? When the purpose of the digital artefact is to initiate dialogue, what is the researchers' responsibility? Would it for example be to adjust the representation? (p. 55)

Gready (2010) points out how this becomes an ethical dilemma 'with questions raised over ownership of knowledge and control over representation (p. 180).'

A seemingly simple issue such as identifying and choosing music as soundtrack for the digital artefact contains the question of power and ownership. Who gets to choose the music, or even who gets to create the music? In almost all of the digital artefacts described above, we as researchers ended up choosing, the music keeping in mind specific ideas about some of the audiences that we saw as crucial. This meant that we were actually excluding the participants from another aspect of our participatory visual research process.

Who Owns It?

Researchers usually have the necessary resources to carry out the research, are usually constructed – in the eyes of the participants – as experts who know the area under study, who understand the methods used, and who own and bring the equipment to the research site. In participatory visual research it is therefore important to engage with the participants in such a way that they see themselves positioned not as 'the researched' but as 'trustworthy researchers themselves' (Berry, 2004, cited in Gubrium & Harper, 2013, p. 55), as the keepers of insider knowledge, producers of expert knowledge, and as autonomous agents of change, able to see and reflect on their own lives and the value of what they bring. It is when they are positioned as owning the knowledge that they would be able to act as agents of change when the research team is no longer in the community.

It is therefore important for participants not only to own the knowledge, but also for them to see themselves as owners of the digital artefact produced. We have seen how the handing over of copies of the digital dialogue tools – which contain their knowledge – for use in the community and with different stakeholders brings a sense of elation and taking ownership of the task ahead.

Who Gets to Use It?

In producing digital artefacts participatory visual research is disseminated in other ways beyond the conventional ways of publishing an article or chapter and importantly penetrates the community and other public spaces. This, according to Gubrium and Harper (2013, p. 13) 'allows for greater access to social research knowledge beyond the academy'. Such new opportunities have been made possible in a context of 'visual gluttony' (Haraway, 1991, cited in Rose, 2007, p. 5) combined with new opportunities in digital scholarship.

While it is commendable that participatory visual researchers make a point of distributing copies of the digital artefacts to the participants, the use thereof is not without problems, as access and lack of access to digital opportunities could seem to increase hierarchies (Haraway, 1991, cited in Rose, 2007, p. 5). A basic challenge for example, is whether the participants have the equipment, such as a laptop, speakers, a screen (even power) to screen the video, or access to the internet to upload or download the digital artefact. Equally important is whether the participants are prepared for the screening and facilitating of the dialogue, or to respond to difficult questions, and are safe when they disseminate the work and dialogue about difficult issues.

Who Gets to Initiate and Facilitate the Dialogue?

As we have indicated in Chapter 2 we as researchers 'begin with the end in mind' and have an idea of who the key dialogue partners are who could make a difference in the issue under study. A question that we need to ask ourselves is whether we are targeting the most appropriate stakeholders? Have we listened carefully enough to the participants to hear their issues and to identify appropriate stakeholders? Are we willing to shift from the list of stakeholders we had in mind at the outset of the research?

In participatory visual work the importance of heightening participation should never be underestimated and the participants should initially be supported (if necessary) to initiate and facilitate the dialogue, and use the digital artefacts. As we have argued (De Lange & Mitchell, 2012b), 'we contend that in a public showing, meaning can be found through active engagement with the public and the filmmakers when the latter are on hand to engage with and to challenge the audience' (p. 327). For example, MacEntee and Mandrona (2015), when working with teachers in addressing HIV and AIDS within a rural school and community, helped the teachers to set up the venue and equipment, and then encouraged the teachers to facilitate dialogues with school children and later with other teachers and parents from the community. As researchers we contributed to financing refreshments for the gathering of people for the various activities (see Chapter 5). With time, however, these local activities may continue without the intervention of the research team (see also De Lange, Mitchell, & Moletsane, 2015). It is only then when we can imagine that the dialogue will continue in our absence from the field, or 'when we are gone' (Mitchell & De Lange, 2012b). We draw on Tochon's (2007, cited in Mitchell & De Lange, 2012b) 'notion of the third construct to frame the importance of participatory video in a post-video production milieu, showing a possible means of sustaining the momentum of change' (p. 328).

From Dialogue to Taking Action

The purpose of creating digital artefacts is to initiate and sustain continued dialogue with appropriate stakeholders and in communities, but it is also important for the dialogue to go over into taking action. We therefore ask ourselves how the dialogue is captured, how it is turned into action, and how we keep track of the process and ensuring change comes about. We have been astute in setting up and recording the various dialogic engagements, and recently, we have included the dialogue with the audience in our ethical clearance applications, ensuring that we have the necessary permissions to undertake but also research the dialogic engagements as well. For example, in a Canada-South African project[3] where we were studying how the use of innovative approaches to knowledge-production, policy-making, and communication could address sexual violence against girls and young women

---

[3]Networks for Change and Well-being: Girl-led 'From the Ground Up' Policy-making to Address Sexual Violence in Canada and South Africa, a Project Funded by SSHRC, Canada, and IDRC, South Africa.

in the two countries, we also applied for ethics separately to examine how the girls could engage with an audience of community practitioners and policy makers. In so doing, the project aimed to shift the boundaries of knowledge-production and inform policy change.

Working with digital artefacts and in a digital age it is possible to keep track of when, where, and how the digital artefacts have been used and to map it out as a holistic dialogic engagement process. We can keep field notes, take photographs and video record the events, and so visually document the processes. Gubrium and Harper (2013) however, point out that such documentations are also socially constructed, as Ruby (1996) argues that the camera is 'constrained by the…culture of those who filmed…and those who are filmed' (p. 345). It thus makes sense to also encourage the participants to document the events, and in so doing enable a co-reflexivity to deepen an understanding of what happened. What is even more difficult is to track change, or what difference the research and the dialogues have made. What did the context look like and how has policy been changed, and how has it changed for the people on the ground? Monitoring and evaluation is necessary, and for us it means that researchers should track policy change, but also track change on the ground, for example through using participatory methods to 'monitor' what has changed for the people on the ground and in the community.

Interpreting Data through the Digital

Strong-Wilson et al. (2014) ask how participants, communities, and other researchers interpret the presence of multimedia and various digital forms in scholarship. As they observe:

When data is collected, archived, analyzed and disseminated through multimedia/ digital forms, the tendency may be to privilege these accounts as more truthful or trustworthy, based on the positive social prejudice towards digital formats, which are associated with relevancy and innovation. In the wake of poststructuralist frameworks, we know that truth is relational and that words, representations, and subjects are unstable and often contradictory. (p. 687)

While the authors are specifically speaking about autobiographical/autoethnographic research, the meanings conveyed through digital artefacts that are meant to be dialogic may seem as fixed, and as such require even more of a need to create an open space for critical commentary. As they go on to observe:

We need to be careful not to take the image/visual at face value as evidence of truth, and instead contextualize it as a version of an event or experience. We need to begin from the premise that just like print text, multimedia data forms are value laden, are subject to interpretations as diverse as those who view/listen/experience them, and may even be commercially or politically driven (e.g., by relying on particular programs or software). (p. 687)

Sensitive and Provocative Material

Producing digital artefacts for use with participants and various communities may, in and of themselves, be provocative and perhaps troubling to view all in one short digital text. In a post-apartheid era in South Africa, for example, these include lingering legacies of the past such as widespread social and economic inequities, impoverished schools, as are many of the images produced by the children in the informal settlements of Nairobi. But this was also the case for many of the drawings and photographs of bullying and harassment that children in schools in Montreal produced. As Strong-Wilson et al. (2014) note: 'This work may demand that participants engage in the process of "picturing atrocity" as Batchen et al. (2012) term the idea of photography in/of crisis. Batchen et al. (2012) are speaking of pictures of atrocity in public journalism, offering close readings of images depicting atrocities in the Congo in the early 20th century (Twomey, 2012), the "iconography of famine" (Campbell, 2012), images of the civil rights movement in the US (Abel, 2012) through to the mushroom cloud of Hiroshima (Hariman & Lucaites, 2012). However, their work anticipates, we would argue, the types of digital representations that might also be produced in digital photovoice and participatory video projects' (pp. 685–686). Batchen et al. (2012) argue that photographs of atrocity bring with them 'a particular set of ethical responsibilities' (p. 15). As they observe:

The media (photographer) has a responsibility to contextualize and caption the atrocity photography correctly. We have a responsibility to read the image closely – perhaps not immediately to trust what we see in the image. If an atrocity has been committed, someone is responsible. This matter of responsibility gave rise to the first humanitarian campaigns that worked with atrocity photographs. Do we also have a responsibility to respond to the photograph beyond simply reading it? What is the question that atrocity photographs ask of us? (p. 15)

RESEARCHER REFLEXIVITY/DISCUSSION

Perhaps the greatest value of producing and using these digital dialogue tools comes back to our role as researchers using participatory visual methods. As we highlight in Chapter 1, reflexivity becomes key in this work – both for advancing the work, particularly in relation to digital production (i.e., what data are we going to use, why and how?) and then extending the study through community engagement (how are audiences responding to this data? Why and so what?). Reflecting on our work done since 2004 we realize that the current digital era opens up more and more opportunities to engage participants and communities in dialogue – using digital artefacts. At the same time, this work places new demands in terms of tracking the screening process: who are the viewers for each screening? What have we learned? How do we incorporate the feedback and comments into later projects? How does this work advance fieldwork studies?

This shift is also seen in creating, maintaining, and using a digital archive. In creating our first archive we wanted teachers and community health workers – all older adults – to use the archive in their daily work (Mnisi, De Lange, & Mitchell, 2010) but also to engage in some participatory analysis processes (De Lange & Mitchell, 2012a). In this work we had to revert to working with the archive in a blended way – the digital archive along with pen and paper – to ensure that the participants from the rural areas could provide input into the archive. As we describe in Chapter 5 (Screening), Casey Burkholder (2016) provides an example of how a YouTube-based digital archive (*We Are HK Too*) was set up and maintained by participants – all young adults from Hong Kong – to preserve but also to share and engage others with the cellphilms they had made.

CONCLUSION

The area of digital scholarship is constantly expanding as the range of digital software and digital spaces develop and as access to these increases, opening up endless possibilities for research teams and participants to try out new ways of inquiry, representation, and dissemination, in participatory visual research. We see this in our own work where we have adopted and adapted as we forged ahead in our participatory visual research – trying to ensure that the visual data produced were making the voices of the often ignored participants heard, but also that the work moves beyond the data production process with the participants, towards extending the dialogue, in this instance, to various stakeholders and policy makers. Doing participatory visual research is clearly not a quick way of doing research, nor will it facilitate social change by itself, as it requires time, and commitment from the researchers and the participants to the cause. The range of digital artefacts we created, however, can help to sustain the dialogue and enable the researchers and the participants separately or together, to do it over and over again (Mitchell, 2016b) until the required change is brought about. We concur with Wheeler's (2012), conclusion from her policy engagement processes through community-produced participatory video that 'a single space for debate is not enough – there needs to be ongoing pressure on different fronts' (p. 376) to ensure that social change happens. As tools, the digital artefacts are key in creating such spaces for dialogue and engagement.

KEY POINTS OF THE CHAPTER

- A digital artefact – a researcher-produced and data-driven tool – can be used to raise public awareness about a critical issue under study and engage audiences in dialogue to facilitate policy change.
- Consider and understand the policy context in which the critical issue under study and requiring addressing is located.

- Producing and using the digital tool is a process which requires careful thinking.

  o Gather all the data (visual and other) together for analysis and identify emerging themes in response to the research question and prompt.

  o Develop a storyline and use a storyboard to plan the flow and content of digital dialogue tool.

  o Screen the digital dialogue tool first to participants for member checking, comment, and responding in terms of offering their from the ground up solutions to the issue represented.

  o Screen the video to relevant audiences to deepen an understanding of the issue, to stimulate dialogue, and taking action to change policy.

- Consider issues of power such as who gets to produce it, own it, use it, initiate and facilitate the dialogue; and who and how the dialogue is captured so that participants, community members, and policy makers act upon it.

- Participants' visual data should be interpreted with care ensuring principles of rigour and trustworthiness.

- An important tenet of participatory visual work is that researchers should maintain a reflexive stance and continue to ask what difference the participatory visual research makes within the community.

7

ENGAGING POLICY MAKERS

CHAPTER CONTENTS

INTRODUCTION

This chapter focuses on specific approaches in participatory research that might engage policy makers to effect sustainable social change. The chapter responds to what critics commonly identify as gaps between research and engagement with policy and policy makers. In particular, it engages with examples from participatory research that illustrate the different pathways that researchers have utilized to engage policy makers in dialogue about the issues impacting on the lives of participants in communities and institutions. As noted in Chapter 1, many have decried the limited impact that research often has on policy dialogue or the way in which attention to policy dialogue appears to be an after-thought. Subject to criticism, too, is the failure to take into consideration questions such as: What policy? Which policy makers?' While there is a rich body of work on what might be described as activist strategies in such key areas as girl-led and youth activist research (MacKay, 2011; Rentschler, 2003; Stuart & Mitchell, 2013; Taft, 2010; Trigg, 2010; Tuck & Yang, 2014a), and in relation to environmental and health issues (Laverack, 2013), to date many of those working in the area of participatory visual research have not necessarily aligned themselves with this work. Linked to work in areas such as girlhood, as Taft (2010) observes, very few studies focus specifically on girls' own politics or polit-ical identities. To what extent and in what ways are girls and young women provided with political education and opportunities that adequately and appropriately prepare them for engaging policy makers on issues that affect them such as, for example, sexual violence and safety and security in schools and on university campuses? Might the use of participatory visual methods enable such an education and activism? How might this activism be applied to other marginalized groups such as community health-care workers or rural extension workers?

We acknowledge that there are a number of challenges and barriers to engaging with policy makers. A key issue that often faces researchers working in resource-poor communi-ties in particular, is the imbalance in power; as outsiders they are regarded as more knowledgeable and, therefore, more powerful by the communities they research. A second issue is that engaging policy makers often proves difficult for research participants, particu-larly those who reside, work, or learn in rural contexts. Factors that make policy makers inaccessible to them include, too, unequal power relations based on the rural-urban divide, social class (we are thinking, here, for example, of the cost of travel for poor rural dwellers), age (particularly in the case of learners), gender, poverty, and other factors. Often, research participants are unable to access policy makers to communicate their needs and are, there-fore, marginalized and rendered voiceless. In our research projects over the years, we have used participatory research to address these power imbalances. In essence, our research uses participatory visual methods to achieve three aims. We want to produce knowledge so as to deepen our understanding of the phenomena/issues under study (for example, sexual violence, HIV-related stigma, and poverty); communicate the research findings and their implications to policy makers and decision-makers and ensure that participants themselves are enabled to use their understanding of the issues to initiate action directed towards resolving the issues; and ensure that policy makers, other stakeholders (and participants) are in a position to use such findings to effect social change. With these objectives in mind, we locate this work within the broad framework of transformative pedagogy that views participants as critical thinkers, as well as participatory and active learners who are capable of imagining alternative possibilities of social reality (Nagda et al., 2003, in Ngidi and Moletsane, 2015), and in Paulo Freire's (1985) terms, of imagining alternative ways of being and acting. Of particular interest to our work, particularly with young women in relation to sexual violence, is the elimination of oppressive hierarchies, and the democratization of the research process. Informed by this framework, and using participatory visual research, our work aims to

...[create] safe spaces for [participants]; encouraging [them] to think about their experiences, beliefs and biases; promoting engagement and participation; posing real world problems that address societal inequalities; and helping [participants] to implement action-oriented solutions. (Meyers, 2008, p. 219)

Transformative pedagogy tries to encourage participants to reflect critically on their own assumptions, and to not only imagine, but actively take part in social action and contribute to social change (Ngidi & Moletsane, 2015).

Another critical issue, closely related to the first is access. Very few young people or other participants who are typically involved in visual participatory projects routinely have direct access to policy makers or decision-makers in an organization. As our work and that of others (for example, Rivard, 2015) demonstrates, a lot of effort (on the part of the researcher in most cases) goes into getting the research findings to policy makers and other decision-makers. In our own work on sexual violence with young women at a South African university, it took Naydene's networking advantages and position in the university to secure meetings with different decision-makers, at least at the beginning (see De Lange, Mitchell, and Moletsane, 2015). In the case of Rivard's (2015) work described in this chapter with girls in Rwandan schools, as the researcher, and an outsider, it was relatively easy for her to secure meetings with different stakeholders. Her mentor, also an outsider, was also able to connect her with different policy makers in the Rwandan system. However, other masters or doctoral students, with fewer resources and lacking the necessary support, including financial resources, time and political authority, would be unable to access policy makers. It seems then, that visual researchers must build into their design strategies for engaging with decision-makers at different stages of the research process as well as for communicating findings to this group of stakeholders.

As a third point, we have noted the incredulity of some elite audiences towards what participants (for example young people, women farmers, community health-care workers) have produced in their photos, drawings, and videos. This of course is also linked to power and about who can possess and represent knowledge. One of our first experiences dates back to 2000. Claudia was involved in a project on educational leadership that included attention to safety and security in schools and especially the legal responsibility of senior administrators (such as Directors General, Deputy Directors General) to address gender-based violence (GBV) in schools. One of the components of the project included asking school children to draw their ideas about GBV. Ultimately the drawings became part of a seven-minute video called *Unwanted Images*. Claudia recalls that the facilitated discussions with these senior policy makers after the screening were tricky. As Mak (2006, 2011) writes, the responses of the policy makers when this video was first screened were of disbelief. Who drew these pictures, anyway? Were they making this up? Did this really happen? The drawings were highly graphic and the re-representation of the images into a video production complete with a haunting sound track rendered the production all the more dramatic. But the music and placement of the images did not change what was in them. The responses of the leaders provided a stark reminder that seeing is not necessarily believing.

A second example of local officials expressing disbelief can be seen in the work of Gervais and Rivard (2013) in two photovoice projects with women farmers in Rwanda. In the first project, two groups of rural women farmers (each made up of eight women) in Kicukiro and Kayonza districts used photovoice to investigate the obstacles they face in agricultural production. In the second, women explored 'how photovoice might help to better reveal and integrate women farmers' perspectives about scientific farming practices in seed production and to generate practical results grounded in the reality of all stakeholders' (Gervais & Rivard, 2013, p. 504). The photovoice images were exhibited to various stakeholders (women parliamentarians, elected senators, gender specialists, researchers, donors, and government representatives working in agriculture). While these audiences eventually acknowledged the significance of the women farmers' views and the depth of their analysis of the issues, some of the stakeholders' initial responses indicated skepticism, astonishment, and some level of disbelief. Did these women farmers know how to use the camera and did they really take these pictures? Few of the audience members themselves took photos and perhaps did not believe that the women could possibly operate a camera. One of the women, to prove that she could do this, demonstrated, on the spot, her knowledge of how to use the camera. The stakeholders were surprised both at the women's mastery of the camera as well as the clarity with which, through photovoice, they were able to communicate issues.

Finally, audiences such as policy makers might see visual productions but not actually engage with the work. In such circumstances participatory visual work may seem tokenistic. Bober (2011) draws attention to this problem in relation to the use of children's drawings in the publications of large international NGOs aimed at policy makers. Drawings may simply be dismissed with comments like 'Oh they are children! How cute.'

Taking into account these barriers, this chapter highlights the ways in which visual productions have been used to engage policy makers and in particular to challenge some of these concerns. We start with policy posters, drawing on work with girls with disabilities, community health-care workers, and young women in university. We then go on to consider the use of action briefs, again based on a participatory visual project with young women that focused on addressing sexual violence on a university campus. Then we examine the use of participatory visual tools in communicating new knowledge vertically (from communities to policy makers/decision-makers). To do this, we explore the use of action-oriented PowerPoint presentations and photo-documents in which the researcher or the community members (or both) *occupy* the offices of ministry officials or policy makers in institutions to make them view the visual data (De Lange, Moletsane, & Mitchell, 2015; Rivard & Mitchell, 2013). As a third example and following Rogers's (2014a) work on critical film-making with young people, we examine the ways in which participatory video and digital story-telling has been used with very specific policy makers.

PARTICIPANT-LED TOOLS FOR ENGAGING POLICY MAKERS

Several examples of the possible ways in which participatory visual research might be used to engage policy makers and other decision-makers in dialogue for social change in various cultural and geographical contexts are offered. As we highlight, much of this work falls under the umbrella of cultural production and reflects an agenda of popular education and one of reaching different audiences through the materiality of documents and other texts like policy posters, action briefs, action-oriented PowerPoint presentations and photo-documents, alongside DVDs or web-based productions such as participatory video (PV).

Policy Posters
Biography of the Policy Poster

No one on our team now quite remembers exactly the sequence of events in the workshop in Vietnam leading up to the birth, for us, of the policy poster. We recall that the workshop had been hectic and sometimes we were flying by the seat of our pants to ensure the meaningful participation of the 21 girls with disabilities involved in a two-day workshop which took place in Hanoi. But this is the overarching narrative of many such events. You plan ahead. You think it is going to go this way or that and then as you go along you realize that there is a need for some re-jigging. This is the stuff of participatory workshops. Sometimes it feels as though you make it up as you go along, following a plan but thinking after every activity, is this going to work? Where are we going to display the images? Are participants going to sit in a circle or theatre style during the presentations? Have we left enough time? Is it too rushed? Do we complete the caption writing before the break or after? In this case we are trying out the use of photovoice and drawing as methods of monitoring rights. After several days of training on photovoice and drawing with a group of women with disabilities who will become the workshop facilitators, we are deeply engaged with the girls who, in the workshop, produce a series of drawings following the prompt *me and my community* and a series of photos with captions on *feeling included and not included*. The girls have worked hard and they know that on the third day they are going to be participating in a forum with policy makers (from the ministries and from several national and international NGOs dealing with disability). The girls have produced their drawings, discussed them in small groups, and presented them to the whole group and even exhibited them. They have finished their photovoice activity and the images and captions have been discussed, presented to each other, and exhibited. Now is yet another moment of decision. Time is working well. Are we going to do another round of drawings or photos, or more discussion, or...or? What is clear is that the girls are excited about their work and they are excited about meeting the policy makers who are going to see their productions the next day. Serendipitously in the back and forth of team members, we start thinking of recommendations. The girls have all these wonderful ideas about next steps and so we put it to them and ask, 'What are your recommendations?' As if by magic the girls are back in their small groups to come up with one recommendation per group. They have loved both the drawing and photovoice aspects so we realize that this is the moment to combine them.

Select one or two of your photos (or take one new photo) that best represents your recommendation (that is, what would you like to tell the policy makers?). As a group come up with a slogan or recommendation. Design your poster to include (1) the message, slogan or recommendation, (2) the photo, and (3) drawings. This is the birth of the policy poster for our team. (Reflective notes, Claudia)

The idea of policy (or media posters as they are sometimes called) with a social message targeting a particular audience is not new, and we are greatly indebted to Buckingham and Sefton-Green's (1994) work with identity posters along with Stuart's (2007) work with pre-service teachers on AIDS awareness posters. Walton's (1995) work with sixth-grade children focusing on gender violence in schools similarly uses this idea. What is so compelling about the idea of the policy poster is the activity of using participatory visual methods to move the work to the level of *so what?* as seen through the eyes of the participants. What needs to be done? This of course can be achieved in photovoice activities through poster narratives (Mitchell, 2011; Moletsane, Mitchell, De Lange, Stuart, Buthelezi, & Taylor, 2007), or as part of a discussion following participatory analysis. The idea in the work with the girls with disabilities captured both the immediacy of next steps but also the recognition that there are real policy makers out there who will be seeing the girls' productions and not just some vague group of audience observers. By way of illustration, we offer several examples.

Girls with Disabilities in Vietnam

The first example is based on work that we carried out with girls with disabilities in Vietnam (Nguyen, Mitchell, De Lange, & Fritsch, 2015). As Claudia's Reflective Field Notes above indicate, in our workshops with the girls, we facilitated a session during which they designed policy posters. As our work in Vietnam and elsewhere makes clear, working with participants in addressing local issues needs to go beyond understanding their individual experiences in order to seek collective action. The policy poster activity aimed to bring the collective voice of girls with disabilities to policy makers. Several issues emerged: the need for solidarity and collectivity; transformation of access to education; participation in the community and public spaces; and the significance of the voice of those with disabilities. For example, the poster below, 'Listen to what disabled people say', is a powerful message from these disabled girls about their right to education. See Figure 7.1.

Figure 7.1   *"Listen to what disabled people say"* Policy poster produced by a group of girls with disabilities in the photovoice workshop, Hanoi, 2014

Policy posters developed by workshop participants

MRDG. (2014). *Listen to what disabled people say* [Policy poster]. Hanoi, Vietnam: MRDG.

This policy poster demonstrates how girls with disabilities have thought about what needs to be put in place in order for the school to become more accessible to them. The poster shows the road to the school with images of cheerful children holding hands. On the other side of the road, we see a mother getting her daughter to school in a wheelchair. The title at the top reads 'anti-illiteracy class'[1] and stands out as a symbol of educational

---

[1]Anti-illiteracy is an educational campaign in the Education for All movement in Vietnam. An anti-literacy class refers to a form of continuing education reserved primarily for adults and children who have never been in school to help them pursue basic education.

transformation. The photos, emphasizing pride and happiness, depict girls with disabilities participating in educational activities. Their anti-illiteracy class, represented symbolically through letters A, B, C, D, E, is a vivid sign of basic education. This is the site where the girls feel included. As the group proposed in their policy recommendations, they would like the government to establish a literacy class for children with disabilities. They also proposed a program of action for themselves to help other children with disabilities in schools. This is a strong message about changing the traditional culture of schooling to one where all children are equal. Thus, what is conveyed through the poster 'Listen to what disabled people say' is not just *about* girls with disabilities. Rather, it is the work done by disabled girls that conveys powerful messages to society about disability rights, gender equality, and social justice for all.

Community Health-Care Workers in South Africa

A second example comes from our work with community health-care workers (CHW) in a rural South African community. In a qualitative participatory arts-based study with five female community health workers working from a clinic in a rural district of South Africa, we facilitated a series of workshops that led to the production of what we termed then as media posters (De Lange and Mitchell, 2016), but which seem to fit with the notion of policy. Our visual research process involved, first, screening an existing video, *Our Stories* that drew on one of the short participatory videos produced by young secondary school learners from the same community that focused on their experiences of GBV in and around the school. Second, the CHW brainstormed key issues concerning GBV which they saw as needing attention (such as, for example, children not respecting older people, grandmothers being raped, domestic violence perpetrated by men and boys against women and girls, and keeping silent when it is the breadwinner who is the abuser, the danger of having many sex partners, and the effects of alcohol abuse). They then discussed how they might represent the issues in media posters through which they would be able to engage with their communities. The third step involved the women taking carefully planned photographs that would enable them to represent the issues. In the fourth step, the photographs were printed and mounted on charts. Captions or slogans (in both isiZulu, the local language, and English) were created for each of the images. Finally, ten posters were produced and then digitized and reproduced for the CHWs by our research assistant.

In an article that appears in a special issue on participatory visual methods in the journal *Global Public Health* (2016) we trace their process of becoming cultural producers and taking action through a series of processes we have called 'data moments' (De Lange and Mitchell, 2016). Following Tobin (2000) in using a close reading approach, we analysed the transcripts from the workshop, the posters, and our field notes. Our analysis suggests that in the first data moment, *Community health workers with insider cultural knowledge*, in an expression of this knowledge informed by what Vaughan (2014) calls their 'historically, socially and psychologically situated lived experience' (p. 184), the CHWs identified key issues that required attention in relation to sexual violence in the community. In the second, *Constructing the messages*, in creating the messages and slogans and developing images for their media posters, the CHWs had to consider carefully who their audience would be. In so doing, they used their insider cultural knowledge and lived experiences to train fresh eyes, as it were, on the issues. This enabled them to produce messages and slogans that spoke to local issues and context rather than those usual government or even NGO produced generic messages. For example, their messages included: 'Violence affects everyone in the family', 'Teach your children to respect people', 'Being beaten by your husband, brother, son or grandson is violence, SPEAK OUT!'; 'Any abuse in the family must be reported even if it is [by] the breadwinner'; 'Think before you do things, your choices have consequences'; 'A real man has only one partner'; 'Having sex with elderly women (*gogos*) does not cure AIDS and it affects the *gogos*' health'; and 'Alcohol and drug abuse contributes to violence and destroys the community. DO NOT DRINK TOO MUCH!'

In the third data moment, *Taking action and the significance of audience texts*, we discussed how the CHWs might use the posters they had created. As the first audience of their own creations, the women talked about how the packages would enhance their work in communities. Further, they proposed to extend the reach of the productions and recommended that the packages be reproduced and distributed to all CHWs working in the same clinic. These were handed to clinic authorities in a ceremonial manner that included a photographer taking pictures of the handover as a way of documenting the value of the work of the CHWs.

Young Women and Sexual Violence on a University Campus in South Africa

As a third example of policy posters, we draw on the project discussed in detail in Chapter 2 in our work with 14 young women of rural origin studying at an urban university in South Africa (see De Lange et al., 2015), to address sexual violence on campus as a critical policy issue. As we noted earlier, our participatory research process with the young women involved creating cellphilms to further our and the participants' understanding of sexual violence on campus, particularly from the latter's perspective, and policy posters aimed at creating awareness of sexual violence on campus.

In the first series of workshops or digital retreats as these came to be known, we facilitated cellphilm workshops, out of which the participants, in small groups of three or four, created four productions (see De Lange et al., 2015). The cellphilms were viewed in one session and from the discussions that followed, the participants added several other issues which they felt negatively affected their safety and security on campus including date rape and sexual harassment by other groups of on-campus staff.

From there we began to embark upon what Taft (2010) might refer to as politicization through an educational process of having the young women envision creating policy posters and action briefs, two types of text that are typically used to reach audiences as the next step. We had seen the effectiveness of participants creating media/policy posters in the work in Vietnam and also with the community health-care workers discussed above. Thus, we embarked upon a policy poster production process with the young women during which they translated the six key issues into a visual artefact that could be used on campus.

Designing a Policy Poster

- Think of your issue for which you also have a solution.
- Discuss how to present it in the form of a poster.
- Plan and create a first draft policy poster:

  o   Who is the main audience?
  o   What do you want to get across?
  o   Or: What do you want to have happen?

(Photograph? Drawing? Slogan or message…)

- Present to whole group for critique.
- Refine your poster and slogan.
- Present to whole group for critique.

Each poster was made up of a visual (either a photograph the participants took or a drawing they created to depict the issue) and a message or slogan aimed at communicating why and how each is a problem so as to create awareness among various stakeholders on campus. To enhance the image created by the participants, our research assistant, using MS publisher, digitized the six handmade policy posters and printed several sets to hand to the policy makers and other stakeholders.

We take a closer look at one of these policy posters: *Date rape. No one is above the law. It is still rape, report it!* This poster has a hand drawn image of a young couple holding hands, obviously in love. The man has a thought bubble that says '*ha ha ha! I'm getting some*', while the woman's has three hearts and says: '*Oh, I trust him*'. The poster aimed to raise awareness about date rape on campus and the need to report it since it is obviously a crime. Considering the fact that date rape often goes unreported since the common perception is that one cannot be raped by one's date, boyfriend, or husband, it was encouraging to see the participants willing to interrogate their own assumptions, and to challenge their target audience to do the same. For us, this was what Taft (2010) sees as political activism in action and what Ngidi and Moletsane (2015) describe as a potentially transformative pedagogical opportunity. The more people who saw the posters, the more conversations could take place and the higher the chances for social change among those reached, even if it just involves reporting such rapes to authorities. See Figure 7.2.

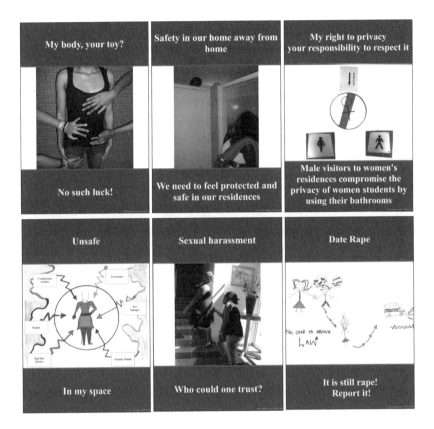

Figure 7.2 Policy posters

Policy posters developed by *Girls Leading Change*

Girls Leading Change. (2015). *Digital media for change and well-being: Girl-led 'from the ground up' policy-making in addressing sexual violence at a South African university* [Policy posters]. Port Elizabeth: Nelson Mandela Metropolitan University.

The opportunity to present their draft policy poster to the whole group, for criticism and refinement encouraged further clarifying of their ideas, preparing them for the final phase of dialogue with the policy makers.

Based on these three projects, we see far-reaching possibilities for using policy posters in visual research in which participants are involved in creating messages and images aimed at transforming policy and/or society. For us, this offers a fertile pedagogical space for addressing that 'So what?' question that is (or should be) ever-present in social research. Through the images and messages they create, participants are able to reach not only audiences in their own communities, but those who make decisions. Put another way, the posters they create both inform and mobilize them as participants and reach various research audiences, including policy makers who are to take action to address the issues identified.

Action Briefs

Another text that can reach various policy makers is the action brief, a short targeted document that maps out a particular social issue and offers recommendations for change. The idea of an action brief (as a type of policy brief) produced by participants in a social action project offers a tool that serves as a type of counter-text to the direction of conventional policy work.

The example we use here draws, too, on the project with the 14 young women who tackled campus-based sexual violence. As noted above, they had spent many hours identifying the issues through their cellphilm productions and of course they were able to screen these narrative productions to various audiences. Producing the posters described above and the action briefs allowed the young women to both reflect on the changes that were required and create something tangible that they could leave with the policy makers on campus. In workshops, the participants created these action briefs in which they themselves engaged in or worked towards taking action, or in which they made a call to action to the various constituencies they were targeting with their visual productions. While the action briefs use the format of the usual information pamphlet in its structure, the content of the action briefs developed by the participants in this project differed from the norm. Here, action briefs were understood as a concise document that sketches out the background to the problem that requires addressing, the nature of the problem itself, and some solutions, particularly in relation to who is most suited to implement the suggested solution. Thus, in their action briefs, in a 'short, crisp, clear, convincing and persuasive' manner, the participants described the issue depicted in the cellphilm and represented in the policy poster. In short, their aim was to persuade the policy makers at the university to bring about changes to ensure women's safety in and around campus.

Developing an Action Brief

- An action brief is a concise document which sketches the background to a problem which requires attention, clearly explains the nature of the problem, and puts forward steps on how and who to address the problem.
- Work with the transcript of your cellphilm.
- Develop an action brief which sketches the situation, the problem to be addressed, and specific pointers on how to address the problem (brief, crisp, clear, convincing, persuasive).

The template included the following: (1) a brief situational analysis; (2) a description of the problem; and (3) a suggested solution or solutions for addressing it. Informed by the work of Taft (2010) that focuses on girls and young women and political activism, the solution involved what they themselves could do, or what others in the university, particularly those with the power and resources, could do (see Figure 8.3, Action Briefs). The action briefs had the same titles and images as the policy posters. In the latter, these were on the front cover of the pamphlet. The three inside pages of the folded piece included the project title and abstract; the situational analysis; the problem; and the solution To illustrate, the front cover of the action brief, *My right to privacy, your responsibility to respect it: Male visitors to women's residences compromise the privacy of women students by using their bathrooms* had a picture of the male and female icons usually found on doors of toilets/restrooms for the two sexes. Above the signs was a crossed-out male sign and a 'Restroom' sign pointing to the two toilets/bathrooms. The issue here was that women's expectation of safety and security when they first move into university residences is quickly shattered as the people tasked with protecting them are often the perpetrators of the violence against them. The problem is described as involving male visitors using the women's toilets in the residences, and how this compromises the security of the women. The suggested solution involves hiring female security personnel for women's residences; displaying clear guidelines and rules where all residents and staff would see them; establishing complaints procedures, including the contact numbers of available staff members displayed in a visible spot; and setting up CCTV cameras in strategic places. The back cover of the brief includes the names of the authors/producers/creators.

TAKING RESEARCH TO POLICY MAKERS

As we noted in the Introduction to this chapter, access to policy makers is one of the challenges to be overcome in this kind of *from the ground up* policy-making. What if policy makers never see the visual productions created in participatory research? Delgado (2015) in his comprehensive study of photovoice work with urban youth, acknowledges the significance of the exhibiting phase in photovoice work. As he observes, 'Having an exhibition boycotted because of its controversial content, or, even worse, simply ignored, with minimal attendance and no media coverage, can have a long lasting impact on the participants' (p. 99). Perhaps the most compelling point is one that he shares from the work of Haw (2008) and the idea that the opposite of having a voice is being silenced. Failure (on the part of researchers) to come up with a way for photos or other visual images to reach appropriate audiences is part of that silencing. How to use the various artefacts that are produced then is another matter. What does it mean to mobilize? What are the most effective strategies? What people or offices or institutions are the targets? While these questions are perhaps less well developed in the literature on participatory visual research, they are questions that are obvious ones in the rich body of literature on social movements, popular education, and resistance related to activism and community mobilization, ranging from in-depth studies of learning activism (Choudry, 2015) through to work that looks specifically at youth activism and resistance as we see in Tuck and Yang (2014a), alongside work that looks at specific movements and campaigns such as the Treatment Action Campaign in South Africa (Geffen, 2010) and the Idle No More movement (Wotherspoon & Hansen, 2013) among Indigenous youth in Canada.

Being 'In the Right Place'

One solution is to take the images, exhibitions, policy posters, and action briefs to the policy makers. Mitchell (2011) refers to the idea of being 'in the right place' (p. 184) and uses several examples to make the point. Jen Thompson (2009), in studying environmental concerns in Sierra Leone through an intergenerational photovoice project, set up an exhibition of the participants' photos in the lobby of the Ministry of Agriculture in Freetown so that government officials had to pass the exhibition every day to get to their offices. Thompson, as the researcher, seized the opportunity to confront policy makers. In another project based on her own photovoice work with Grade 7 children on GBV Claudia found an opportunity to exhibit some of the work of the girls on the problem of safety and security in toilets at the UN where policy makers were looking at issues concerning water and sanitation. Building on examples such as these, we have begun to document when and where policy makers are most likely to respond/act on/engage with participant-produced photos, videos, drawings, and digital stories.

We might also refer to this approach as something of an 'occupy' strategy. In the case of the young women who created the policy posters and action briefs described in the previous sections, the group which they had named Girls Leading Change, embarked upon a series of dialogues with key stakeholders and decision-makers in the university itself, given that the setting is a university campus and the context is the high rates of sexual violence on campus. The actual officials targeted ranged from the Deputy Vice Chancellor for Research and Engagement through to those whose dossiers apply to the everyday lives of students: the Dean of Students, the Residence Manager, the Head of Protection Services, and the Student Representative Council, and other student organizations on campus. Overall the feedback from the stakeholders was positive and encouraging, as many felt that what the Girls Leading Change had presented to them was important and useful in gaining an understanding of women students' lived experiences in residence and on campus; others indicated that they had been completely unaware of what the women students were experiencing and felt that they too should be addressing the issues the women students raised. At one presentation, however, the group and Naydene who was present for each of these meetings were taken by surprise when a stakeholder pointed out that should this information be made public it would be detrimental to the university's good name. As Naydene observes:

The GLC wanted the stakeholders to address the concerns, not ignore them or pretend they did not exist! And so as a group we met after the presentation to reflect on the response, and decided to include this very issue – the threat to the reputation of the university – in subsequent presentations and make it clear that these lived experiences had been silenced for too long, and that it was time for honest engagement with the women students' concerns. The GLC realized that the presentations would not always be received positively, but that did not deter them, but strengthened their motivation to be activists for women's rights. (Naydene's Reflective notes)

In a related way Lysanne Rivard (2015) describes the strategy of the researcher occupying the offices of key policy makers. Her doctoral research focusing on girls, sport, and physical activity in Rwanda was an attempt to address the lack of tools that can bridge the distance between stakeholders implementing and experiencing the programme and those responsible for policy-making and programme development. The project aimed to challenge what counts as policy when it comes to girls' physical activity and to confront the question of what would happen if we engaged girls and young women. In a photovoice project with a total of 196 Rwanda schoolgirls, Rivard aimed to understand the girls' lived experiences of physical activity and sport in school and to discuss these with key local decision-makers. Typically in a photovoice project there is some sort of public exhibition. However, in Rivard's case, a number of circumstances intervened and it was not possible to organize school or community-based exhibitions. Instead she created what she called a photo-report, a PowerPoint which she also printed out and compiled as a booklet of the most important images and related findings. Armed with these photo-reports which she used both as dissemination and interview tools, she went out and occupied offices of various policy makers in the Rwandan system to both inform them about the schoolgirls' perspectives and lived experiences of physical education, as well as interview them about their own perspectives on the issues. In her study she targeted several key policy makers; for each she made an appointment to meet the person in his or her office, and arranged to have a significant period of time for each meeting. Unlike the participants, 14-to-16-year-old girls who would have had difficulty making an appointment and gaining access to these officials because of such factors as the cost of travel, their age, and the official positions and status of these officials relative to them, Rivard had many factors that counted in her favour. Among others, she was a white outsider, a PhD student, and she had networks that enabled her access to officials that ordinary Rwandan people, and in particular young schoolgirls, could not access. In reflecting on the value of the occupy approach as both a tool for data collection and for dissemination and engaging policy makers, Rivard cautions that further research is needed that will 'shift feminist debates in PES [Physical Education & Sport] from body to voice and from discourse analysis to a participatory analysis taking place directly with key stakeholders [particularly policy makers]' (Rivard, 2015, p. 198).

That the girls were able to articulate their experiences through photovoice and the captions they created made it possible for these to be communicated directly to policy makers, albeit via an intermediary (the researcher), through a PowerPoint presentation, printed and packaged as a photo-report. As discussed in the previous sections, participants, particularly those in poor resource contexts, often do not have direct access to policy makers. It is through researcher-facilitated opportunities such as photovoice exhibitions, PowerPoint presentations, or through the occupy strategies in government or decision-maker offices that the voices of local people are heard by those who can effect social change.

A third example of occupying comes out of a project in Kenya on barriers to the participation of women from informal settlements in the paid labour force.[2] Close to 50 women participated in a photovoice project in Korogocho, in which they took photos of challenges and solutions to childcare. As described (Mitchell et al., 2016) there were numerous barriers identified including safety and security issues and financial insecurity. Their photos, mounted as an exhibition and exhibition catalogue called *Through the Eyes of Mothers* have travelled to a number of locations, but started with an exhibition that included policy makers and stakeholders from national and international organizations interested in childcare and women's labour, members of the Ministry responsible for early childhood education, and other policy makers in health and social development. Five of the women attended the launch exhibition; they confidently circulated throughout the exhibition hall and engaged with the audience. As Claudia observes:

What was fascinating about the presence of the five women is that the audience could not simply take the event as a social occasion to meet and chat with peers as so often happens in launch events. Each of the women from Korogocho in her own way 'forced' people to look at the images closely. I overhear one of the women commenting to two viewers 'See that electrical outlet. And look at that child. That's dangerous'. She also goes on to explain that this is a perfect example of community members not looking out for others sometimes, even if a child's life might be at risk. Finally I overhear one viewer to her colleague observe after now carefully looking at the image of the electrical outlet and the child nearby 'this is better than any sociology textbook I have ever read on informal settlements and poverty. The exhibition should be required viewing'. Privately I think the fact that it took one of the photographers to point out what needs to be seen suggests that there is need for visual literacy among policy makers. (Claudia's Reflective Field Notes, June 22, 2016)

It is worth noting that following the launch of the exhibition, the director of one of the key ministries asked if he might exhibit the photos in the lobby of the office building in which he works.

---

[2]The photovoice project is part of a large project 'Creating Better Economic Opportunities for Women in Nairobi Slums through Improved Childcare Options' funded by IDRC through McGill University and the African Population Health Research Centre, Nairobi, Kenya.

USING PARTICIPATORY VIDEO AND DIGITAL STORY-TELLING TO ENGAGE POLICY MAKERS

As discussed in the Introduction, researchers working in resource-poor communities are often confronted with power imbalances between themselves and the research participants and the communities with which they are working. Engaging policy makers brings with it another layer of unbalanced power, rendering the participants even more powerless. One of the transformative pedagogies we have identified in our work to address such power imbalances and marginality is participatory video (PV). PV involves a group of people or members of a community developing and making a film about their own lives (Lunch and Lunch, 2006; Milne, Mitchell, & De Lange, 2012). Further, through PV, community members are enabled to communicate community issues to policy makers and other decision-makers (Duncan and Cullen, 2012). PV has been used as a vertical communication tool to enhance dialogue between communities and policy makers. For example, Tremblay (2013) reports on a project that used a participatory action research approach and a collaborative research design to co-produce, with participants, participatory videos aimed at promoting dialogue and inclusive approaches to waste management in a Brazilian community. While PV is often celebrated as key to democratizing the research space and for its counter-hegemonic possibilities (Rogers, 2014b), Tremblay (2013) and others have reflected on the relationship between power and knowledge and the theoretical and methodological value of using PV in research to enhance dialogue and shift power imbalances between researchers, policy makers, and community members.

We offer an example here from Wheeler's (2012) work in the *favelas* (informal settlements) of Rio de Janeiro, Brazil, in which PVs were created. While acknowledging the possibilities created by the use of PV in communicating research to a wider audience than the immediate community, the author raises questions about how such productions might be interpreted and used in policy spaces and processes related to addressing violence in the communities. In particular, she asks 'how participatory video, as a medium for communicating particular forms of knowledge, interacts with the power dynamics, political interests, and other competing forms of knowledge within these spaces' (p. 365). During the PV processes, participants made three videos, each with its own theme, about their views on violence and how it might be addressed. Using these as well as existing videos on violence, the research process included facilitated debates as spaces in which residents of the *favelas*, two of whom were involved in the PV project, and another two who were not, could dialogue with government officials. Screenings of the videos in the participating *favelas* involved participants talking about their work and this created opportunities for open debate that involved the video productions from the project.

In her analysis, Wheeler (2012) examines how relationships of power and knowledge unfolded during the debates intended to facilitate dialogue between residents of the *favelas* and government officials; the video productions were used as additional ammunition to lend weight to community perspectives on violence and the lack of security in the communities, as well as the participants' views on how this could be addressed. The author notes that the debates revealed how political identities and imperatives influenced the ways in which people responded to what they saw and heard. Of particular significance is her observation that the video productions (both the processes and the productions themselves) seemed to have failed to address the unequal power dynamics in terms of who could speak, what they could say, and to whom. Further, their screenings to the rest of the city failed to address the power dynamics between residents of the *favelas* and the city and this often led to social exclusion in terms of whether and how the *favela* residents could speak about their experiences of violence and how the state could respond. From these observations, she concludes that the video productions and the community dialogues and debates that followed were, to a certain extent, successful in enabling state players to see the residents of the *favelas* in a different light, to hear their perspectives on violence and how it might be addressed, and to take into account how these perspectives and local knowledge might influence how policies are made. In essence, the participatory research processes and PV in particular opened up dialogue and made it possible to insert different, often marginalized, forms of knowledge into policy debates. However, the ways in which the dialogues unfolded also illustrated the complexity of attaining significant changes in power relations in communities and society. Most importantly, the author concludes that a single engagement with policy makers and other community stakeholders cannot realistically be expected to significantly change the ways in which policies are made. Rather, it would take sustained engagements with policy makers for them to fully recognize the significance of citizens' perspectives and knowledge expressed through participatory processes.

This idea of sustained engagement is nicely highlighted in an interview with Sarah Flicker based on her work with Indigenous youth in Canada and the uses of digital story-telling in addressing youth leadership in addressing HIV and AIDS (See Flicker et al., in press). She comments in the interview on how the youth often talked directly about the impact of colonization and less about condoms and safer sex.[3] When their digital stories were screened for community members, including a public health nurse, it became clear that sustained dialogue is very important:

This was a screening out east in a reserve community. And the public health nurse came. She was like, 'Oh they're doing an HIV film night. Great, HIV is in my portfolio. Great.' And she went and she was just like, 'This was a waste of time. I can't believe I came. This has nothing to do with HIV. I flew in for this and I really thought you were going to do, like, harm reduction… and I brought condoms.' And our team said, 'Well, we put out the condoms. You know, but that wasn't the point here.' And, you know, she was kind of a little bit rude. And we were like, 'Well, I'm sorry you feel this way.' And then team members saw her the next day on the plane. They were all flying out together. And she was like, 'You know, I was up all night thinking about it,

---

[3]We are grateful to Pamela Lamb for her work in conducting these interviews.

and I really want to thank you. And I'm sorry that I was so rude yesterday, because you helped me see things that I hadn't seen before. And I feel like we need to do public health differently in this community.' And I'm *so* glad that they ran into her again, because I was so disturbed after hearing about the first interaction. This approach seemed to get to her in a way that none of us had anticipated, and opened up the possibility, I think, for a different conversation, which is what this community desperately needed. So I think, you know, they [the films] have that kind of power too. (Personal Communication, Sarah Flicker, February 2017)

More than anything this interview highlighted the need for a more complex approach to understanding impact on policy-makers, and certainly one that sets aside time for policy makers and other stakeholders to process the viewings.

Another researcher, Liz Miller, from Concordia University, leading the *Mapping Memories* project with refugee youth in Montreal observed that although she identifies herself first and foremost as a film maker and facilitator (as opposed to a policy lobbyist or strategist), she has a deep appreciation for the ways in which the various productions created by the youth contributing to building alliances with groups who are policy makers. As she commented in an interview:

Mapping Memories[4] a participatory media project working with youth with refugee experience, and using video, storytelling and mapping as a way to facilitate young people sharing difficult stories. Different than some projects, one of the important aspects of *Mapping Memories* was helping young people take their stories public. So it wasn't simply about facilitating a space where people with different lived experiences could feel less alone, and could have an opportunity to share and shape their story, but it was also about thinking about how that story could also be useful in the world. There's a risky component to building in outreach or advocacy or that kind of public place in storytelling workshops, but I think the flip side of it is that it facilitates a process that says there's a reason that we revisit difficult stories. That they can in fact move others – who are in policy, in education, or in different contexts. That lived experience, and especially lived experiences that are sometimes socially considered shameful or difficult, can really serve to help others. It was important to think about how we could integrate these stories into a larger framework that spoke to some of the political and legal advocacy that our partners were working on. We weren't going to ministers, or advocating ourselves, but we were in communication with this organization that was either using the stories individually or simply consulting with us. (Personal Communication, Liz Miller, February 2017)

---

[4]Mapping Memories: Participatory Media, Place-based stories & refugee youth is SSHRC funded study led by Liz Miller (2007–2012). A description of the project and the stories produced by the youth can be found in Miller, L., Luchs, M., & Dyer Jales, G. (2011). *Mapping memories: Participatory media, place-based stories & refugee youth*. Montreal, QC: Marquis Book Printing Inc.

STUDYING PATHWAYS TO IMPACT

The different tools and artefacts described above take into consideration groups of participants whose voices and perspectives are often marginalized in research and policy-making processes. Further, they take into consideration very specific audiences of visual productions created by participants who do not typically get involved in knowledge-production – policy makers and decision-makers. As Rose (2012) and others highlight, audience research has many complexities to it. How do we know audiences are looking? And how do we know what audiences really think? Clearly the field of audience reception is vast and is an issue that forms the basis for study in television, film, advertising and so on. John Fiske's (1994) work is particularly relevant because he, like Rose, includes in his work the idea of three sites of production – the primary text (the image); the production text (or what the producers say and experience as part of image-making); and the audience text. But how do we think of policy makers as an audience? This was a question that our research team encountered when we submitted a proposal to the Research Ethics Board of one of our universities. As Claudia observes:

What caught me off guard when I heard back from the Research Ethics Board was a comment about the audience participants (adult policy makers and community members) and the fact that they could be at risk in viewing the images. As the review panel noted, 'Given the sensitive nature of the photographs or other visual images, how will you ensure that the vulnerability of audience members, who may themselves have experienced trauma, is addressed?' Aside from the slight irritation at having to resubmit the application with an amendment on how I would address 'Why the visual?' and the potential impact of the visual, this was the first time that a committee had gone beyond challenging the risks involved in taking the photos (or producing a video) to the risks of seeing the photos (or viewing the video). (Mitchell, 2015b)

The examples we offer in this chapter illustrate how engaging policy makers as audiences of our research and visual productions might, while providing opportunities for community members to speak directly, as it were, to them, also raises ethical issues regarding the vulnerability not only of the participants, but of the decision-makers as well. To ensure that we take this into consideration in audience research, we have embarked upon a series of interviews with policy makers and other audiences using participatory visual methods, including questions such as the following:

---

1   What is the main message (or messages) in the exhibition/videos?
2   How are these images the same (or different) from the images that one typically sees in local media on the issue being represented?
3   Which images have an impact on them and why?

---

4 How do they feel about the images and the image-making?

5 Are there certain images that offer new perspectives?

6 What do they intend to do (if anything) as a result of seeing an exhibition or screen-ing of a video?

7 Are there questions that they would like to pose to the producers about image-making?

In many projects which are meant to engage young people, this final question may of course be explored more directly through face-to-face contact between producers and audiences. However this may not always be possible, and depending on the issues, the situation may not even be desirable. Kindon, Hume-Cook, and Woods (2012) in their work with PV offer an example of audience members being very unreceptive to the participants' video, even though the producers and the audience were from the same community. MacEntee and Mandrona (2015) in their discussion of audiences and visual productions talk about how rural South African teachers as producers of cellphilms dealing with content related to sexuality chose their own students as audience even though in the study context they could have chosen parents, other teachers, school board members or various other policy makers. They speculate that perhaps the children were a safer audience, or at least a known audience. Alongside this, one might think of what Alexandra (2015) refers to as political listening in work with the digital story-telling productions of asylum seekers and refugees in Ireland. As we have explored in more detail in Chapter 2, Alexandra builds on the work of Bickford (1996) who talks about the idea of 'democratic communication' that is based 'not on the possibility of consensus but the presence of listening' (p. 18).

Finally, if we are to take seriously the idea of impact in relation to audiences, and especially the idea of engaging policy makers, it is important to look at actions and what has changed as a result of the students voicing their concerns through image-making and the policy makers viewing the images. The point is that engaging policy makers also involves some accountability for doing something about the issues raised. As Wheeler (2012) points out, sustainable long-term change is not easy to document. As we highlight in Chapter 8, we might even use the tools of participatory visual research – the visual – as a significant feature of documentation.

CONCLUSION

In this chapter we have explored the ways in which visual productions have been used to engage policy makers in challenging some of the barriers to direct communication between communities and policy makers on issues that affect their lives. In the work with the different groups, we see participants 'testing out' a form of political activism through creating messages and images aimed at transforming social conditions and changes in policy. While some critics have argued that in such populations community health-care workers or girls and young women with disabilities often have little input into community efforts aimed at addressing the social issues that negatively affect their lives because of their low status in the community, lack of support, and lack of formal recognition in the field, our engagement with them in these projects suggested that the opposite was true, at least as far as their agency was concerned. For example, illustrating the ways in which participatory research can function as transformative pedagogy, participants in the various projects we highlight above, often demonstrated that they were in a position to change the conditions in their communities or institutions. While we cannot conclusively claim that the participants in these projects can operate as 'agents of community empowerment' (Schneider, Hlophe, & Van Rensburg, 2008, p. 108), our analysis suggests that they do have the capacity to raise awareness and act on critical issues affecting their own communities.

At the same time, Rogers (2014a) cautions that knowing more about the issues and informing policy makers does not necessarily change the power relations that produce the negative conditions in the first place. His work with the New Brunswick students' films illustrates how, while they drew on counter-hegemonic discourses, they also reflected oppressive gender constructs, heterosexism, homophobia, heteronormativity, and ableism. Invoking the work of Lather (1992) and Ellsworth (1992), the author reminds us that 'power operates through all pedagogical practices, even those claiming to be critical' (p. 282). Unless we continually strive to interrogate and address such unequal power relations, our participatory visual research processes will be tokenistic at best, and will not be able to significantly alter the unequal power relations that create conditions that marginalize some forms of knowledge and those who produce it.

KEY POINTS OF THE CHAPTER

- Participatory visual research highlights the importance of the voices of participatory research participants in policy-making and the role of participatory visual methods in addressing the challenges or barriers to engaging policy makers.
- Participatory visual research aims to produce knowledge that leads to a better understanding of issues; communicate this to various audiences, including policy makers and decision-makers and other stakeholders; empower participants to take action; and ensure that all stakeholders can use the knowledge to effect social change.
- As a form of transformative pedagogy, participatory visual research seeks to address the gap between research and policy impact by reaching and engaging various audiences, including policy makers.

- Participant-led tools (developed and used by research participants) can be used to engage policy makers: policy posters (posters that inform audiences, including policy makers about a problem) and action briefs (brief documents which describe the problem and identify possible steps that can be taken to address it); photovoice exhibitions; and screenings of visual productions.
- Access to policy makers is often not easy: issues of power, resources, and distance must be addressed, through for example, an intermediary (someone in a position of authority and with easy access to policy makers such as the researcher, a community leader, and so on) occupying or physically visiting the offices of the policy makers.
- Policy makers' reception/response to the various productions and texts used to engage them varies reflecting the power differentials between them and the participants or producers.
- There is a need to understand the empowerment of participants in engaging policy makers, but also their vulnerability to various forms of backlash from their own communities, from external audiences and the policy makers themselves.
- It is important to challenge (and where possible) change unequal power relations that create conditions that marginalize research participants and the knowledge they produce.

8

WHAT DIFFERENCE DOES THIS MAKE?

━━ CHAPTER CONTENTS ━━━━━━━━━━━━━━━━━━━━━━━━━━━━━━━━

INTRODUCTION

When everything changes, from the small and immediate, to the vast and abstract –
the object of study, the world immediately around it, the student immediately around
him [her] and the world immediately around both – there seems to be no place to
stand to locate what has altered and how. (Geertz, 1995, p. 2)

The words of the anthropologist Clifford Geertz serve as a reminder of the challenge of
locating change. As the previous chapters have demonstrated, it often depends on who
is looking and on where, how and why this is taking place; this is why we need studies
in Critical Audience Engagement. It is only when we turn our attention to something of
a sociology of producing, showing, looking, and doing that we get a more nuanced picture of what it is that we might capture as impact or difference or change. Thus, we
acknowledge here the importance of some type of monitoring and evaluation in
research, recognizing, at the same time, that there are some inherent contradictions. It
may seem strange to end this book by looking into change, especially since in the earlier
chapters we say that participatory visual research should begin with the end in mind.
But can we always anticipate the end, and are there tools and methods that might allow
for this? Two illustrative cases are worth noting. In the first, a group of college deans in
Ethiopia, as we described in Chapter 4, spend 45 minutes discussing one photograph, a
picture of a half-eaten plate of food displayed on a chair in the cafeteria, produced by a
group of students to represent the living conditions on the campus. Several are fine with
the photograph being exhibited but one is not and feels that this girl, a young woman
really, should clear up the mess. It is only after this lengthy conversation that the group
as a whole agrees that the photograph can be exhibited. The conversation charts change
and of course the decision itself represents change. But how do we capture such conversations and how does this demonstrate impact? In the second case, referred to in
Chapter 7, a group of community health-care workers, all older women, working in rural
South Africa produce, through photovoice activities, a poster that highlights the vulnerable lives of older women in relation to sexual violence. Three years later, it is an issue
that is highlighted in a research report 'Long lives aren't necessarily happy ones in
Africa, particularly for women' (see Ngalomba & Harpur, 2016).[1] As researchers we cannot prove that those who produced this report ever saw the poster and they probably
did not, but there is still, we would argue, something that needs to be recognized as a

---

[1]S. Ngalomba and P. Harpur (2016). Long lives aren't necessarily happy ones in Africa, particularly for
women. *The Conversation, Africa Pilot.* https://theconversation.com/long-lives-arent-necessarily-happy-
ones-in-africa-particularly-for-women 66140?utm_medium=email&utm_campaign=Latest%20from%20
The%20Conversation%20for%20October%2011%202016%20-%205782&utm_content=Latest%20
from%20The%20Conversation%20for%20October%2011%202016%20 %205782+CID_382d6028266fe
3858082ce9dde09e780&utm_source=campaign_monitor_africa&utm_term=Long%20lives%20
arent%20necessarily%20happy%20ones%20in%20Africa%20particularly%20for%20women

precursor. Why is it important that a group of older women, walking from house to house doing their work as community health-care workers in a rural area, know, three years before researchers from universities and other organizations that something needs to be done? How do we document this as change?

THEORIES OF CHANGE

Theory of Change: 'a theory of how and why an initiative works' (De Silva, Breuer, Lee, Asher, Chowdhary, Lund, & Patel, 2014, p. 2).

Following Tuck and Yang's (2014b) contestation of the idea of organizational models of change based primarily on pre-determined outcomes, in favour of theories and ideas of change that draw on community-led and youth-led self-determined initiatives, we recognize the complexity of conversations about the question 'What difference does this make?' This is particularly pertinent in a context that is often about research and sometimes about interventions and sometimes about both at the same time. A theory of change is meant to highlight 'the assumptions about the process through which change will occur, and specifies the ways in which all of the required early and intermediate outcomes related to achieving the desired long-term change will be brought about and documented as they occur' (Anderson, 2006, p. 1). According to De Silva et al. (2014), key to the effectiveness and usefulness of a theory of change, and in line with participatory research, is that it must be developed in collaboration with the participants and other stakeholders and must involve continuous reflection to identify the nature of and the ways in which change occurs. Such continuous reflection must involve revision of any earlier failure that occurred in the project or when other unanticipated factors are found to have played a role. In participatory research, a theory of change assists the research team and participants to describe and analyse the issues affecting the community, taking into account the assumptions about what is needed to address them so as to effect change.

In practice, how might this work? Specifically, what might we, as researchers, working with the participants and other stakeholders in communities do differently to realize change? To offer an example from participatory visual research, we refer to a six-year project with girls and young women in Canada and South Africa focused on addressing sexual violence.[2] Informed by the case study described in Chapter 2, the project examines the co-creation of knowledge about sexual violence in relational and institutional settings from

---

[2]Funded by IDRC and SSHRC, the Networks for Change and Wellbeing is an international partnership project (under the IPASS program) which aims to study and advance the use of innovative approaches in knowledge-production, policy-making, and communication, in addressing sexual violence against girls and young women in South Africa and Canada. This international and interdisciplinary partnership is co-led by the University of KwaZulu-Natal (South Africa) and McGill University (Canada), and involves universities, government agencies, and community-based organizations, and girls and young women from communities in the two countries.

the perspectives of girls and young women themselves. Methodologically, the project draws on approaches to learning from the ground up through the use of digital story-telling, participatory video, cellphilms, drawing and mapping, and community radio along with social media. As such, it is located within several broad areas of design: youth-led media making, community-based research, participatory visual research, research-as-intervention, and research-as-social-change. How might we assess and track change in this project during its six-year lifetime and beyond using an approach based on a theory of change? Looking at just one of five sites as a case, we refer to a community in rural KwaZulu-Natal. Following the work of Laing and Todd (2015), we have adopted a collabo-rative model in the development of a theory of change. Our approach is informed by available research on what works to address sexual violence against girls and young women, as well as approaches to developing a theory of change, along with contributions from our community partners (the two local NGOs) and members of the community. In our workshops with the communities, we brainstormed and debated the various aspects of change that the participants and other stakeholders would like to see emanating from the project. Specifically, in our first community engagement event, in addition to introducing the project to the community, we set out to understand the context in which we were intending to work. We, together with the stakeholders (community members, staff from community NGOs, young women and girls) analysed the situation in the community in relation to the safety of young women and girls generally and to sexual violence in particu-lar. In the second and third workshops, using the various participatory digital tools we have described in the chapters of this book, we worked with a group of young women and girls from the community to examine their experiences of safety and sexual violence and to determine what change they would like to see so as to ensure their safety. From these work-shops, we have identified the goal of the project and the focus of the change we seek: it is to catalyse girl-led change to address sexual violence at a material, sociocultural, and policy level in two rural communities in KwaZulu-Natal by 2020. Figure 8.1 summarizes the various aspects of our theory of change.[3]

A second aspect covered in our workshops involved hearing from the participants about what they believed could be done, and what the community as a collective, and members as individuals would need to do differently to address the issues they identified, and about what resources are available in the community to achieve the change. From our initial mapping exercise, we identified four stakeholders who could potentially stimulate change: 1) the participants themselves (girls and young women); 2) parents and teachers; 3) com-munity organizations (e.g., local NGOs, Faith-based organizations, 'war rooms' or local forums focusing on identifying and solving community challenges, traditional leaders); 4) and government departments. Figure 8.2 illustrates.

---

[3]We acknowledge Lisa Wiebesiek for her leadership, as well as the rest of the research team, the partici-pants and community members in the continuing development of the Theory of Change for the KwaZulu-Natal community sites.

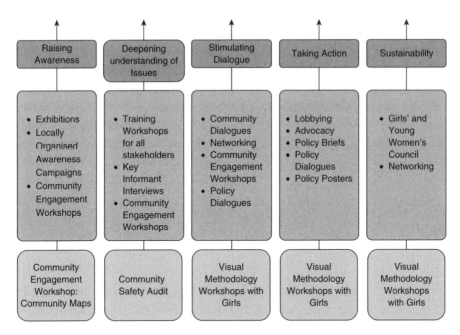

Figure 8.1 Theory of change, *Networks for Change and Well-being*

Diagram developed by Lisa Wiebesiek

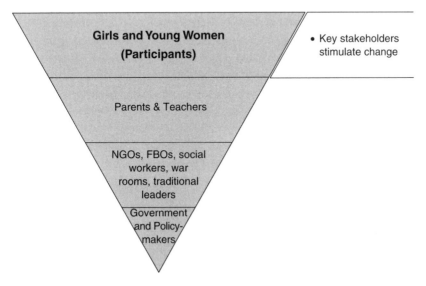

Figure 8.2 Stakeholders, *Networks for Change and Well-being*

Diagram developed by Lisa Wiebesiek

What is clear to us is that as this project develops, our theory of change will continue to evolve, and that the significance of continuous monitoring and adapting or changing our strategies to address emerging challenges cannot be underestimated.

TRACKING CHANGE

Concerned with how we might track and assess the influence of our work on change very broadly and on policy-making in particular, we have been interested in the literature on tracking policy. We know that the role of research in policy decision-making is complex and messy (Lewis, 2011) and that monitoring and evaluation to track research influence on policy-making is challenging (Jones, 2011). As Jones (2011) observes, this is because of the fact that 'policy change is a highly complex process shaped by a multitude of interacting forces and actors … and the work that does influence policy is often unique and rarely repeated or replicated, [and] many incentives [are] working against the sharing of "good practice"' (p. 1). Lewis (2011) argues that to understand how research influences policy makers, it is necessary to investigate their prior understanding and views about the importance of the issues being addressed. It is also important to understand 'their assessment of the policymaking environment, whether they had formed a provisional or strong opinion on policy direction; the extent to which the [research] changed their understanding and in which direction; and have a nuanced understanding of what they mean by [research] "use"' (p. 2).

Jones (2011) identifies a number of specific approaches that can be used to track the influence of research on policy change, warning that the key is for research teams to recognize the value of monitoring and evaluation in their work, and to incorporate it throughout the research process. According to him, some useful strategies include using the most significant change approach, and interviewing policy makers about their work and the extent to and ways in which they use research evidence in policy-making. These strategies help to set up the framework for monitoring, and evaluation, and knowing in advance and throughout the duration of a project what to assess and how to make sense of the evidence.

Picturing Change

One set of practices that we see as particularly beneficial in tracking change in relation to participatory visual research is the use of the visual to picture change and to explore the question 'can we see change?' Throughout this book we have been arguing for studying the ways in which participatory visual research lends itself to supporting dialogue, first among the participants themselves, and then with the community and policy makers. At the same time, we might also think about how the visual – producing visually verifiable data – can be a critical component of studying the difference we want to make (Mitchell, 2011). In this section, then, we consider a variety of strategies for what we describe as picturing change.

As an example of generating visually verifiable evidence of change, we might consider the exhibition briefly described in Chapter 4, *Seeing, Believing, and Acting for Change in HIV and AIDS, Integrating HIV and AIDS in Higher Education Curricula*, an initiative involving the members of the HEAIDS HIV and AIDS Education Community of Practice in South Africa, all university teachers and researchers representing the various higher education institutions in that country. Most of the members had been focusing on different ways of integrating HIV and AIDS education into the teacher-education curriculum for several years, so an activity of picturing change was a way to visually evaluate what was happening. To assess change in their work, members of the Community of Practice used the following prompt: *What does change look like? Take two photographs of what has changed for you (or your faculty or school) in terms of integrating HIV and AIDS into your academic curriculum.*

When the members came together with their images, the resulting exhibition illustrated a variety of ideas. Some of the photographs reflected the change the members saw in themselves, some were about the increased awareness of the challenges in their institutions, and some reflected what they had changed in terms of the content and the ways in which they engaged their students and colleagues. For example, a photograph of the sun rising over a mountain (Figure 8.3), with a caption *Change is on the horizon*, showed that these members had managed to solicit more financial support for the integration work, and that they had succeeded in getting other academics to buy into the integration approach and into teaching sexuality education since 'we are beginning to see a lot of political will from management'.

CHANGE IS ON THE HORIZON
We are on the brink of a revolution and curriculum integration is our weapon!
Financial support, active involvement of academic staff are just some of the positive factors which contribute to a renewed hope

Figure 8.3 Change is on the horizon

Photograph by Athol Kleinhans

Kleinhans, A. (Photographer). *Change is on the horizon* [Photograph]. Pretoria, South Africa: HEAIDS.

Their views on HIV testing had also changed as they pointed out that they now advocate for testing with their students. The photograph (Figure 8.4) shows a notice on the inside of the door of a teacher educator's office, stating, 'After leaving this office, make sure you get tested.'

The photographs also show how teacher educators, although having to work against the odds, integrate HIV and AIDS into the curriculum using innovative methods, and giving assignments focusing on HIV and AIDS.

Some photographs showed that teacher educators now ensure that they build caring and sharing relationships with students, and that they are focused on teaching to achieve change in sexual behaviour. The assumption that students have enough knowledge gave way to their ensuring that the students have appropriate and correct knowledge. The participants also showed how they created spaces for students to share openly, and how they changed from seeing HIV as a private matter to viewing it as a public one. One part of the photograph set shows a woman sitting on her own, writing down her thoughts. In a second part the photograph shows a group of students working together in a circle and sharing their thoughts, fears, and emotions and being supported by the others.

A second example of using visually verifiable data comes out of our project with a group of women university students of rural origin we had been working with using participatory visual methods to address sexual violence on campus. In Chapters 2 and 7 we describe the participatory processes and methods we engaged the young women in, as well as how they used their digital productions from these to engage the policy makers on their campus to

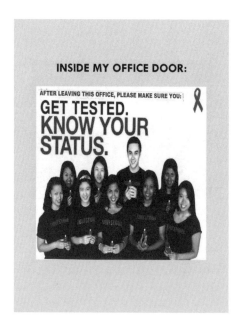

Figure 8.4 Inside my office door

Photograph by Misheck Ndebele

Ndebele, M. (Photographer). (2014). *Inside my office door* [Photograph]. Pretoria, South Africa: HEAIDS.

work towards change. After their various meetings to engage policy makers on campus, we asked the young women (and ourselves) three related questions: 'So what?'; 'How will we know that anything is happening?'; and 'Can we picture transformation and what would we see in such a picture?' (De Lange, Moletsane, & Mitchell, 2015, p. 169).

From their meetings around the various campuses of the university, the young women created visual images of what they saw as change emanating from their engagement with policy makers and the university community. These portraits of change (see De Lange et al., 2015) included, among others, a general clean up around the areas they had identified as unsafe, more lighting being provided, and broken furniture removed. For example, one portrait of change presents the before and after images of a corridor near the campus post office (Figure 8.5), leading one of the participants to comment:

Figure 8.5 *Picturing Change,* Lights in the passage to post office

Photograph by Takatso Mohlomi

Mohlomi, T. (Photographer). (2014). *Lights in the passage to post office* [Photograph]. Port Elizabeth: Girls Leading Change.

… by the post office. These used to be dark painting, no lights and broken chairs which were carelessly kept…they have now changed the painting, it's white. There has been lights [put up] and that makes the place to look safer for us… (quoted in De Lange et al., 2015, p. 171)

Other portraits of change included modified rules in residences accompanied by better communication to all the residents so as to make it easy for them to comply with these changed rules. See Figure 8.6.

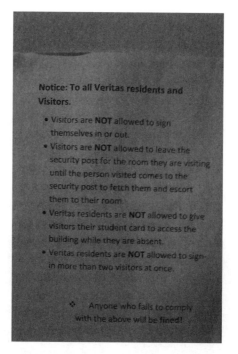

Figure 8.6 *Picturing Change,* Residence rules printed in bold and displayed

Photograph by Asisipho Mntonga

Mntonga, A. (2014). *Residence rules printed in bold and displayed* [Photograph]. Port Elizabeth: Girls Leading Change.

We acknowledge that this does not represent such extensive social change that sexual violence on campus is eliminated, but the political agency of the Girls Leading Change goes a long way towards extending and sustaining the social change required.

However, for us these portraits of change represent 'movement' (Kumashiro, 2000 cited in Baez, 2002, p. 53). It is from such movement and incremental change, as well as continuous engagement and dialogue among members of the community that we can hope to build sustainable change for the safety of women and men on campus.

Most Significant Change Technique

Furthering the idea of the visual to study the impact of the visual, Lemaire and Lunch (2012) have explored the use of participatory video in a variety of contexts. True to the principles of participatory research and interventions, their focus was on using approaches 'that are engaging, accessible, easy to implement, rigorous and accountable' (p. 303). Their work is premised on the notion that 'to obtain information and learning that truly reflect program impact, beneficiaries [including participants and community members] must play a central role in the [monitoring and evaluation] process, defining their own measures of success and assessing whether the program responds appropriately to the real-life needs and aspirations of the community' (p. 304). For these authors, using participatory video as a tool for monitoring and evaluation enables participants to be at the forefront of information gathering and sharing, and therefore, of immediately spotting change when it occurs, or recognizing when the intervention is not working or is leading to negative consequences for the community. A very specific approach involving participatory video used by Lemaire and Lunch (2012) is the idea of 'the most significant change' technique. Serrat (2009) defines the most significant change technique as 'a qualitative and participatory form of monitoring and evaluation based on the collection and systematic selection of stories of reported changes from development activities' (p. 1). As the author notes, the technique 'facilitates project and program improvement by focusing the direction of work away from less-valued directions towards more fully shared visions and explicitly valued directions, e.g., what do we really want to achieve and how will we produce more of it?'

According to Davies and Dart (2005), most significant change stories 'are collected from those most directly involved, such as participants and field staff… [using questions] such as: "During the last month, in your opinion, what was the most significant change that took place for participants in the program?"' (pp. 10–11) as well as why they regard as so important the change they identify as the most significant.

This work draws on using participatory video as a tool to engage in story-telling as 'sharing and building consensus on what is important to [participants or stakeholders]' (p. 310). Quoting the work of Davies and Dart (2005, p. 8), they define the most significant change technique as:

a form of participatory monitoring and evaluation…[which is participatory] because many project stakeholders are involved both in deciding the sorts of change to be recorded and in analyzing the data…[It] occurs throughout the program cycle… provides data on impact and outcomes that can be used to help assess the performance of the programme as a whole. (Lemaire & Lunch, 2012, p. 311)

These stories are documented in oral or written format. With the increase in the use of digital story-telling in research and interventions, we see an opportunity here for using digital technology to record and document the stories of most significant change in communities.

With visual stories researchers and those charged with implementing interventions in communities can learn about the nature of the changes that occur as a result of their initiative, as well as how and why those changes occur. With stories like these, researchers and government workers might also be able to identify challenges in the initiative, revisit their plans and implementation strategies, and improve effectiveness. The stories also make it possible for them to revisit the project and the lessons it offers long after it has ended.

Participatory Evaluation

As Guba and Lincoln (1989) and others have highlighted, the term participatory evaluation refers to a participant-driven strategy for investigating the ways in which the research partners (researchers and participants) working together, come to understand their work, how they use the evaluation to help them to look critically at their own situation, self-reflect, and take action to change the status quo. Further, Guba and Lincoln (1989) address a number of key principles that are often ignored in traditional evaluation research. First, it is premised on the understanding that participants (particularly participants from the community) have a relatively high stake in the outcomes of the project and the evaluation thereof. Thus, to exclude them from the evaluation process (including its design and implementation) is both discriminatory and unethical. Involving them helps them to voice their concerns and to provide information about the outcomes. Second, participatory evaluation is informed by the notion that if knowledge is power, withholding the findings of an evaluation from the participants further marginalizes them. Thus, to ensure that they have access to the information or knowledge produced, which concerns their lived experience in the first instance, participatory evaluation focuses on involving participants in the evaluation process right from design to data collection to data analysis. Third, involving participants throughout the evaluation process ensures mutual learning between them and the researchers, making it highly likely that the knowledge produced is actually used by and for those who most need it, and that the work/intervention is sustained beyond the life of the project.

While there are numerous accounts of participatory evaluation in the research literature, we refer here to a study conducted by Faisal Islam (2010) who both facilitated and documented a participatory evaluation of a partnership project between our research group at the University of KwaZulu-Natal and two rural high schools in the province of KwaZulu-Natal in South Africa. The study aimed to investigate what difference the school-university partnership, which involved a cohort model of practical professional development, the Rural Teacher Education Project (RTEP), was making or could make over a three-year period from 2007 to 2009 'in preparing new teachers in the troubling context of rural schools typified by HIV and AIDS, poverty, and the sense of isolation…' It focused on 'how student teachers as a Community of Practice self-reflect upon their: professional development, identity creation, pre-conceived orientation about teaching and learning in rural schools, and teacher preparation as per their perceived challenges in rural schools' (Islam, 2010, p. iv).

Islam notes that while he could not claim that the evaluation process was fully participatory, it was nevertheless helpful in identifying both the benefits and challenges of the partnership. For him, this suggests 'that a school-university partnership can be mutually beneficial if it is assessed reciprocally [and that] participatory evaluation can help the partners to understand each other's expectations, build trust and negotiate the goals and the processes of the partnership' (2010, p. 196). Informed by this mutual trust and sense of purpose, together, the partners are able to identify what changes linked to the program occur. They are also able to identify challenges that occur early and address these before they get out of control and before the project is derailed as a result. For example, the author identifies one of the outcomes of the participatory evaluation conducted of RTEP as involving teachers reflecting on the changes brought about by the project over the years it had been operational in the schools. He notes a teacher's reflection about the evaluation process during a focus group in 2007:

This [focus group discussion] has helped us to go back and analyze the impact that the student teachers have made on our school through collective discussion. This is the first time that we are getting the opportunity to discuss openly about the project and share our voices. Knowing [other teachers'] point of view and discussing them in detail is helping us to draw conclusions about the project and to understand it clearly. (Islam, 2010, p. 101)

Cautioning that an authentic participatory evaluation process is complex and difficult to organize because of time constraints on the part of participants (after all, they do have their own lives and schedules to attend to), Islam notes that researchers need to go the extra mile in ensuring that participants are involved and informed throughout the process. Thus, any participatory evaluation must take into account issues of engagement and commitment in the context of competing personal (and professional) demands. According to him, the process also needs to pay attention to such issues as the power dynamics within the group of participants, ensuring that all have the opportunity to air their views. For example, reflecting on issues of power during his project in the two schools, he notes the seeming reluctance of female stakeholders (teachers) to participate in the discussions during meetings, and refers specifically to a female deputy principal, who was the only top female manager in the school, who seemed unwilling or unable to participate in the various conversations and reflections about the project. This, as he came to learn from his work, can be addressed through continuous or sustained engagement and equal participation of all stakeholders throughout the process. From his perspective, such power dynamics were addressed 'as a result of our regular visits to the schools with flexible and responsive attitudes towards all stakeholders during the past three years, [and] the trust and confidence started to emerge and the fear started to dissipate' (Islam, 2010, p. 103). For Islam, the free and full participation of a variety of stakeholders from both sides of the partnership in the schools contributed positively not only to the evaluation process, but to the project itself.

INTERPRETIVE AND ETHNOGRAPHIC APPROACHES

A promising area for considering impact and the question, 'What difference does this make?' can be seen in work that uses interpretive and ethnographic approaches. As Bell and Aggleton (2016) note:

Interpretive and ethnographic approaches to monitoring and evaluation seek to apply the analytic methods of interpretive researchers and ethnographers to the purposes of programmatic decision making. They strive to be emic rather than etic in character, focusing in on how participants and stakeholders interpret a program and its effects in the light of local realities and meaning systems. (p. 6)

In advancing this work, the authors highlight such features as being context sensitive, and drawing attention to reflexivity on the part of researchers. 'They encourage reflexivity and critical self-awareness on the part of researchers. Monitoring and evaluation specialists need to question their own behavior, attitudes, values and beliefs in the light of the influence these may have on others'. (Hammersly & Atkinson, 2007, p. 6)

In this section we consider two approaches to carrying out this work – the focused revisit and the autoethnography.

Studying the 'Afterlife' of Participatory Visual Projects

The idea of studying the afterlife of interventions is something that seems particularly relevant to addressing the question 'What difference does this make?' in relation to participatory studies and dialogue. In this section we consider this work in the context of what sociologist Michael Burawoy (2003) refers to as focused or reflexive revisiting and the various permutations of what that could involve. What does it mean to study a site some time later (several years, a decade or even longer), either as the original research team returning to study what has happened to the participants, or returning to the same site years later and studying not the original participants but the current population of the same age or experience (in this case young people between the ages of 16 and 18) in the original setting, or what does it mean for a different team to visit the site? To add to these various permutations recent work by Sefton-Green and Rowsell (2015) involved a whole set of researchers returning to different sites (some as little as a few years later and some several decades later) to study the afterlife of various literacy projects. Indeed it was in this context that Claudia had occasion to revisit the *Soft Cover* project, a literacy-and-creative arts/participatory study focusing on HIV and AIDS carried out in 2001 to 2003 with young people in Khayelitsha and Atlantis in Western Cape, South Africa. Drawing on a series of revisits carried out with the youth participants, here we draw attention to the significance of time and life-events in understanding/evaluating the outcome of a project focusing on youth activism and literacy and the ways that youth interpretations of activism change over time.[4] In this case, the study was one of frequent revisits over a period of ten years, something along the lines

---

[4]The fieldwork for this revisiting study was supported by SSHRC-funded study 'What Difference Does This Make?' (Mitchell, Larkin, Flicker, De Lange, Stuart, and Moletsane).

of the well-known '7 Up, 14 Up' study conducted in the UK.[5] In that study which is still going on (and at the time of writing is at 60 Up) participants were visited. The 'up' in the title Fire + Hope Up signals a particular type of sociological revisit, inspired by this television series mentioned above produced by Britain's Granada Television which followed a group of 14 children first interviewed in 1963 and then filmed at regular seven-year intervals ('7 Plus Seven' was released in 1970, followed by '21 Up' in 1977, 28 Up in 1984, '35 Up' in 1991, '42 Up' in 1999, '49 Up' in 2005, and '56 Up' in 2012). In an article called 'Fire + Hope Up', Claudia describes the frequent visits to meet with some of the original 14 youth that either she or her co-researcher Shannon Walsh carried out (Mitchell, 2015a). As part of the study, five of the original group participated in a symposium that the three of us convened in 2011 called 'What difference does this make?' The panel on which the five presented at the symposium was called 'Ten years later'. The question being studied was this: What difference did it make to participate in an arts and media project where a group of young people developed books, created various art forms, created a book of poetry and so on? Some of the follow-up interviews were conducted as one-on-one conversations, while others were more like focus groups based on who was available.

The revisiting interviews of the Fire + Hope study are particularly revealing for what they say about the variability and shifting nature of impact over time. 'Time', as Neale (2010) writes 'is a complex and endlessly fascinating phenomenon, not simply the medium through which we do research, but an important topic of enquiry in its own right' (p. 3). Had we severed contact with the main participants in June, 2003 when the funding more or less ended, the research team (Shannon and Claudia) might have simply had the idea that youth empowerment was quite straightforward in this project, and that the kind of literacy-and-creative arts work we were doing with youth is exactly what is needed to engage youth in social activism in relation to HIV and AIDS. Three years later however, the findings and impact would have been seen to be quite different as can been seen in Claudia's account of a revisit in 2006:

It is a cold wet windy and thoroughly miserable Cape Town winter day in July of 2006. As my colleague, Shannon, and I make our way on foot through Section R of Khayelitsha with Jordie, the former youth worker who helped us to convene the *Soft Cover* project, a school-based literacy and creative arts-focused HIV&AIDS awareness initiative several years earlier, we wonder who will actually show up for the interviews we plan to conduct with former participants in the project. It is just over 3 years since the launch of their publication, *'In My Life': Youth Stories and Poems on HIV/AIDS* and the release of a short documentary *Fire + Hope* that Shannon has directed and that includes many of the participants from the project speaking about how they see their role as youth activists in addressing HIV&AIDS.

---

[5]The series was originally part of The World in Action, and was directed by Paul Almond. Michael Apted, his assistant, was the one who proposed to visit the children every seven years, with the idea of exploring the links between class and life success in Britain. Apted is now the series director.

We plan to meet up at a café later in the evening with as many of the original 14 youth who can come, but decide that perhaps we might be able to do some of the interviews in the day time as well. We are not quite sure who will still be around, especially in the middle of a week-day afternoon when you would think that most nineteen- or twenty-year-olds would probably be in university or training or at work. This day there are four of the original group (sometimes called the Soft Cover group and sometimes referred to as the Fire + Hope group) who show up at the house of Gene,[6] one of the group members. They are not at work, they are not studying or in training, and really it turns out that mid-afternoon is a perfect time to meet because they are doing nothing that afternoon or most week-day afternoons. We gather in the small two room house which closely resembles all the other small two room houses of Section R of Khayelitsha. We hear many things that afternoon. Some, like Gene, the one whose peers would have voted most likely to succeed in 2003, hasn't actually been able to complete his Matric [Grade12] even though 3 years ago he was on the verge of writing his final exams. Laura feels discouraged. She is still talking about the piece she wrote for *In My Life*, but now that she has part-time work as a cashier in Checkers, a supermarket chain, she can't figure out how she can do any more writing, the one activity that has given her some personal satisfaction. Daniel is working on a building site quite close to Gene's and we go to visit him on his break, but even there we hear the frustration in his voice about having a low-paying unskilled job and uncertain hours, and then working out in the rain and wind and cold this Cape Town winter day. Gene would like to get something going in drama and performance in the community. In the intervening years he has had a chance to participate in an arts-based workshop in Europe for which he has received funding but is not sure how to go about getting the project off the ground. Later in the evening when we go to the café, we meet up with other members of that original group of 14. Some are working, or taking up training, or are attending university. More of the ones who are now working or studying are from Atlantis, the township that always seemed somewhat more prosperous than Khayelitsha. Sheena from Atlantis, for example, is studying to become a social worker. Greg is in a first year arts program at one of the local universities. Reshma is working in a bank – but then when Gene and Daniel and Laura and others join in, there is a sense that on balance this is a very uncertain time. (Mitchell, 2015a, p. 34)

And then when we meet up with members of the original group at the 'What difference does this make? The arts, youth and HIV&AIDS' conference where we have the benefit of the hindsight of the youth-now-adults, we could reach other conclusions. Jordie, the project leader in particular, now in his early 30s is particularly discouraged:

---

[6]All names of participants are pseudonyms.

I mean the reality of the matter is that I need money to live on. And activism is not going to give me this. I mean, not now. Like, here we are fighting for the future, but I'm hungry now, I'm starving now. So I kind of needed a solution to that. So I think for me, for me the change started to happen there, is like, now I'm empowered enough, I understand things and I understand, the vigour that I had to change things, that was not going to happen overnight. It was kind of defeating really when you actually see what you have been working hard for. It didn't make any difference. I mean, just a very small difference, but you would have hoped that people would have understood things the way that you do, and changed things the way you want things to change for all of us. So it's kind of defeating to see, actually, things are getting worse. So all the knowledge, all the education, the workshops, kind of went to waste. It was a drop in the ocean. (Cited in Walsh, 2012, p. 412)

When we first completed the *Soft Cover* project our focus was on HIV awareness and we hoped that the various arts-based activities would contribute to making a space for dialogue about HIV and AIDS. When the group came to the 'What difference does it make' symposium, many of the participants in the session were very interested in posing that exact question to them. The answers were fascinating. Sheena, for example, says she remembers really none of the specific activities in which she participated as part of the *Soft Cover* project; she only remembers the open-endedness of discussing and indeed, that it is this that she has carried over in to her social work practice. Greg recalls that it was in the *Soft Cover* project that he learned about condoms, and indeed credits being alive today to the in-depth discussions about condoms. At 17, he was not publically out as a gay youth, but during the video interviews we did for the *Fire + Hope* documentary he discussed what sexuality meant for him, and the need for a safe space:

I think one of the biggest challenges is this whole thing about sexuality, who you are. When am I ready for sex? Should I do it? Shouldn't I? They've thrown, like, the whole subject of sex in our face and now we have to deal with it. And in between that we still have to find out who we are too, so, it's like, kind of complicated. It just complicates life! (Walsh, Fire + Hope, 2003)

In a group interview session in 2011, Greg explains the link for him between his identity when in drag and the creative work we did in the *Soft Cover* project that allowed him to find his own way of self-expression and activism.

I think coming out in drag and being out in drag, is really a tool for expressing myself, and in that way, also showing that it's okay to be yourself and to express yourself in a way that might not be a social norm. ...where Soft Cover fits into that is that I came to understand that process led to [this expression]. I can see it as a platform, because of the way that we took things, ... [like] the writing about everyday life experience. The Soft Cover Project showed that we can, [and that] it actually means something to some other people. The stories we wrote, other people could relate to. I think that is the biggest thing that I take from the Soft Cover Project is coming to feel comfortable with working with different mediums, and not just thinking that standing on a pedestal and saying a speech is the sum total of activism or doing your bit...there is a whole creative process. I am not a painter or poet, but [drag] is my creative outlet. (As cited in Walsh, 2012, p. 411)

The 'Ten Years Later' reminds us of the multiple truth factor in social research. At the end of her revisiting chapter (Mitchell, 2014), Claudia notes that her colleague, Shannon Walsh, offers a different, though not totally dissimilar narrative in her article. "We grew as we grew": Visual methods, social change and collective learning over time (Walsh, 2012), observing, 'While we began the work of literacy, meaning-making and AIDS activism at exactly the same point, we entered the project itself at very different points in our careers and so the question of where revisiting this project takes us is itself a component of revisiting.' (p. 37) It also suggests the use of autoethnography which, as we note in the next section, is a critical component of the question 'What difference does this make?'

A Case for Autoethnography

A theme running throughout this book has been the significance of reflexivity, our own as researchers, the reflexivity of participants, and reflexivity as a key feature of Critical Audience Engagement. Here we take our own reflexivity as researchers one step further, and propose a more robust consideration of positioning, not at the expense of the participants and the social issues they deem significant, but alongside their voices. It is not always easy to fit in all the narratives that need to be heard into any one article, chapter, conference presentation, community gathering, or policy forum, and if there can only be one set it should certainly be the voices of the participants and not the reflections of the researcher. So often absent from bodies of literature that are about best practices or good practices and lessons learned that satisfy donors or funders, are instances of findings about the visual and about participation that do not seem to have immediate relevance to the intended outcomes of an intervention on food security, public health or safety and security in schools, and so they may get left out of a report or article.

Methods of autoethnography seem ideally suited to taking up this aspect of the field-work. As various authors have noted (e.g., Chang, 2008; Hamilton, Smith, & Worthington, 2008), autoethnography is a methodology that allows for critically examining the self to better understand experiences in a broader social context. The work of Caroline Ellis and Art Bochner (2003) on the idea of the wide-angle lens seems particularly apt. As they write, 'Auto-ethnography is an autobiographical genre of writing that displays multiple layers of consciousness, connecting the personal to the cultural. Back and forth ethnographers gaze, first through an ethnographic *wide-angle lens*, focusing on social and cultural aspects of their personal experience; then they look *inward*, exposing a vulnerable self that is moved by and may move through, refract and resist cultural interpretations…' (p. 209, emphasis added). It is their idea of both the wide-angle lens and looking inward that frames the use of the visual in autoethnography (for example taking or working with photographs, creating cellphilms or videos and working with other digital media forms). Other scholars have used critical autoethnography in their work on racial justice education to deconstruct white racial privilege (Adams, Bell, & Griffin, 2007; Bishop, 2002).

What could be gained by taking something of the wide-angle lens approach of autoethnography in order to engage more critically across our own participatory visual projects and studies? Elsewhere, Claudia draws from several sources to create a set of six propositions about the value of autoethnography in teaching and research (Mitchell, 2016a). Notwithstanding the more obvious ones related to ethics and positionality, she includes one on social justice and one on advocacy. Adams, Holman Jones, and Ellis (2013) in the *Handbook of Autoethnography* argue that it helps us turn our attention to 'experiences of exclusion, degradation and injustice, and in so doing create work that not only makes the case for change but also embodies the change it calls into being' (p. 669). Turning finally to the notion of advocacy, Adams et al. (2013) in their call to action ask researchers to '[t]urn [their] attention to the harm being done to us and to others and use autoethnographic research to tell, and write stories of injustice' and '[w]rite stories of compassion, of solidarity and communion, of change and justice and hope' (adapted from Adams et al., 2013, p. 676).

Working with the visual and the arts, as Cole (2004) highlights, can provoke critical examination of the self. While much of this work is often framed in the context of ethical dilemmas, they are more than that or at least about more than ethics only in relation to what satisfies an institutional REB. Indeed, as we have found in numerous ethics 101, as it were, community discussions in preparation for a photovoice or cellphilm workshop, that session and follow-up discussions could become the basis for the entire project: What can be shown? Who can show it? To whom? But these are also discussions that we have as researchers and practitioners. A powerful example of this work can be seen in Alessandra Papi's (2009) autoethnographic study of the visual images used in UNICEF fund-raising campaigns. Taking a leave of absence from her position as a development practitioner in an international organization providing humanitarian aid to carry out graduate work at McGill University, she uses the tensions of 'looking inward' on the images that are used in a series of four fund-raising proposals submitted as part of her work in supporting programs for children orphaned by AIDS in Rwanda, Malawi, and the Democratic Republic of Congo. For her analysis of each campaign she includes the official photo that has been taken by a UNICEF photographer, the official 300-word narrative that goes with the image, and then her own reading as informed by postcolonial theory, theories of childhood, and visual studies. In her work she juggles two competing agendas: the critiques of 'othering' offered by theorizing in works such as Lutz and Collins' (1993) *Reading the National Geographic* and Holland's *Picturing Childhood,* and the recognition that the funds raised support local staff in international NGOs as well as the direct beneficiaries (the children and their families) of the projects. Unlike the work carried out by Lutz and Collins, and Holland, who are writing from the outside, Papi is able to place herself in the middle of the tensions. Her critiques are about being white and Western and privileged, but they are also about the project of attempting to do most good and least harm, an agenda that we think is significant in all research and interventions, and more importantly, in participatory work in communities.

As an example, one important finding, particularly in relation to the exhibition and curation literature, is the observation in Chapter 4 that community members in an informal settlement attending an exhibition of local women's photographs were reluctant to circulate in a public venue because they seemed unsure of whether just walking around and looking as much as they pleased was allowed. However, this finding which is an important one in relation to visual display and the politics of exhibiting does not really relate so much to literature on women's economic empowerment and as such is something that is unlikely to be reported – even though we would see it as important to understanding the cultural context of participatory research. Another finding relates to the very nature of having this exhibition of images of the informal settlement in the informal settlement itself. As Claudia observes in a set of field notes from the day:

As the researcher more or less responsible for this aspect of the project and for this particular event, I suddenly feel an awkwardness about the whole thing: spending all those hours before coming to Kenya trying to think of the best way of displaying the images, choosing to have the images reproduced on a special fabric so they could be easily transported, but also so that they would capture an element of the everyday-ness perhaps of clothing/images hanging on a clothesline. But such symbolism seems more appropriate now to an art gallery in Montreal than to this community centre. The photos the women take are visually stunning but then I start to question why it is more satisfying to look at the images of poverty in photos mounted on cloth hanging from a make-shift clothesline than to see the same scenes in real life. Everyone had to walk by these scenes of real life to get to the exhibition. As it turns out the community centre is double booked. When we arrive to mount the exhibition, women from the community are already heating up huge pots over charcoal to cook for a youth function. Something is happening behind the scenes and I go off with a couple of the gate keepers of the community, young men who have been hired to protect us, to look for a different venue. Then I learn that we can stay but it means a major removal to get those red hot pots transported to another venue. The fact that this exhibition, full of its symbols, takes precedence over some sort of income generation worries me but of course I am pleased that the work of the local women photographers will finally be acknowledged by their friends and family. But I am wondering if people think that the money that is going to support the exhibition could have been used for something else. I know I shouldn't think that way and the alternative in most research projects is that the participants are interviewed or surveyed [but] never see any aspect of the findings, participate in none of the analysis, and receive no recognition whatsoever. There are even refreshments but I see that they are sweets and cold drink. Wouldn't people have preferred proper chipatis and tea, something hot on this cool June morning, and something of a little more substance for [the] rest of the day, especially since so many of the pictures taken by the women highlight the struggle to feed one's children? (Claudia's Reflective Field Notes June, 2016)

Looking at the event through this lens serves as a reminder to us, as the researchers, of the implications of Western, or academic or middle-class notions of display.

CONCLUSION

We started this book by suggesting that there were stories to be told about stories being generated. Fourteen years after our somewhat naïve beginnings where we launched into work in rural South Africa with photovoice to take on challenges and solutions to addressing HIV and AIDS 'through the eyes of teachers and community health care workers', we find ourselves occasionally daunted, but mostly inspired to take this work further. We have drawn together these stories of stories in this book as a way to advocate for asking new questions and new issues in relation to participatory visual research and social change. As we come to the end of this book we find ourselves 'landing' on the uses of reflexivity and autoethnography as critical to asking new questions.

At the broadest level, our focus on community and policy dialogue, throughout the book highlights the need for further work in the area of picturing change and picturing social justice. Susan Sontag (2003) more than a decade ago was concerned about the proliferation of images in the media of human suffering and the ways in which audiences might become immune to this suffering. In many ways the examples we use in this book suggest a different path for thinking about the visual because of who is creating the images (local communities) and the close relationship, often, to those who are viewing the images (other community members, along with other stakeholders and policy makers). This is, in some ways, a radical shift in thinking about the visual and about audiences, particularly in contrast to work that is framed within the world of the Humanities: Fine Arts, Museum Culture, and related areas. How might visual artists, visual theorists and social scientists work in ways that are complementary? Where possible we have drawn on this literature that is often outside social research, seeking to bring it into the realm of social change, and we propose stronger alliances between these various disciplinary areas. We are heartened by the idea that four of the research students attached to the Participatory Cultures Lab of McGill University are contributing a panel on curation and social change 'Who frames the picture? Curation as social interaction' at the 2017 Annual Conference of the International Visual Studies Association (IVSA).

One of the areas that has been most critical in writing this book has been the recognition that participatory visual research offers such rich possibilities for the co-creation of knowledge. Although the idea of the co-creation of knowledge has been central, at least in theory, to participatory visual research, what we are seeing is that some of the most compelling questions about the power of images, the challenges to ethics and the politics of representation can be most effectively explored through the various participatory studies. The speaking back work we describe in Chapter 3 acknowledges that involving participants as audiences of their own productions offers rich possibilities for rethinking and repositioning. A critical feature of the fieldwork we are currently carrying out with girls and young women who are producing media texts related to sexual violence is work on speaking back and the ways in which the project seeks to disrupt rather than reproduce dominant narratives of gender and violence. Too often research studies do not last long enough to do the kind of revisiting and speaking back over time that is so critical. This is something that we regard as a challenge for masters and doctoral students in their research and a strong rationale for research teams that include both established scholars and new scholars and projects that can operate over time.

Returning to landing in the area of autoethnography and reflexivity, we see the need for stronger 'meta' work in the area of studying impact and social change and an increasing need to adopt a 'go ask' approach in our fieldwork. By that we refer to building in a meta-level to our work with participants and also with other researchers. One example of this 'go ask' approach responds to issues of ethics and working with Research Ethics Boards in carrying out participatory visual research. Often we are challenged by the responses of REBs at our respective institutions. As noted in Chapter 7 where we write about the responses of an REB at one of our institutions to the impact of images on audiences, this prompted us to include more nuanced questions about impact and affect in interviews and focus groups. What happens if we build in a 'go ask' approach to our work with young people by asking what they see as some of the challenges in the politics of representation? How do they feel about issues of ownership of visual productions? How might their perspectives shift over time? This meta-level of 'go ask' of course also requires ethical approval but in asking such questions we contribute to altering (and improving we would argue) the co-producer relationships and at the same time we deepen an understanding of the issues and theories of the visual. We also recognize that just as participants in research projects can be resources to each other, participatory visual researchers can also be resources to each other. Gubrium and Harper (2013) highlighted this when they embarked upon 'go ask' interviews with other researchers about issues of process in participatory visual research. In Chapter 7 'Engaging Policy Makers' we draw attention to the types of focus group and interview questions that we are currently using with policy makers to engage explicitly with questions of impact in a study on girl-led arts-based approaches to addressing sexual violence in Canada and South Africa noted earlier (see note 43). As part of that same project we are carrying out 'go ask' fieldwork where we are following up with other visual researchers on how they see the power of images in their fieldwork, and on the ways in which they see images as having an impact on communities. Again highlighting the notion of audience, as visual researchers we are audiences, but we are also in the position to observe and document audiences. In taking a practice-based approach, we are continuing to explore theoretical frameworks which draw together audience studies, political listening, reflexivity, and community dialogue. Ultimately such frameworks can help us theorize the ways in which participatory visual methodologies can be key to leveraging change through community and policy dialogue.

KEY POINTS OF THE CHAPTER

- The question 'What difference does this make?' should be one that frames our research.
- Although there may not be just one 'theory of change', the idea of a theory of change can help to situate our thinking about change in participatory research.
- A key feature of participatory visual work is that we can use the visual to document or 'picture' change.
- Visual researchers might consider the use of interpretive and ethnographic approaches such as reflexive revisiting and autoethnography to studying change.

REFERENCES

Abel, E. (2012). History at a standstill: Agency and gender in the image of civil rights. In
G. Batchen, M. Gidley, N. K. Miller, & J. Prosser (Eds.), *Picturing atrocity: Photography in crisis* (pp. 105–114). London, UK: Reaktion Books.

Abrahams, N., Jewkes, R., Martin, L. J., Mathews, S., Vetten, L., & Lombard, C. (2009). Mortality of women from intimate partner violence in South Africa: A national epidemiological study. *Violence and Victims, 24*(4), 546–556.

Adams, M., Bell, L. A., & Griffin, P. (2007). *Teaching for diversity and social justice* (2nd ed.). New York, NY: Routledge.

Adams, T., Holman Jones, S., & Ellis, C. (2013). Conclusion: Storying our future. In
S. Holman Jones, T. Adams, & C. Ellis (Eds.), *Handbook of autoethnography* (pp. 659–668). Walnut Creek, CA: Left Coast Press.

Adams Tucker, L., George, G., Reardon, C., & Panday, S. (2016). 'Learning the basics': Young people's engagement with sexuality education at secondary schools. *Sex Education: Sexuality, Society and Learning, 16*(4), 337–352. doi: 10.1080/14681811.2015.1091768

Akesson, B., Denov, M., D'Amico, M., Khan, F., Linds, W., & Mitchell, C. A. (2014). 'Stepping back' as researchers: Addressing ethics in arts-based approaches to working with war-affected children in school and community settings. *Educational Research for Social Change (ERSC), 3*(1), 75–89.

Aldridge, J. (2007). Picture this: The use of participatory photographic research methods with people with learning disabilities. *Disability & Society, 22*(1), 1–17. doi: 10.1080/09687590601056006

Alexandra, D. (2015). Are we listening yet? Participatory knowledge production through media practice: Encounters of political listening. In A. Gubrium, K. Harper, &
M. Otañez (Eds.), *Participatory visual and digital research in action* (pp. 41–55). Walnut Creek, CA: Left Coast Press.

Anderson, A. A. (2006). *The community builder's approach to theory of change: A practical guide to theory development*. New York, NY: The Aspen Institute Roundtable on Community Change.

Arnstein, S. R. (1969). A ladder of citizen participation. *Journal of the American Institute of Planners, 35*(4), 216–224. Ashcroft, B., Griffiths, G., & Tiffin, H. (1989). *The empire writes back: Theory and practice in post-colonial literature*. London, UK: Routledge.

Baez, B. (2002). Confidentiality in qualitative research: Reflections on secrets, power and agency. *Qualitative Research, 2*(1), 35–58. doi: 10.1177/1468794102002001638

Bal, M. (1996). *Double exposures: The subject of cultural analysis*. New York: Routledge.

Balfour, R. J., Mitchell, C., & Moletsane, R. (2008). Troubling contexts: Toward a generative theory of rurality as education research. *Journal of Rural and Community Development, 3*(3), 100–111.

Barndt, D. (2009). Touching minds and hearts: Community arts. In G. J. Knowles & A. Cole (Eds.), *Handbook of the arts in qualitative research: Perspectives, methodologies, examples, and issues* (pp. 351–362). Thousand Oaks, CA: Sage.

Bashir, S. A. (2002). Home is where the harm is: Inadequate housing as a public health crisis. *American Journal of Public Health, 92*(5), 733–738. doi: 10.2105/AJPH.92.5.733

Batchen, G., Gidley, M., Miller, N. K., & Prosser, J. (Eds.). (2012). *Picturing atrocity: Photography in crisis*. London, UK: Reaktion Books.

Bell, S., & Aggleton, P. (2016). *Monitoring and evaluation in health and social development: Interpretive and ethnographic perspectives*. Abingdon, UK: Routledge.

Bennett, G. G., McNeill, L. H., Wolin, K. Y., Duncan, D. T., Puleo, E., & Emmons, K. M. (2007). Safe to walk? Neighborhood safety and physical activity among public housing residents. *PLOS Medicine, 4*(10), e306. doi: 10.1371/0040306

Bennett, J. (2009). Policies and sexual harassment in higher education: Two steps forward and three steps somewhere else. *Agenda: Empowering Women for Gender Equity, 23*(80), 7–21.

Bhana, D. (2012). "Girls are not free" – In and out of the South African school. *International Journal of Educational Development, 32*(2), 352–358. doi: 10.1016/j.ijedudev.2011.06.002

Bhana, D., De Lange, N., & Mitchell, C. (2009). Male teachers talk about gender violence: "Zulu men demand respect". *Educational Review, 61*(1), 49–62. doi: 10.1080/00131910802684771

Bickford, S. (1996). *The dissonance of democracy: Listening, conflict and citizenship*. Ithaca, NY: Cornell University Press.

Bishop, A. (2002). *Becoming an ally: Breaking the cycle of oppression in people* (2nd ed.). New York, NY: Zed Books.

Bober, L. (2011). Visualizing justice: The politics of working with children's drawings. In L. Theron, C. Mitchell, A. Smith, & J. Stuart (Eds.), *Picturing research: Drawing as visual methodology* (pp. 63–76). Rotterdam, Netherlands: Sense.

Bohm, D. (1990). *On dialogue*. Ojai, CA: David Bohm Seminars.

Boler, T., & Archer, D. (2009). *The politics of prevention: A global crisis in AIDS and education*. London, UK: Pluto Press.

Boler, M., & Zembylas, M. (2003). Discomforting truths: The emotional terrain of understanding difference. In P. Pericles Trefonas (Ed.), *Pedagogies of difference: Rethinking education for social change* (pp. 110–136). New York, NY: RoutledgeFalmer.

Borland, K. (1991). 'That's not what I said': Interpretive conflict in oral narrative research. In S. B. Gluck & D. Patai (Eds.), *Women's words: The feminist practice of oral history* (pp. 63–75). New York, NY: Routledge.

Bowe, R., Ball, S., & Gold, A. (1992). *Reforming education and changing schools:* London, UK: Routledge.

Bucher, H. J., & Niemann, P. (2012). Visualizing science: the reception of PowerPoint presentations. *Visual Communication, 11*(3), 283–306. doi: 10.1177/1470357212446409

Buckingham, D. (2009). Creative visual methods in media research: Possibilities, problems and proposals. *Media, Culture & Society, 31*(4), 633–652. doi: 10.1177/0163443709335280

Buckingham, D., & Sefton-Green, J. (1994). *Cultural studies goes to school.* New York, NY: Routledge.

Burawoy, M. (2003). Revisits: An outline of a theory of reflexive ethnography. *American Sociological Review, 68*(5), 645–679.

Burgess, J. (2006). Hearing Ordinary Voices: Cultural Studies, Vernacular Creativity and Digital Storytelling. *Continuum: Journal of Media & Cultural Studies, 20*(2), 201–214.

Burkholder, C. (2016). We are HK too: Disseminating cellphilms in a participatory archive. In K. MacEntee, C. Burkholder, & J. Schwab-Cartas, (Eds.), *What's a cellphilm? Integrating mobile phone technology into participatory visual research and Activism* (pp. 153–170). Rotterdam, Netherlands: Sense.

Burns, C. (2011, April). *Putting us in the picture: Persuasion and plausibility in HIV/AIDS higher education.* Keynote presentation at the HIV and AIDS Education Community of Practice Symposium, Nelson Mandela Metropolitan University, Port Elizabeth.

Burton, P., & Leoschut, L. (2013). *School violence in South Africa: Results of the 2012 National school violence study.* Cape Town: Centre for Justice and Crime Prevention.

Buthelezi, T., Mitchell, C., Moletsane, R., De Lange, N., Taylor, M., & Stuart, J. (2007). Youth voices about sex and AIDS: Implications for life skills education through the 'Learning Together' project in KwaZulu-Natal, South Africa. *International Journal of Exclusive Education, 11*(4), 445–459. doi: http://dx.doi.org/10.1080/1360311070 1391410

Butler, S. R., & Lehrer, E. (Eds.). (2016). *Curatorial dreams: Critics imagine exhibitions.* Montreal, Canada: McGill Queens University Press.

Campbell, C., & MacPhail, C. (2002). Peer education, gender and the development of critical consciousness: Participatory HIV prevention by South African youth. *Social Science & Medicine, 55*(2), 331–345. doi: 10.1016/S0277-9536(01)00289-1

Campbell, D. (2012). The iconography of famine. In G. Batchen, M. Gidley, N. K. Miller, & J. Prosser (Eds.), *Picturing atrocity: Photography in crisis* (pp. 79–92). London, UK: Reaktion Books.

Caron, C., Raby, R., Mitchell, C., Thewissen-Leblanc, S., & Prioletta, R. (2016). From concept to data: Sleuthing social change-oriented youth voices on YouTube. *Journal of Youth Studies, 20*(1), 47–62. doi: http://dx.doi.org/10.1080/13676261.2016. 1184242

Carpentier, N., Schröder, K. C., & Hallett, L. (Eds.). (2013). *Audience transformation: Shifting audience positions in late modernity.* Abingdon, UK: Routledge.

Chalfen, R., Sherman, L., & Rich, M. (2010). VIA's visual voices: The awareness of a dedicated audience for voices in patient video narratives. *Visual Studies, 25*(3), 201–209. doi: 10.1080/1472586X.2010.523271

Chang, H. (2008). *Autoethnography as method*. New York, NY: Routledge.

Chege, F., Maina, L., Mitchell, C., & Rothman, M. (2014). A safe house? Girls' drawings on safety and security in slums in and around Nairobi. *Girlhood Studies, 7*(2), 130–135. doi: 10.3167/ghs.2014.070209

Choudry, A. (2015). *Learning activism: The intellectual life of contemporary social movements*. Toronto: University of Toronto Press.

Choudry, A., & Kapoor, D. (2010). Learning from the ground up: Global perspectives on social movements and knowledge production. In A. Choudry & D. Kapoor (Eds.), *Learning from the ground up: Global perspectives on social movements and knowledge production* (pp. 1–13). New York, NY: Palgrave Macmillan.

Church, K. (2008). Exhibiting as inquiry: Travels of an accidental curator. In G. Knowles & A. Cole (Eds.), *Handbook of the arts in qualitative research: Perspectives, methodologies, examples, and issues* (pp. 421–434). London, UK: Sage.

Clacherty, G., with the Suitcase Storytellers and Welvering, D. (2006). *The suitcase stories: Refugee children reclaim their identities*. Cape Town, South Africa: Double Storey Books.

Clandinin, D.J., & Connelly, F.M. (1992). Teacher as curriculum maker. In P. Jackson (Ed.), *Handbook of research on curriculum* (pp. 363–401). New York, NY: Macmillan.

Clark, A., & Moss, P. (2011). *Listening to young children: The mosaic approach* (2nd ed). London, UK: NCB.

Clowes, L., Shefer, T., Fouten, E., Vergnani, T., & Jacobs, J. (2009). Coercive sexual practices and gender-based violence on a university campus. *Agenda: Empowering Women for Gender Equity, 23*(80), 22–32.

Coffey, J., Budgeon, S., & Cahill, H. (2016). Introduction. In J. Coffey, S. Budgeon, & H. Cahill (Eds.), *Learning bodies: The body in youth and childhood studies* (pp. 1–19). Singapore: Springer.

Cole, A. L. (2004). *Provoked by art: Theorizing arts-informed research*. Halifax, NS: Backalong Books; Toronto, ON: Centre for Arts-Informed Research.

Cole, A. L., & McIntyre, M. (2006). *Living and dying with dignity: The Alzheimer's project*. Halifax, NS: Backalong Books.

Corbett, M. (2007). *Learning to leave: The irony of schooling in a coastal community*. Halifax, NS: Fernwood.

Cotton, T. (2007). What is it it like to be here? A methodology. *For the Learning of Mathematics, 27*(2), 40–44.

Csikszentmihalyi, M. (1990). *Flow: The psychology of optimal experience*. New York, NY: Harper and Row.

D'Amico, M., Denov, M., Khan, F., Linds, W., & Akesson, B. (2016). Research as intervention? Exploring the health and well-being of children and youth facing global adversity through participatory visual methods. *Global Public Health: An International Journal for Research, Policy and Practice, 11*(5–6), 528–545. doi: 10.1080/17441692.2016.1165719

Daniels, L. (2013). Expressions of policy effects: Hearing memories of Indian residential schools. In T. Strong-Wilson, C. Mitchell, S. Allnutt, & K. Pithouse (Eds.), *Productive remembering and social agency* (pp. 31–48). Rotterdam, Netherlands: Sense.

Darroch, F., & Giles, A. (2014). Decolonizing health research: Community-based participatory research and postcolonial feminist theory. *The Canadian Journal of Action Research, 15*(3), 22–36.

Dartnall, E., & Gevers, A. (2015). Violence can be prevented. *SA Crime Quarterly,* (51), 3–4.

Davies, R., & Dart, J. (2005). *The 'most significant change' (MSC) technique: A guide to its use.* Retrieved from www.mande.co.uk/docs/MSCGuide.pdf

Davison, K. K., Werder, J. L., & Lawson, C. T. (2008). Children's active commuting to school: Current knowledge and future directions. *Preventing Chronic Disease: Public Health Research, Policy and Practice, 5*(3), 1–11.

De Lange, N. (2012). Researching to make a difference: Possibilities for social science research in the age of AIDS. *SAHARA-J: Journal of Social Aspects of HIV/AIDS: An Open Access Journal, 9*(Sup 1), 3–10. doi: 10.1080/17290376.2012.744897

De Lange, N., Buthelezi, T. M., Mazibuko, M. N., Mitchell, C., Moletsane, R., Stuart, J., & Taylor, M. (2004). *Learning together: Towards an integrated participatory approach to youth, gender and HIV/AIDS interventions in rural KwaZulu-Natal schools.* South Africa: NRF Project.

De Lange, N., & Combrinck, M. (2011). What will we do with 24 ducks? Building community partnerships. In F. Islam, C. Mitchell, N. De Lange, M. Combrinck, & R. Balfour (Eds.), *School-university partnerships for educational change in rural South Africa: Particular challenges and practical cases* (pp. 231–243). New York, NY: Edwin Mellon Press.

De Lange, N., & Mitchell, C. (2012a). Community health workers working the digital archive: A case for looking at participatory archiving in studying stigma in the context of HIV and AIDS. *Sociological Research Online, 17*(1), 1–14.

De Lange, N., & Mitchell, C. (2012b). Building sustainability into work with participatory video. In E. J. Milne, C. Mitchell, & N. De Lange (Eds.), *Handbook of participatory video* (pp. 318–330). Lanham, MD: AltaMira Press.

De Lange, N., & Mitchell, C. (2014). Building a future without gender violence: Rural teachers and youth leading community dialogue. *Gender and Education, 26*(5), 584–599. doi: 10.1080/09540253.2014.942257

De Lange, N., & Mitchell, C. (2016). Community health workers as cultural producers in addressing gender-based violence in rural South Africa. *Global Public Health, 11*, 5–6, 783–798. doi: 10.1080/17441692.2016.1170867

De Lange, N., Mitchell, C., & Bhana, D. (2012). Voices of women teachers about gender inequalities and gender-based violence in rural South Africa. *Gender and Education, 24*(5), 499–514. doi: 10.1080/09540253.2011.645022

De Lange, N., Mitchell, C., & Moletsane, R. (2012). Anyway, what difference does this make? Arts-based methodologies in addressing HIV and AIDS. *Educational Research for Social Change, 1*(2), 1–7.

De Lange, N., Mitchell, C., & Moletsane, R. (2015). Girl-led strategies to address campus safety: Creating action briefs for dialogue with policy makers. *Agenda: Empowering Women for Gender Equity, 29*(3), 118–127.

De Lange, N., Mitchell, C., & Stuart, J. (Eds.). (2007). *Putting people in the picture: Visual methodologies for social change.* Rotterdam, Netherlands: Sense.

De Lange, N., Mitchell, C., & Stuart, J. (2011). Learning together: Teachers and community health care workers draw each other. In L. Theron, C. Mitchell, A. Smith, & J. Stuart (Eds.), *Picturing research: Drawings as visual methodology* (pp. 177–189). Rotterdam, Netherlands: Sense.

De Lange, N., Moletsane, R., & Mitchell, C. (2015). Seeing how it works: A visual essay about critical and transformative research in education. *Perspectives in Education, 33*(4), 151–176.

De Lange, N., Nguyen, L. A., & Nghiem, T. T. (2016). Creating dialogue on inclusion in Vietnam: Girls with disabilities exhibiting their work. *Girlhood Studies, 9*(1), 104–117. doi: 10.3167/ghs.2016.090108

De Lange, N., Nguyen, X. T., Mitchell, C., & Nguyen, T. L. A. (2014). *Our voices, our hopes: Girls with disabilities and participatory visual methodologies.* Hanoi, Vietnam: MRDG Project.

De Lange, N., Olivier, T., & Wood, L. (2008). Participatory video documentary: Just for whom? *Education as Change, 12*(2), 109–122.

Delgado, M. (2015). *Urban youth and photovoice: Visual ethnography in action.* New York, NY: Oxford University Press.

DeMartini, A., & Mitchell, C. (2016). Cellphilms, teachers, and HIV and AIDS education. In K. MacEntee, C. Burkholder, & J. Schwab-Cartas (Eds.), *What's a cellphilm? Integrating mobile phone technology into participatory visual research and activism* (pp. 103–118). Rotterdam, Netherlands: Sense.

Denzin, N. K., & Lincoln, Y. S. (2000). *Handbook of qualitative research* (2nd ed.). Thousand Oaks, CA: Sage.

Department of Education (DoE). (2001). *Opening our eyes: Addressing gender-based violence in South African schools. A module for educators.* Pretoria, South Africa: Canada–South Africa Education Management Programme. Retrieved from www.thutong.doe.gov.za/ResourceDownload.aspx?id=44564

Department of Education (DoE). (2008). *Guidelines for the prevention and management of sexual violence and harassment in public schools.* Pretoria, South Africa: Department of Education.

De Ridder, S., Vesnic-Alujevic, L., & Romic, B. (2016). Challenges when researching digital audiences: Mapping audience research of software designs, interfaces and platforms. *Participations: Journal of Audience and Reception Studies, 13*(1), 374–391.

De Silva, M. J., Breuer, E., Lee, L., Asher, L., Chowdhary, N., Lund, C., & Patel, V. (2014). Theory of change: A theory-driven approach to enhance the Medical Research Council's framework for complex interventions. *TRIALS, 15*(267). doi: 10.1186/1745-6215-15-267

Dockney, J., & Tomaselli, K. G. (2009). Fit for the small (er) screen: Films, mobile TV and the new individual television experience. *Journal of African Cinemas, 1*(1), 126–132.

Dowler, L., Cuomo, D., & Laliberte, N. (2014). Challenging 'The Penn State Way': A feminist response to institutional violence in higher education. *Gender, Place & Culture: A Journal of Feminist Geography, 21*(3), 387–394. doi: 10.1080/0966369X.2013.802676

Doyon, P. (2009). *Girls don't do wires: An exploration of adolescent girls' media production* (Doctoral dissertation). McGill University, Montreal, Canada.

Duncan, A., & Cullen, B. (2012). *Participatory video: A novel mechanism for sharing community perceptions with decision makers* [CPWF innovation funds project completion report]. Colombo, Sri Lanka: CGIAR Challenge Program on Water and Food.

Durham Community Research Team. (2011). *Community-based participatory research: Ethical challenges.* Durham, UK: Centre for Social Justice and Community Action.

Eberts, D., & Cotton, H. (Directors), Cotton, H., Cotton, A., & Eberts, F. (Producers). (2008). *Where the water meets the sky* [Motion Picture]. UK: Camfed.

Edwards, E. (2002). Material beings: Objecthood and ethnography of photographs. *Visual Studies, 17*(1), 67–75. doi: 10.1080/14725860220137336

Eisner, E. W. (2005). *Reimagining Schools: The selected works of Elliot W. Eisner.* New York, NY: Routledge.

Eliot, T. S. (1942). *The four quartets: Collected poems, 1909 – 1962.* London, UK: Faber and Faber.

Ellis, C., & Bochner, A. (2003). Autoethnography, personal narrative, reflexivity: Researcher as subject. In N. K. Denzin & Y. S. Lincoln (Eds.), *Collecting and interpreting qualitative materials* (2nd ed.) (pp. 199–258). London, UK: Sage.

Ellsworth, E. (1992). Why doesn't this feel empowering? Working through the repressive myths of critical pedagogy. In C. Luke & J. Gore (Eds.), *Feminisms and critical pedagogy* (pp. 90–119). New York, NY: Routledge.

Escarpit, R. (1958). *Sociology of literature* (Sociologie de la littérature). Paris: Presses Universitaires de France.

Ewald, W. (2000). *Secret games: Collaborative works with children 1969-1999.* New York, NY: Scalo Publishers.

Farrington, J., Bebbington, A., Wellard, K., & Lewis, D. J. (1993). *Reluctant partners: Non-governmental organisations, the state and sustainable agricultural development.* London, UK: Routledge.

Feld, S. (1987). Dialogic Editing: Interpreting how Kaluli read sound and sentiment. Cultural Anthropology, 2 (2), 190 – 210.

Fine, M., & McClelland, S. (2006). Sexuality education and desire: Still missing after all these years. *Harvard Educational Review, 76*(3), 297–338. doi: 10.17763/haer.76.3.w5042g23122n6703

Finlay, L. (2002). Negotiating the swamp: The opportunity and challenge of reflexivity in research practice. *Qualitative Research, 2*(2), 209–230. doi: 10.1177/146879410200200205

Fiske, J. (1987). British cultural studies. In R. Allen (Ed.), *Channels of discourse reassembled: Television in contemporary criticism* (pp. 284–326). Chapel Hill, NC: University of North Carolina Press.

Fiske, J. (1994). Audiencing: Cultural practices and cultural studies. In N. K. Denzin & Y. S. Lincoln (Eds.), *The SAGE handbook of qualitative research* (pp. 189–198). London, UK: Sage.

Flicker, S., Danforth, J., Konsmo, E., Wilson, C., Oliver, V., Jackson, R., Prentice, T, Larkin, J., Restoule, J-P., & Mitchell, C. (2014). Because we are Natives and we stand strong to our pride: Decolonizing HIV prevention with Aboriginal youth in Canada using the Arts. *Canadian Journal of Aboriginal Community-Based HIV/AIDS Research*, *5*, 4–24.

Flicker, S., Danforth, J., Wilson, C., Oliver, V., Larkin, J. Restoule, J-P., Mitchell, C., Konsmo, E., Jackson, R., & Prentice, T. (2014). "Because we have really unique art": Decolonizing research with Indigenous youth using the arts. *International Journal of Indigenous Health*, *10*(1), 16–34. doi: 10.18357/ijih.101201513271

Flicker, S., Wilson, C., Native Youth Sexual Health Network., Prentice, C., Oliver, C., Jackson, R., Larkin, J., Restoule, J-P., & Mitchell, C. (in press). Stay strong, stay sexy, stay native: Storying, Indigenous youth, and HIV prevention activism. *Action Research Journal*.

Flyvbjerg, B. (2001). *Making social science matter: Why social inquiry fails and how it can succeed again*. Cambridge, UK: Cambridge University Press.

Francis, D. (2010). Sexuality education in South Africa: Three essential questions. *International Journal of Educational Development*, *30*(3), 314–319. doi: 10.1016/j.ijedudev.2009.12.003

Francis, D. (2012). Teacher narratives on the teaching of sexuality and HIV/AIDS education [Special issue]. *Communitas*, *17*, 45–59.

Freiler, C., Hurley, S., Canuel, R., McGahey, B., Froese-Germain, B., & Riel, R. (2012). *Teaching the way we aspire to teach: Now and in the future*. Ottawa, ON: The Canadian Education Association and the Canadian Teachers' Federation.

Freire, P. (1985). *The politics of education: Culture, power and liberation*. South Hadley, MA: Bergin & Garvey.

Froese-Germain, B., & Riel, R. (2012). *Understanding teachers' perspectives on student mental health: Findings from a National Survey*. Ottawa, ON: Canadian Teachers' Federation.

Gaventa, J., & Cornwall, A. (2001). Power and knowledge. In P. Reason & H. Bradbury (Eds.), *Handbook of action research: Participative inquiry and practice* (pp. 70–90). London, UK: Sage.

Geertz, C. (1995). *After the fact: Two countries, four decades, one anthropologist*. Cambridge, MA: Harvard University Press.

Geffen, N. (2010). *Debunking delusions: The inside story of the Treatment Action Campaign*. Auckland Park, South Africa: Jacana Media.

Gelber, K. (2002). *Speaking back: The free speech vs hate speech debate*. Amsterdam, Netherlands: John Benjamins.

Geldenhuys, M. (2016). *Addressing gender-based violence in the age of aids: Rural youth engaging peers through social media* (Doctoral dissertation). Nelson Mandela Metropolitan University, Port Elizabeth, South Africa.

Gender Links. (2012). *The war @ home: Findings of GBV prevalence study in South Africa*. Retrieved from www.genderlinks.org.za/article/the-warhome-findings-of-the-gbv-prevalence-study-in-south-africa-2012-11-25

Gervais, M., & Rivard, L. (2013). 'SMART' Photovoice agricultural consultation: Increasing Rwandan women farmers' active participation in development. *Development in Practice, 23*(4), 496–510. doi: 10.1080/09614524.2013.790942

Gillander, G. K. (2013). Violence, gender equality and the millennium series. In S. Fahlgren, A. Johansson, & E. Soderberg (Eds.), *Eight gender scientific readings of the Swedish welfare state by Stieg Larsson's Millennium trilogy* (pp. 27–36). Sundsvall: Mid-Sweden University.

Gott, R. (2008, July 20). Olando Fals Borda. *The Guardian*. Retrieved from www.theguardian.com/world/2008/aug/26/colombia.sociology

Grace, S. (2001). *Canada and the idea of North*. Montreal, Canada: McGill-Queen's University Press.

Gready, P. (2010). Introduction – 'Responsibility to the Story'. *Journal of Human Rights Practice, 2*(2), 177–190. doi: 10.1093/jhuman/huq008

Greene, M. (1994). Carpe diem: The arts and school restructuring. *Teachers College Record, 95*(4), 494–507.

Guba, E., & Lincoln, Y. (1989). *Fourth generation evaluation*. Newbury Park, CA: Sage.

Gubrium, A. (2009). Digital storytelling: An emergent method for health promotion research and practice. *Health Promotion Practice, 10*(2), 186–191. doi: 10.1177/1524839909332600

Gubrium, A., & Harper, K. (2013). *Participatory visual and digital methods*. Walnut Creek, CA: Left Coast Press.

Gubrium, A., Harper, K., & Otañez, M. (2015). *Participatory visual and digital research in action*. Walnut Creek, CA: Left Coast Press.

Gubrium, A., Krause, E. L., & Jernigan, K. (2014). Strategic authenticity and voice: New ways of seeing and being seen as young mothers through digital storytelling. *Sexuality Research and Social Policy, 11*(4), 337–347. doi: 10.1007/s13178-014-0161-x

Guillemin, M., & Drew, S. (2010). Questions of process in participant-generated visual methodologies. *Visual Studies, 25*(2), 175–188. doi: 10.1080/1472586X.2010.502676

Guishard, M., & Tuck, E. (2014). Youth resistance research methods and ethical challenges. In E. Tuck & K. W. Yang (Eds.), *Youth resistance research and theories of change* (pp. 181–194). New York: Routledge.

Haalboom, B. J., Robinson, K. L., Elliott, S. J., Cameron, R., & Eyles, J. D. (2006). Research as intervention in heart health promotion. *Canadian Journal of Public Health, 91*(4), 291–295.

Halasz, J. R. (2010). Cultural icons/Moving viewers: American film and the spectator's experience. *Visual Studies, 25*(1), 101–103. doi: 10.1080/14725861003607058

Hale, C. R. (2001). What is activist research? *Social Science Research Council, 2*(1–2), 13–15.

Hamilton, M. L., Smith, L., & Worthington, K. (2008). Fitting the methodology with the research: An exploration of narrative, self-study and auto-ethnography. *Studying Teacher Education: A Journal of Self-Study of Teacher Education Practices, 4*(1), 17–28.

Hampl, P. (1996). Memory and imagination. In J. McConkey (Ed.), *The anatomy of memory: An anthology* (pp. 201–211). New York, NY: Oxford University Press.

Hariman, R., & Lucaites, J. (2012). The iconic image of mushroom cloud and the Cold War nuclear optic. In G. Batchen, M. Gidley, N. K. Miller, & J. Prosser (Eds.), *Picturing atrocity: Photography in crisis* (pp. 135–146). London, UK: Reaktion Books.

Hart, R. (1992). *Children's participation: From tokenism to citizenship*. Florence, Italy: UNICEF.

Hartmann, W., Silvester, J., & Hayes, P. (1999). *The colonising camera: Photographs in the making of Namibian history*. Cape Town, South Africa: University of Cape Town Press.

Haw, K. (2008). 'Voice' and video: Seen, heard, and listened to. In P. Thompson (Ed.), *Doing visual research with children and young people* (pp. 192–207). London, UK: Routledge.

HEAIDS. (2010). *Curriculum-in-the-making: Being a teacher in the context of the HIV and AIDS pandemic*. Pretoria, South Africa: Higher Education South Africa.

Helleve, A., Flisher, A. J., Onya, H., Mukoma, W., & Klepp, K-I. (2009). South African teachers' reflections on the impact of culture on their teaching of sexuality and HIV/AIDS. *Culture, Health & Sexuality: An International Journal for Research, Intervention and Care, 11*(2), 189–204.

Hines, B. (2002). *Photobooth*. New York, NY: Princeton Architectural Press.

Holland, P. (2004). *Picturing childhood: The myth of the child in popular imagery*. London: I.B. Tauris.

Holliday, R. (2007). Performances, confessions, and identities: Using video diaries to research sexualities. In G. Stanczak (Ed.), *Visual research methods: Image, society, and representation* (pp. 255–280). Thousand Oaks, CA: Sage.

hooks, b. (1989). *Talking back: Thinking feminist, thinking black*. Boston, MA: South End Press.

hooks, b. (1994). In our glory: Photography and black life. In D. Willis (Ed.), *Picturing us: African American identity in photography* (pp. 43–54). New York, NY: The New Press.

Horowitz, C. R., Robinson, M., & Seifer, S. (2009). Community-based participatory research from the margin to the mainstream: Are researchers prepared? *Circulation, 119*(19), 2633–2642. doi: 10.1161/CIRCULATIONAHA.107.729863

Hubbard, J. (1994). *Shooting back from the reservation: A photographic view of life by Native American youth*. New York, NY: New Press.

Hughes, I., & Seymour-Rolls, K. (2000). Participatory action research: Getting the job done. *Action Research E-Reports, 4*. Retrieved from www.fhs.usyd.edu.au/arow/arer/004.htm

Human Rights Watch (HRW). (2012). *Human rights of women and children with disabilities.* Retrieved from www.hrw.org/sites/default/files/related_material/0912_disabilities_brochure.pdf

Ingham, R. (2005). 'We didn't cover that at school': Education against pleasure or education for pleasure? *Sex Education, 5*(4), 375–388. doi: 10.1080/14681810500278451

InsightShare. (n.d.). *Global participatory video hub network.* Retrieved from www.insightshare.org/hubs/list.html

Islam, F. (2010). *New teachers for new times? A participatory evaluation of a school-university partnership to improve novice teacher education in rural South Africa in the age of AIDS* (Unpublished doctoral dissertation). McGill University, Montreal, Canada.

Jenkins, H., Purushotma, R., Weigel, M., Clinton, K., & Robison, A. (2006). *Confronting the challenges of participatory culture. Media education for the 21st Century.* London, UK: MIT Press.

Jewitt, C. (2013). Multimodal methods for researching digital technologies. In S. Price, C. Jewitt, & B. Brown (Eds.), *The SAGE handbook of digital technology research* (pp. 250–265). London, UK: Sage.

Jewkes, R. (2010). Preventing sexual violence in the 21st century: Using research to shape the agenda for prevention. *Injury Prevention, 16*(Sup 1), A282–A282. doi: 10.1136/ip.2010.029215.1003

Jewkes, R. K., Dunkle, K., Nduna, M., & Shai, N. (2010). Intimate partner violence, relationship power inequity, and incidence of HIV infection in young women in South Africa: a cohort study. *The Lancet, 376*(9734), 41–48. doi: 10.1016/S0140-6736(10)60548-X

Jones, H. (2011). *A guide to monitoring and evaluating policy influence* [Background Note]. London, UK: Overseas Development Institute.

Khan, F. (2015). Combating sexual violence using community-based intervention tools in informal settlements. *Agenda: Empowering Women for Gender Equity, 29*(3), 128–133.

Kindon, S., Hume-Cook, G., & Woods, K. (2012). Troubling the politics of reception within participatory video discourse. In E. J. Milne, C. Mitchell, & N. de Lange (Eds.), *Handbook of participatory video* (pp. 349–364). Lanham, MD: AltaMira Press.

Knowles, J. G., & Cole, A. L. (2008). *Handbook of the arts in qualitative research: Perspectives, methodologies, examples, and issues.* London, UK: Sage.

Kraidy, U. (2003). Digital media and education: Cognitive impact of information visualization. *Journal of Educational Media, 27*(3), 95–106.

Kress, G. (2008). Meaning and learning in a world of instability and multiplicity. *Studies in Philosophy and Education, 27*(4), 253–266. doi: 10.1007/s11217-007-9070-2

Kress, G. (2010). *Multimodality: A social semiotic approach to contemporary communication.* London, UK: Routledge.

Kuhn, A. (1995). *Family secrets: Acts of memory and imagination*. London, UK: Verso.

Kumashiro, K. K. (2002). *Troubling education: Queer activism and antioppressive pedagogy*. London, UK: Routledge.

Kumashiro, K. K. (2015). *Against common sense: Teaching and learning towards social justice* (3rd ed). New York, NY: Routledge.

Kutcher, S., & McDougall, A. (2009). Problems with access to adolescent mental health care can lead to dealings with the criminal justice system. *Paediatrics & Child Health, 14*(1), 15–18.

Laing, K., & Todd, L. (Eds.). (2015). *Theory-based methodology: Using theories of change in educational development, research and evaluation*. Newcastle-upon-Tyne, UK: Newcastle University Research Centre for Learning and Teaching.

Lambert, J. (2006). *Digital storytelling: Capturing lives, creating community*. Berkeley, CA: Digital Diner Press.

Lassiter, L. E. (2005). Collaborative ethnography and public anthropology. *Current Anthropology, 46*(1), 83–106.

Lather, P. (1992). Post-critical pedagogies: A feminist reading. In C. Luke & J. Gore (Eds.), *Feminisms and critical pedagogy* (pp. 120–137). New York, NY: Routledge.

Laverack, G. (2013). *Health activism: Foundations and strategies*. London, UK: Sage.

Leach, F. M., & Mitchell, C. (2006). *Combating gender violence in and around schools*. Stoke-on-Trent, UK: Trentham Books.

Lee, L. (Ed.). (2013). *Jo Spence: The final project*. London, UK: Ridinghouse.

Lemaire, I., & Lunch, C. (2012). Using participatory video in monitoring and evaluation. In E. J. Milne, C. Mitchell, & N. De Lange (Eds.), *Handbook of participatory video* (pp. 303–317). Lanham, MD: AltaMira Press.

Lewis, D. (2003). Editorial. *Feminist Africa, 2*, 1–7. Retrieved from http://agi.ac.za/sites/agi.ac.za/files/fa_2_editorial.pdf (accessed on 3 July, 2017)

Lewis, D. (2003). Editorial. *Feminist Africa, 2*, 1–7. Retrieved from http://agi.ac.za/sites/agi.ac.za/files/fa_2_editorial.pdf (accessed on 19 July, 2017)

Lewis, S. (2011). Editorial: How research influences policy makers: Still hazy after all these years. *JNCI: Journal of the National Cancer Institute, 103*(4), 286–287.

Lick, E. (2015). Print advertising in anglophone and francophone Canada from a critical discourse analytical point of view: establishing different relations between the producer and viewer of advertisement images. *Visual Communication, 14*(2), 221–241.

Lobinger, K., & Brantner, C. (2015). Likable, funny or ridiculous? A Q-sort study on audience perceptions of visual portrayals of politicians. *Visual Communication, 14*(1), 15–40. doi: 10.1177/1470357214554888

Low, B. (2016, June). *Building a tripartite urban arts high-school partnership: School, university, and community*. Paper presented at the annual Canadian Society for Studies in Education, Calgary, Alberta.

Low, B., Rose, C. B., Salvio, P. M., & Palacios, L. (2012). (Re)framing the scholarship on participatory video: From celebration to critical engagement. In E. J. Milne, C. Mitchell, &

N. De Lange (Eds.), *Handbook of participatory video* (pp. 49–66). Lanham, MD: AltaMira Press.

Low, B., Carter, M. R., Wood, E., Mitchell, C., Proietti, M., & Friedman, D. (2016). Building an urban arts partnership between school, community artists, and university. *Learning Landscapes, 10*(1), 153–171.

Luce, K. (2011). The viewer and the printed image in late medieval Europe. *Visual Studies, 26*(3), 275–276. doi: 0.1080/1472586X.2011.610964

Lunch, N., & Lunch, C. (2006). *Insights into participatory video.* Oxford, UK: InsightShare.

Lunt, P., & Livingstone, S. (2013). Media studies' fascination with the concept of the public sphere: critical reflections and emerging debates. *Media Culture Society, 35*(1), 87–96 doi: 10.1177/0163443712464562

Lutz, C., & Collins, J. L. (1993). *Reading National Geographic.* Chicago, IL: University of Chicago Press.

Lykes, M. B., & Crosby, A. (2013). Feminist practice of action and community research. In S. N. Hesse-Biber (Ed.), *Feminist research practice: A primer* (pp. 145–181). London, UK: Sage.

MacEntee, K. (2013, March). *Cellphones and rural schools: Stories of challenges and possibilities* [Report]. Durban, South Africa: Centre for Visual Methodologies for Social Change.

MacEntee, K. (2016a). Facing responses to cellphilm screenings of African girlhood in academic presentations. In K. MacEntee, C. Burkholder, & J. Schwab-Cartas (Eds.), *What's a cellphilm? Integrating mobile phone technology into participatory visual research and activism* (pp. 137–152). Rotterdam, Netherlands: Sense.

MacEntee, K. (2016b). Girls, condoms, tradition, and abstinence: Making sense of HIV prevention discourses in rural South Africa. In C. Mitchell & C. Rentschler (Eds.), *Girlhood and the politics of place* (pp. 315–332). New York, NY: Berghahn.

MacEntee, K., Burkholder, C., & Schwab-Cartas, J. (Eds.). (2016). *What's a cellphilm? Integrating mobile phone technology into participatory visual research and activism.* Rotterdam, Netherlands: Sense.

MacEntee, K., & Mandrona, A. (2015). From discomfort to collaboration: Teachers screening cellphilms in a rural South African school. *Perspectives in Education, 33*(4), 43–56.

MacEntee, K., & Mitchell, C. (2011). Lost in translation. In L. Theron, C. Mitchell, A. Smith, & J. Stuart (Eds.), *Picturing research: Drawing(s) as visual methodology* (pp. 89–102). Rotterdam, Netherlands: Sense.

MacKay, F. (2011). A movement of their own: Voices of young feminist activists in the London Feminist Network. *Interface: A Journal for and About Social Movements, 3*(2), 152–178.

Mail & Guardian (2016, April 20). *Rhodes University shuts down as anti-rape protests continue.* Retrieved from http://mg.co.za/article/2016-04-20-rhodes-university-shut-down-as-anti-rape-protests-continue

Mak, M. (2006). Unwanted images: Tackling gender based violence in South African schools through youth artwork. In F. E. Leach & C. Mitchell (Eds.), *Combating gender violence in and around schools* (pp. 113–123). Stoke-on-Trent, UK: Trentham Books.

Mak, M. (2011). The visual ethics of using children's drawings in the documentary 'Unwanted Images'. In L. Theron, C. Mitchell, A. Smith, & J. Stuart (Eds.), *Picturing research: Drawing as visual methodology* (pp. 77–88). Rotterdam, Netherlands: Sense.

Masinga, L. (2009). An African teacher's journey to self-knowledge through teaching sexuality education. In K. Pithouse-Morgan, C. Mitchell, & R. Moletsane (Eds.), *Making connections: Self-study and social action* (pp. 237–248). New York, NY: Peter Lang.

Maslow, A. (1987). Maslow's hierarchy of needs. Retrieved from www.researchhistory. org/2012/06/16/maslows-hierarchy-of-needs/

McLuhan, M. (1964). *Understanding media: The extensions of man.* Retrieved from http:// beforebefore.net/80f/s11/media/mcluhan.pdf

McNay, M. (2009). Immigrants, labourers, "others": Canada's home children. In L. Lerner (Ed.), *Depicting Canada's children* (pp. 153–172). Waterloo, ON: Wilfred Laurier University Press.

Merriam, S. B. (1998). *Qualitative research and case study applications in education* (2nd ed.). San Francisco, CA: Jossey-Bass.

Mertens, D. M. (2009). *Transformative research and evaluation.* New York, NY: Guilford Press.

Meyers, S. A. (2008). Using transformative pedagogy when teaching online. *College Teaching, 56*(4), 219–224. doi: 10.3200/CTCH.56.4.219-224

Miller, E., & Smith, M. (2012). Dissemination and ownership of knowledge. In E. J. Milne, C. Mitchell, & N. De Lange (Eds.), *The handbook of participatory video* (pp. 331–348). Lanham, MD: AltaMira Press.

Miller, L., Luchs, M., & Dyer Jales, G. (2011). *Mapping memories: Participatory media, place-based stories & refugee youth.* Montreal, QC: Marquis Book Printing Inc.

Mills, K. A. (2010). A review of the "digital turn" in the new literacy studies. *Review of Educational Research, 80*(2), 246–271. doi: 10.3102/0034654310364401

Milne, E. J., Mitchell, C., & De Lange, N. (Eds.). (2012). *Handbook of participatory video.* Lanham, MD: AltaMira Press.

Mitchell, C. (2006a). Taking pictures, taking action. Visual arts-based methodologies and research as social change. In T. Marcus & A. Hofmänner (Eds.), *Shifting the boundaries of knowledge: A view on social sciences, law and humanities in South Africa* (pp. 227–245). Scottsville, South Africa: University of KwaZulu-Natal Press.

Mitchell, C. (2006b). "In my life": Youth stories and poems on HIV/AIDS: Towards a new literacy in the age of AIDS. *Changing English: Studies in Culture and Education, 13*(3), 355–368. doi: 10.1080/13586840600971919

Mitchell, C. (2008). Taking the picture, changing the picture: Visual methodologies in educational research in South Africa. *South African Journal of Educational Research, 28*(3), 365–383.

Mitchell, C. (2009). Geographies of danger: School toilets in sub-Saharan Africa. In O. Gershenson & B. Penner (Eds.), *Ladies and gents* (pp. 62–74). Philadelphia, PA: Temple University Press.

Mitchell, C. (2011). *Doing visual research*. London, UK: Sage.

Mitchell, C. (2014, April). *Children and housing in several Nairobi slums: Tools and methods for interpreting with children their drawing on safety, security and well-being.* Paper presented at CEREV: Children's Art from the Past and Present: An Interdisciplinary Symposium. Concordia University, Montreal, Canada.

Mitchell, C. (2015a). Fire+hope up: On revisiting the process of revisiting a literacy for social action project. In J. Sefton-Green & J. Rowsell (Eds.), *Revisiting learning lives – longitudinal perspectives on researching learning and literacy* (pp. 32–45). Abingdon, UK: Taylor & Francis.

Mitchell, C. (2015b). Looking at showing: On the politics and pedagogy of exhibiting in community based research and work with policy makers. *Educational Research for Social Change*, 4(2), 48–60.

Mitchell, C. (2016a). Autoethnography as a wide-angle lens on looking (inward and outward): What difference can this make to our teaching? In D. Pillay, I. Naicker, & K. Pithouse-Morgan (Eds.), *Inside teaching in higher education: South African academic autoethnographies* (pp. 175–190). Rotterdam, Netherlands: Sense.

Mitchell, C. (2016b, July 16). *Looking into the futures: Problematizing socially engaged research in visual sociology.* Keynote presentation at the Third International Sociology Association Forum, Vienna.

Mitchell, C., & Allnutt, S. (2008). Photographs and/as social documentary. In G. Knowles & A. Cole (Eds.), *Handbook of the arts in qualitative research: Perspectives, methodologies, examples and issues* (pp. 251–264). London, UK: Sage.

Mitchell, C., & De Lange, N. (2008). Through our eyes: Using photovoice to address stigma in the age of AIDS. *Girlhood Studies* 1(1), 138–142.

Mitchell, C., & De Lange, N. (2011). Community-based participatory video and social action in rural South Africa. In E. Margolis & L. Pauwels (Eds.), *The SAGE handbook of visual research methods* (pp. 171–185). London, UK: Sage.

Mitchell, C., & De Lange, N. (2013). What can a teacher do with a cellphone? Using participatory visual research to speak back in addressing HIV&AIDS. *South African Journal of Education*, 33(4), 1–13.

Mitchell, C., & Pithouse-Morgan, K. (2014). Expanding the memory catalogue: Southern African women's contributions to memory-work writing as a feminist methodology. *Agenda: Empowering Women for Gender Equity*, 28(1), 92–103. doi: 10.1080/10130950.2014.883704

Mitchell, C., & Sommer, M. (2016). Participatory visual methodologies in global public health. *Global Public Health: An International Journal for Research, Policy and Practice*, 11(5–6), 521–527. doi: 10.1080/17441692.2016.1170184

Mitchell, C., & Weber, S. (1999). *Reinventing ourselves as teachers: Beyond nostalgia.* London, UK: Falmer Press.

Mitchell, C., De Lange, N., & Moletsane, R. (2011). *Digital voices of rural teachers: Participatory analysis, 'being a teacher in the age of AIDS' and social action* [Study]. Retrieved from www.mcgill.ca/dise/research/facultyresearchprojects/voices

Mitchell, C., De Lange, N., & Moletsane, R. (2015). Me and my cellphone: Constructing change from the inside through cellphilms and participatory video. *AREA.* doi: 10.1111/area.12142

Mitchell, C., De Lange, N., & Moletsane, R. (2016). Poetry in a pocket: The cellphilms of South African rural women teachers and the poetics of the everyday. In C. Burkholder, K. MacEntee, & J. Cartas-Schwab (Eds.), *What's a cellphilm? Integrating mobile phone technology into participatory arts based research and activism* (pp. 19–34). Rotterdam, Netherlands: Sense.

Mitchell, C., De Lange, N., & Nguyen, X. T. (2016). Visual ethics with and through the body: The participation of girls with disabilities in Vietnam in a photovoice project. In H. Cahill, J. Coffey, & S. Budgeon (Eds.), *Learning bodies.* Dubai, UAE: Springer-Verlag Singapur.

Mitchell, C., DeMartini, A., & Murthuri, S. (2016). *Through the eyes of mothers. Using photovoice to study the barriers women in one Nairobi slum face in balancing work and child care. A brief.* Montreal, Canada: GRoW Project.

Mitchell, C., Mak, M., & Stuart, J. (2005). *Our photos, our videos, our stories* [Video Documentary]. Canada: Taffeta Productions.

Mitchell, C., Walsh, S., & Moletsane, R. (2006). Speaking for ourselves: A case for visual arts-based and other participatory methodologies in working with young people to address sexual violence. In F. Leach & C. Mitchell (Eds.), *Combating gender violence in and around schools* (pp. 103–112). Stoke-on-Trent, UK: Trentham Books.

Mitchell, C., Walsh, S., & Weber, S. (2007). Behind the lens: Reflexivity and video documentary. In G. Knowles & A. Cole (Eds.), *The art of visual inquiry* (pp. 281–294). Halifax, NS: Backalong Press.

Mitchell, C., Weber, S., & Pithouse, K. (2009). Facing the public: Using photography for self-study and social action. In D. Tidwell, M. Heston, & L. Fitzgerald (Eds.), *Research methods for the self-study of practice* (pp. 119–134). New York, NY: Springer.

Mitchell, C., Chege, F., Maina, L., & Rothman, M. (2016). Beyond engagement in working with children in eight Nairobi slums to address safety, security, and housing: Digital tools for policy and community dialogue. *Global Public Health: An International Journal for Research, Policy and Practice, 11*(5–6), 651–665. doi: 10.1080/17441692.2016.1165720

Mitchell, C., Strong-Wilson, T., Pithouse, K., & Allnutt, S. (Eds.). (2011). *Memory and pedagogy.* Abingdon, UK: Routledge.

Mitchell, C., Theron, L., Smith, A., & Stuart, J. (2011). Picturing research: An introduction. In L. Theron, C. Mitchell, A. Smith, & J. Stuart (Eds.), *Picturing research: Drawing as visual methodology* (pp. 1–16). Rotterdam, Netherlands: Sense.

Mitchell, C., De Lange, N., Moletsane, R., Stuart, J., & Buthelezi, T. (2005). Giving a face to HIV and AIDS: On the uses of photo-voice by teachers and community health care workers working with youth in rural South Africa. *Qualitative Research in Psychology*, *3*(2), 257–270. doi: 10.1191/1478088705qp042oa

Mitchell, C., Theron, L., Stuart, J., Smith, A., & Campbell, Z. (2011). Drawings as research method. In L. Theron, C. Mitchell, A. Smith, & J. Stuart (Eds.), *Picturing research: Drawings as visual methodology* (pp. 19–36). Rotterdam, Netherlands: Sense.

Mitchell, C., Stuart, J., De Lange, N., Moletsane, R., Buthelezi, T., Larkin, J., & Flicker, S. (2010). What difference does this make? Studying South African youth as knowledge producers in the age of AIDS. In C. Higgins & B. Norton (Eds.), *Language and HIV/AIDS* (pp. 214–232). Toronto, ON: Multilingual Matters.

Mnisi, T. (2014). *Digital storytelling to explore HIV- and AIDS-related stigma with secondary school learners in a rural community in KwaZulu-Natal* (Doctoral dissertation). Nelson Mandela Metropolitan University, Port Elizabeth, South Africa.

Mnisi, T., De Lange, N., & Mitchell, C. (2010). Learning to use visual data to 'save lives' in the age of AIDS? *Communitas*, *15*(1), 183–202.

Moletsane, R. (2011). Culture, nostalgia, and sexuality education in the age of AIDS in South Africa. In C. Mitchell, T. Strong-Wilson, K. Pithouse, & S. Allnutt (Eds.), *Memory and pedagogy* (pp. 193–298). New York, NY: Routledge.

Moletsane, R., & Mitchell, C. (2007). On working with a single photograph. In N. De Lange, C. Mitchell, & J. Stuart (Eds.), *Putting people in the picture: Visual methodologies for social change* (pp. 131–140). Rotterdam, Netherlands: Sense.

Moletsane, R., Mitchell, C., & Smith A. (Eds.). (2012). *Was it something I wore? Dress, materiality, identity*. Cape Town, South Africa: HSRC Press.

Moletsane, R., Mitchell, C., De Lange, N., Stuart, J., Buthelezi, T., & Taylor, M. (2007). Photovoice as an analytical tool in the fight against HIV and AIDS stigmatization in a rural KwaZulu-Natal school. *Journal of Child and Adolescent Mental Health*, *19*(1), 1–10.

Moletsane, R., Mitchell, C., Smith, A., & Chisholm, L. (2008). *Methodologies for mapping a Southern African girlhood in the age of AIDS*. Rotterdam, Netherlands: Sense.

Moletsane, R., Mitchell, C., & Lewin, T. (2015). Gender violence, teenage pregnancy and gender equity policy in South Africa. In J. Parkes (Ed.). *Gender violence in poverty contexts: The educational challenge* (pp. 183–197). Abingdon, UK: Routledge.

Moletsane, R., Mitchell, C., De Lange, N., Stuart, J., Buthelezi, T., & Taylor, M. (2009). What can a woman do with a camera? Turning the female gaze on poverty and HIV and AIDS in rural South Africa. *International Journal of Qualitative Studies in Education*, *22*(3), 1–36. doi: 10.1080/09518390902835454

Molnar, B. E., Gortmaker, S. L., Bull, F. C., & Buka, S. L. (2004). Unsafe to play? Neighborhood disorder and lack of safety predict reduced physical activity among urban children and adolescents. *American Journal of Health Promotion, 18*(5), 378–386. doi: 10.4278/0890-1171-18.5.378

Monitoring Educational Rights for Girls with Disabilities (MRGD). (2016). *Final report on the educational rights of girls with disabilities in Vietnamese schools.* Halifax, NS: Mount Saint Vincent University.

Morrell, R., & Makhaye, G. (2006). Working not blaming: Masculinity work with young African men in KwaZulu-Natal. In F. E. Leach & C. Mitchell (Eds.), *Combating gender violence in and around schools* (pp. 153–162). Stoke-on-Trent, UK: Trentham Books.

Morrell, R., Jewkes, R., & Lindegger, G. (2012). Hegemonic masculinity/masculinities in South Africa: Culture, power, and gender politics. *Men and Masculinities, 15*(1), 11–30. doi: 10.1177/1097184X12438001

Mudaly, R., Pithouse-Morgan, K., Van Laren, L., Singh, S., & Mitchell, C. (2015). Connecting with pre-service teachers' perspectives on the use of digital technology and social media to teach socially relevant science. *Perspectives in Education, 33*(4), 23–41.

Neale, B. (2010). Foreword: Young lives and imagined futures. In M. Winterton, G. Crow, & B. Morgan-Brett (Eds.), *Young lives and imagined futures: Insights from archived data* (pp. 4–6). Retrieved from www.timescapes.leeds.ac.uk/assets/files/secondary_analysis/working papers/WP6-final10Oct.pdf

Ngalomba, S., & Harpur, P. (2016). Long lives aren't necessarily happy ones in Africa, particularly for women. *The Conversation, Africa Pilot.* Retrieved from http://theconversation.com/long-lives-arent-necessarily-happy-ones-in-africa-particularly-for-women-66140

Ngidi, N. D., & Moletsane, R. (2015). Using transformative pedagogies for the prevention of gender-based violence: Reflections from a secondary school-based intervention. *Agenda: Empowering Women for Gender Equity, 29*(3), 66–78.

Nguyen, X. T., Mitchell, C., De Lange, N., & Fritsch, K. (2015). Engaging girls with disabilities in Vietnam: Making their voices count. *Disability & Society, 30*(5), 773–787. doi: 10.1080/09687599.2015.1051515

North York Community House. (2016). *Digital storytelling.* Retrieved from nych.ca/digital-stories/#thestories

O'Fallon, L. R., Tyson, F. L., & Dearry, A. (2000). *Successful models of community-based participatory research: Final report.* Research Triangle Park, NC: National Institute of Environmental Health Sciences.

Papi, A. (2009). *What whiteness has to do with looking at UNICEF visual images? An autoethnographic exploration by a development practitioner.* (Unpublished Master's thesis). Montreal, Canada: McGill University.

Paulus, T., Woodside, M., & Ziegler, M. (2008). Extending the conversation: Qualitative research as dialogic collaborative process. *The Qualitative Report, 13*(2), 226–243.

Pauwels, L. (2002). The video-and multimedia-article as a mode of scholarly communication: toward scientifically informed expression and aesthetics. *Visual Studies, 17*(2), 150–159. doi: 10.1080/1472586022000032224

Pauwels, L. (2006). Representing moving cultures: Expressions, multivocality and reflexivity in anthropological and sociological filmmaking. In L. Pauwels (Ed.), *Visual cultures of science: Rethinking representational practices in knowledge building and science communication* (pp. 120–152). Lebanon, NH: Dartmouth College Press.

Phipps, A., & Smith, G. (2012). Violence against women students in the UK: Time to take action. *Gender and Education, 24*(4), 357–373. doi: 10.1080/09540253.2011.628928

Pillow, W. S. (2002). Confession, catharsis, or cure? Rethinking the uses of reflexivity as methodological power in qualitative research. *International Journal of Qualitative Studies in Education, 18*(2), 175–196. doi: 10.1080/0951839032000060635

Pink, S. (2001). More visualizing, more methodologies: On video, reflexivity and qualitative research. *The Sociological Review, 49*(4), 586–599. doi: 10.1111/1467-954X.00349

Pithouse, K., & Mitchell, C. (2007). Looking into change: Studying participant engagement in photovoice projects. In N. De Lange, C. Mitchell, & J. Stuart (Eds.), *Putting people in the picture: Visual methodologies for social change* (pp. 141–151). Amsterdam, Netherlands: Sense.

Pithouse, K., Mitchell, C., & Weber, S. (2009). Self-study in teaching and teacher development. *Educational Action Research, 17*(1), 43–62.

Pithouse-Morgan, K., Van Laren, L., Mitchell, C., Mudaly, R., & Singh, S. (2015). Digital animation for 'going public' on curriculum integration of HIV and AIDS in higher education. *South African Journal of Higher Education, 29*(2), 237–259.

Pretty, J. N. (1995). Participatory learning for sustainable agriculture. *World Development, 23*(8), 1247–1263.

Proietti, M. (2016, November). *Curating an art exhibition for Black History Month.* Paper presented at the Decolonizing Conference. York University, Toronto, Canada.

Reavey, P., & Johnson, K. (2012). Visual approaches: Using and interpreting images. In J. Hughes (Ed.), *SAGE visual methods: Principles, issues, debates and controversies in visual research* (pp. 167–192). London, UK: Sage.

Reed, J. (2007). *Appreciative inquiry: Research for change.* Thousand Oaks, CA: Sage.

Reinikainen, L., & Zetterström-Dahlqvist, H. (2016). Curating an exhibition in a university setting: An autoethnographic study of an autoethngraphic work. In D. Pillay, I. Naicker, & K. Pithouse-Morgan (Eds.), *Academic autoethnographies: Inside teaching in higher education* (pp. 69–83). Rotterdam, Netherlands: Sense.

Rentschler, C. (2003). Expanding the definition of media activism. In A. Valdivia (Ed.), *Blackwell companion to media studies* (pp. 529–547). Malden, MA: Blackwell.

Ribalta, J. (2008). *Public photographic spaces: Exhibitions of propaganda from Pressa to the Family of Man: 1928–55.* Barcelona, Spain: Museu d'Art Contemporani de Barcelona.

Rist, R. (2003). Influencing the policy process with qualitative research. In N. Denzin & Y. Lincoln (Eds.), *Collecting and interpreting qualitative materials* (pp. 619–644). London, UK: Sage.

Rivard, L. (2015). *Gender, physical education, and sport: Bringing forward Rwandan girls' perspectives on their lived experiences of physical activity and sport in secondary schools* (Doctoral dissertation). McGill University, Montreal, Canada.

Rivard, L., & Mitchell, C. (2013). Sport, gender and development: On the use of photovoice as a participatory action research tool to inform policy makers. In L. Azzarito & D. Kirk (Eds.), *Pedagogies, physical culture and visual methods* (pp. 131–143). Abingdon, UK: Routledge.

Robbins, D. (2010). *Beyond the billboards: The Lovelife story.* Johannesburg, South Africa: Porcupine Press.

Rogers, M. (2014a). *Critical filmmaking: The complexities of addressing social justice issues with youth in New Brunswick schools* (Unpublished doctoral dissertation). University of New Brunswick, Fredericton, Canada.

Rogers, M. (2014b). Problematising participatory video with youth in Canada: The intersection of therapeutic, deficit and individualising discourses. *AREA.* doi: 10.1111/area.12141

Rose, G. (2001). *Visual methodologies: An introduction to researching with visual materials.* Thousand Oaks, CA: Sage.

Rose, G. (2007). *Visual methodologies: An introduction to the interpretation of visual materials.* (2nd ed.). Thousand Oaks, CA: Sage.

Rose, G. (2012). *Visual methodologies: An introduction to researching with visual materials.* (3rd ed.). Thousand Oaks, CA: Sage.

Ross, S. W., Romer, N., & Horner, R. H. (2012). Teacher well-being and the implementation of schoolwide positive behavior interventions and supports. *Journal of Positive Behavior Interventions, 14*(2), 118–128. doi: 10.1177/1098300711413820

Ruby, J. (1996). Antropología visual. *Enciclopedia de Antropología Cultural, 4,* 1345–1351.

Ruby, J. (2000). *Picturing culture: Explorations of film and anthropology.* Chicago, IL: University of Chicago Press.

Rumsey, A. S. (2011). *New-model scholarly communication: Roadmap for change* [Report]. Charlottesville, VA: Scholarly Communication Institute. Retrieved from http://libra.virginia.edu/catalog/libra-oa:3260

Rydstrom, H. (2010). Having 'learning difficulties': The inclusive education of disabled girls and boys in Vietnam. *Improving Schools, 13*(1), 81–98. doi: 10.1177/1365480209352549

Sandeen, E. J. (1995). *Picturing an exhibition: The family of man and 1950s America.* Albuquerque, NM: University of New Mexico Press.

Sartre, J. (1969). *Being and nothingness.* London, UK: Routledge.

Sathiparsad, R., & Taylor, M. (2006). Diseases come from girls: Perspectives of male learners in rural KwaZulu-Natal on HIV infection and AIDS. *Journal of Education, 38*(2), 118–137.

Schaffer, J. (2016, January 26). Inside the culture of sexual violence at America's colleges. *Vice.* Retrieved from www.vice.com/read/inside-the-culture-of-sexual-violence-at-americas-colleges

Shefer, T., Clowes, L., & Vergnani, T. (2012). Narratives of transactional sex on a university campus. *Culture, Health & Sexuality, 14*(4), 435–447.

Schneider, H., Hlophe, H., & Van Rensburg, D. (2008). Community health workers and the response to HIV/AIDS in South Africa: Tensions and prospects. *Health Policy and Planning, 23*(3), 179–187.

Schön, D. A. (1983). *The reflective practitioner: How professionals think in action*. London, UK: Temple Smith.

Schradie, J. (2011). The digital production gap: The digital divide and Web 2.0 collide. *Poetics, 39*(2), 145–168. doi: 10.1016/j.poetic.2011.02.003

Schratz, M., & Walker, R. (1995). *Research as social change: New possibilities for qualitative research*. London, UK: Routledge.

Schwab-Cartas, J. (2012). Learning from communities: Personal reflections from inside. In E-J. Milne, C. Mitchell, & N. De Lange (Eds.), *The handbook of participatory video* (pp. 383–396). Lanham, MD: AltaMira Press.

Schwab-Cartas, J., & Mitchell, C. (2014). A tale of two sites: Cellphones, participatory video and indigeneity in community-based research. *McGill Journal of Education/Revue des sciences de l'éducation de McGill, 49*(3), 603–620.

Sefton-Greene, J., & Rowsell, J. (Eds.). (2015). *Revisiting learning lives – Longitudinal perspectives on researching learning and literacy*. Abingdon, UK: Taylor & Francis.

Serrat, O. (2009). *The most significant change technique*. Washington, DC: Asian Development Bank. Retrieved from http://digitalcommons.ilr.cornell.edu/cgi/viewcontent.cgi?article=1202&context=intl

Skingsley, A., Takuva, S., Brown, A., Delpech, V., & Puren, A. (2014). Monitoring HIV-related mortality in South Africa: The challenges and urgency. *Communicable Diseases Surveillance Bulletin, 12*(4), 116–120.

Smith, A. (2012). Take a picture: Photographs, dress, gender and self-study. In R. Moletsane, C. Mitchell, & A. Smith (Eds.), *Was it something I wore? Dress, identity and materiality* (pp. 57–71). Cape Town, South Africa: HRSC Press.

Smith, K. A., & Harrison, A. (2013). Teachers' attitudes towards adolescent sexuality and life skills education in rural South Africa. *Sex Education, 13*(1), 68–81. doi: 10.1080/14681811.2012.677206

Sontag, S. (2003). *Regarding the pain of others*. New York, NY: Farrar, Strauss & Giroux.

Spence, J. (1986). *Putting myself in the picture: A political, personal and photographic autobiography*. London, UK: Camden Press.

Spence, J., & Martin, R. (1988). Photo-therapy: Psychic realism as a healing art. In L. Wells (Ed.), *The photography reader* (pp. 402–409). Abingdon, UK: Routledge.

Spence, J., & Solomon, J. (1995). *What can a woman do with a camera? Photography for women*. London, UK: Scarlett Press.

Spilt, J. L., Koomen, H. M., & Thijs, J. T. (2011). Teacher wellbeing: The importance of teacher–student relationships. *Educational Psychology Review, 23*(4), 457–477. doi: 10.1007/s10648-011-9170-y

St John Ward, M. (2015). *Exploring the use of digital storytelling in a classroom of girls in an affluent school: Towards HIV and AIDS knowledge production* (Doctoral dissertation). University of KwaZulu Natal, Durban, South Africa.

StoryCenter. (n.d.). *Stories*. Retrieved from www.storycenter.org/stories/

Strangelove, M. (2009). *Watching YouTube: Extraordinary videos made by ordinary people*. Toronto, Canada: University of Toronto Press.

Howe, N., & Strauss, W. (2000). *Millennials rising: The next great generation.* New York, NY: Vintage.

Strong-Wilson, T. (2008). *Bringing memory forward: Teachers, remembrance, social justice.* New York, NY: Peter Lang.

Strong-Wilson, T., Mitchell, C., & Ingersoll, M. (2016). Exploring multidirectional memory-work and the digital as a phase space for teacher professional development. In M. Knoebel & J. Kalman (Eds.), *New literacies and teachers' professional development* (pp. 151–172). New York, NY: Peter Lang.

Strong-Wilson, T., Asghar, A., & Yoder, A. (2015). Éditorial/Editorial. *McGill Journal of Education/Revue des sciences de léducation de McGill, 49*(3). Retrieved from http://mje.mcgill.ca/article/view/9264/7028

Strong-Wilson, T., Mitchell, C., Morrison, C., Radford, L., & Pithouse-Morgan, K. (2014). "Reflecting Forward" on the digital in multidirectional memory-work between Canada and South Africa. *McGill Journal of Education/Revue des sciences de l'éducation de McGill, 49*(3), 675–695. doi: 10.7202/1033553ar

Stuart, J. (2007). *From our frames* (Doctoral dissertation). University of KwaZulu-Natal, Durban, South Africa.

Stuart, J., & Mitchell, C. (2013). Media, participation, and social change: Working within a "Youth as Knowledge Producers" framework. In D. Lemish (Ed.), *The Routledge international handbook of on children, adolescents and media studies* (pp. 359–365). Abingdon, UK: Routledge.

Sultana, F. (2007). Reflexivity, positionality and participatory ethics: Negotiating fieldwork dilemmas in international research. *ACME: An International E-Journal for Critical Geographies, 6*(3), 374–385.

Szorenyi, A. (2006). The images speak for themselves? Reading refugee coffee table books. *Visual Studies, 2*(1), 24–41. doi: 10.1080/14725860600613188

Taft, J. (2010). *Rebel girls: Youth activism and social change across the Americas.* New York, NY: New York University Press.

Taylor, P. C., & Medina, M. N. D. (2013). Educational research paradigms: From positivism to multiparadigmatic. *The Journal of Meaning-Centered Education, 1*(2), 1–13.

Teitelbaum, P. (2012). Online participatory communication: Re-seeing participatory video practices and research. In E-J Milne, C. Mitchell, & N. De Lange (Eds.), *Handbook of participatory video* (pp. 412–426). Lanham, MD: AltaMira Press.

Theron, L., Mitchell, C., Smith, A., & Stuart, J. (Eds.). (2011). *Picturing research: Drawing as visual methodology.* Rotterdam, Netherlands: Sense.

Thomas, V., & Britton, K. (2012). The art of participatory video: Relational aesthetics in artistic collaborations. In E. J. Milne, C. Mitchell, & N. De Lange (Eds.), *Handbook of participatory video* (pp. 208–222). Lanham, MD: AltaMira Press.

Thompson, J. (2009). *How we see this place: Intergenerational dialogue about conservation around Tiwai Island, Sierra Leone* (Master's thesis). McGill University, Montreal, Canada.

Tobin, J. (2000). *Good guys don't wear hats: Children's talk about the media paperback.* New York, NY: Teachers College Press.

Tremblay, C. (2013). Towards inclusive waste management: Participatory video as a communication tool. *Waste and Resource Management, 166*(WR4), 177–186. doi: 10.1680/warm.13.0004

Treseder, P. (1997). *Empowering children and young people: Promoting involvement in decision-making* [Training Manual]. London, UK: Children's Rights Office.

Trigg, M. (Ed.). (2010). *Leading the way: Young women's activism for social change.* New Brunswick, NJ: Rutgers University Press.

Tuck, E. (2009). Theorizing back. An approach to participatory policy analysis. In J. Anyon (Ed.), *Theory and educational research: Toward critical social explanation* (pp. 111–120). New York, NY: Routledge.

Tuck, E., & Yang, K. W. (2012). Decolonization is not a metaphor. *Decolonization: Indigeneity, Education & Society, 1*(1), 1–40.

Tuck, E., & Yang, K. W. (2014a). Introduction to youth resistance research and theories of change. In E. Tuck & K. W. Yang (Eds.), *Youth resistance research and theories of change* (pp. 1–24). Abingdon, UK: Routledge.

Tuck, E., & Yang, K. W. (2014b). R-words: Refusing research. In D. Paris & M. T. Winn (Eds.), *Humanizing research: Decolonizing qualitative inquiry with youth and communities* (pp. 223–248). London, UK: Sage.

Turkle, S. (2011). *Along together: Why we expect more from technology and less from each other.* Cambridge, MA: MIT Press.

Twomey, C. (2012). Severed hands: Authenticating atrocity in the Congo, 1904–13. In G. Batchen, M. Gidley, N. K. Miller, & J. Prosser (Eds.), *Picturing atrocity: Photography in crisis* (pp. 39–50). London, UK: Reaktion Books.

United Nations Children's Funds (UNICEF). (2013). *State of the world's children 2013: Children with disabilities.* Retrieved from www.unicef.org/sowc2013/report.htmlUNICEF

United Nations Educational, Scientific and Cultural Organization (UNESCO). (2015). *Incheon Declaration.* Retrieved from http://en.unesco.org/world-education-forum-2015/incheon-declaration

Van der Riet, M., & Boettiger, M. (2009). Shifting research dynamics: Addressing power and maximising participation through participatory research techniques in participatory research. *South African Journal of Psychology, 39*(1), 1–18. doi: 10.1177/008124630903900101

Van Laren, L., Mudaly, R., Pithouse-Morgan, K., & Singh, S. (2013). Starting with ourselves in deepening our understanding of generativity in participatory educational research. *South African Journal of Education, 33*(4), 1–16.

Van Laren, L., Mitchell, C., Mudaly, R., Pithouse-Morgan, K., & Singh, S. (2015). Connecting with pre-service teachers' perspectives on the use of digital technologies and social media to teach socially relevant science. *Perspectives in Education, 33*(4), 23–40.

Van Laren, L., Mitchell, C., Mudaly, R., Pithouse-Morgan, K., & Singh, S. (2012). Exploring university educators' lived experiences of curriculum innovating through integrating HIV & AIDS. *Alternation: Interdisciplinary Journal for the Study of Arts and Humanities in South Africa, 19*(2), 138–161.

Van Manen, M. (1990). *Researching lived experiences*. Albany, NY: State University of New York Press.

Vaughan, C. (2014). Participatory research with youth: Idealising safe social spaces or building transformative links in difficult environments? *Journal of Health Psychology, 19*(1), 184–192. doi: 10.1177/1359105313500258

Walkerdine, V. (1990). *Schoolgirl fictions*. New York, NY: Verso.

Wallerstein, N., & Duran, B. (2008). The theoretical, historical, and practice roots of CBPR. In M. Minkler & N. Wallerstein (Eds.), *Community-based participatory research for health: From process to outcomes* (2nd ed.) (pp. 26–46). San Francisco, CA: Jossey-Bass.

Walton, K. (1995). Creating positive images: Working with primary school girls. In J. Spence & J. Solomon (Eds.), *What can a woman do with a camera? Photography for women* (pp. 153–158). London, UK: Scarlet Press.

Walsh, A. (2014, March). *To reunite, to honor, to witness: Paintings from Alberni Indian Residential School*. Presentation at the CEREV Conference: Children's Art from the Past and Present. Concordia University, Montreal, Canada.

Walsh, S. (2007). Power, race and agency: Facing the truth and visual methodology. In N. De Lange, C. Mitchell, & J. Stuart (Eds.), *Putting people in the picture* (pp. 241–255). Rotterdam, Netherlands: Sense.

Walsh, S. (2012). "We grew as we grew": Visual methods, social change and collective learning over time. *South African Journal of Education, 32*(4), 406–415.

Walsh, S. (Director), & Mitchell, C. (Producer). (2003). *Fire + Hope* [Motion Picture]. Montreal, Canada: Taffeta Productions.

Walsh, S., & Mitchell, C. (2004). Artfully engaged: Youth, gender and AIDS activism. In A. Cole, I. Nielson, J. G. Knowles, & T. Luciani (Eds.), *Provoked by art*: Theorizing arts-informed research (pp. 191–202). Halifax, NS: Backalong Books.

Walsh, S., & Mitchell, C. (2006). "I'm too young to die": Danger, desire and masculinity in the neighbourhood. *Gender and Development, 14*(1), 57–68.

Walsh, S., Mitchell, C., & Smith, A. (2002). The Soft Cover project: Youth participation in HIV/AIDS prevention. *Agenda: Empowering Women for Gender Equity, 53*, 106–112.

Wang, C. (1999). Photovoice: A participatory action research strategy applied to women's health. *Journal of Women's Health, 8*(2), 185–192. doi: 10.1089/jwh.1999.8.185

Wapikoni. (2017). *Wapikoni: Giving a voice to aboriginal youth*. Retrieved from www.wapikoni.ca

Ward, C. L., Martin, E., Theron, C., & Distiller, G. B. (2007). Factors affecting resilience in children exposed to violence. *South African Journal of Psychology, 37*(1), 165–187.

Watt, J., Dickey, M., & Grakist, D. (2004). *Middle childhood matters: A framework to promote healthy development of children 6 to 12*. Retrieved from www.child-youth-health.net/

Weber, S., & Mitchell, C. (2007). Imaging, keyboarding, and posting identities: Young people and new media technologies. In D. Buckingham (Ed.), *Youth, identity, and digital media* (pp. 25–48). Cambridge, MA: MIT Press.

Weiler, J. M., & Martin-Weiler, C. J. (2012). Addressing HIV/AIDS education: A look at teacher preparedness in Ghana. *Journal of International Social Studies, 2*(1), 14–25.

Wheeler, J. (2012). Using participatory video to engage in policy processes: representation, power and knowledge in public screenings. In E. J. Milne, C. Mitchell, & N. De Lange (Eds.), *The handbook of participatory video* (pp. 365–379). Lanham, MD: AltaMira Press.

White, S. C. (1996). Depoliticising development: The uses and abuses of participation. *Development in Practice, 6*(1), 6–15. doi: 10.1177/1094428116669818

Whiting, R , Symon, G., Roby, H., & Chamakiotis, P. (2016). Who's behind the lens? A reflexive analysis of roles in participatory video research. *Organizational Research Methods*, 1–25. doi: 10.1177/1094428116669818

Wong, L. (2000). *Shootback: Photos by kids from the Nairobi slums*. London, UK: Booth-Clibborn Editions.

Wood, K., Lambert, H., & Jewkes, R. (2007). "Showing roughness in a beautiful way": Talk about love, coercion, and rape in South African youth sexual culture. *Medical Anthropology Quarterly, 21*(3), 277–300. doi: 10.1525/maq.2007.21.3.277

Wood, L. (2012). 'Every teacher is a researcher!': Creating indigenous epistemologies and practices for HIV prevention through values-based action research. *SAHARA-J: Journal of Social Aspects of HIV/AIDS, 9*(Sup 1), S19–S27. doi: 10.1080/17290376.2012.744910

Wotherspoon, T., & Hansen, J. (2013). The "Idle No More" movement: Paradoxes of First Nations Inclusion in the Canadian Context. *Social Inclusion, 1*(1), 21–36. doi: 10.12924/si2013.01010021

Yang, K. (2012). Reflexivity, participation, and video. In E. J. Milne, C. Mitchell, & N. De Lange (Eds.), *The handbook of participatory video* (pp. 100–114). Lanham, MD: AltaMira Press.

Yang, K. (2013). *Participatory video and reflexivity: The experiences of eight adult learners.* (Unpublished doctoral dissertation). Montreal, Canada, McGill University.

Zeller, F., Ponte, C., & O'Neill, B. (Eds.). (2014). *Revitalizing audience research: Innovations in European cultural research*. Abingdon, UK: Routledge.

Zembylas, M. (2015). 'Pedagogy of discomfort' and its ethical implications: The tensions of ethical violence in social justice education. *Ethics and Education, 10*(2), 163–174 doi: 10.1080/17449642.2015.1039274

Zembylas, M., & Boler, M. (2002). On the spirit of patriotism: Challenges of a "pedagogy of discomfort" [Special issue]. *Teachers College Record On-line, 104*(5). Retrieved from http://tcrecord.org

Zembylas, M., & McGlynn, C. (2010). Discomforting pedagogies: Emotional tensions, ethical dilemmas and transformative possibilities. *British Educational Research Journal, 38*(1), 41–59. doi: 10.1080/01411926.2010.523779

Zuromskis, C. (2013). *Snapshot photography: The lives of images*. Cambridge, MA: MIT Press.

INDEX